Citizen Politics in Western Democracies

Citizen Politics
in Western Democracies
Public Opinion and Political Parties
in the United States, Great Britain,
West Germany, and France

RUSSELL J. DALTON
Florida State University

CHATHAM HOUSE PUBLISHERS, INC.
Chatham, New Jersey

CITIZEN POLITICS IN WESTERN DEMOCRACIES
Public Opinion and Political Parties in the United States,
Great Britain, West Germany, and France

CHATHAM HOUSE PUBLISHERS, INC.
Post Office Box One
Chatham, New Jersey 07928

PUBLISHER: Edward Artinian
ILLUSTRATIONS: Adrienne Shubert
COVER DESIGN: Antler & Baldwin, Inc.
COMPOSITION: Chatham Composer
PRINTING AND BINDING: Port City Press

LIBRARY OF CONGRESS CATALOGING-IN-PUBLICATION DATA

Dalton, Russell J.
    Citizen politics in western democracies : public opinion and
political parties in the United States, Great Britain, West Germany,
and France / Russell J. Dalton.
        p.   cm.
    Bibliography: p.
    Includes index.
    ISBN 0-934540-44-6 : $14.95
    1. Political participation. 2. Political parties. 3. Democracy.
4. Public opinion. 5. Comparative government. I. Title.
JF2011.D34   1988
323'.042--dc 19   88-2830
                                                        CIP

Manufactured in the United States of America
10   9   8   7   6   5   4   3   2   1

For
VIRGINIA DEVAUGHN
and BIFF

Contents

Figures

Tables

Preface

The last two decades were ones of tumult and political uncertainty for most Western democracies. The urban riots and student protests in the 1960s evolved into the new social movements of the 1970s: environmentalism, feminism, consumerism, and the peace movement. The stable consensus of democratic party systems was threatened by new issues and new political contenders. Citizen action groups of all political views pressured governments to address their concerns. Many Western political systems faced severe challenges that would determine the future of democratic politics. In short, we live in very interesting, and important times.

To understand these developments we must focus on their source: citizen politics. Until recently, very little was really known about the values, beliefs, and behaviors of the average citizen; hence every new political development was unexpected and unexplained. The advent of scientific survey research has helped fill this void, although there is still considerable disagreement about the nature of citizen politics among researchers in this field.

The intent of this book is to introduce students to the knowledge we have gained, the questions that still remain, and the implications of these findings. This book is also based on the belief that a comparative approach to studying a political process is necessary in order to learn the essentials of that process. The environmental issue, for example, is not limited to the Greens in West Germany; problems about government budget deficits are not limited to the United States. We can better understand these phenomena by looking beyond national borders. This book focuses on citizen politics in four nations: the United States, Great Britain, West Germany, and France. Students of comparative politics can examine the rich variety of public opinion in different democratic systems. Even those interested in only a single nation can benefit from comparisons that highlight the similarities and dissimilarities in national patterns.

I hope that this book will be of value to several audiences, but it was primarily written for classroom use in courses on comparative political parties, public opinion, and West European politics. The first half of the book (chapters 1-6) introduces the principles of public opinion and the broad contours of citizen actions and beliefs in the four nations. The second half of the book (and the school term) could combine the chapters on party alignment (7-10) with other texts on political parties, such as the excellent books by Harmel and Janda, Epstein, or von Beyme. I add a computer research module on comparative public opinion to the first half of the class, based on the SETUPS provided by the American Political Science Association or my own subsets of Eurobarometer surveys. Alternatively, an innovative thematic approach to teaching West European politics could combine this book with texts on comparative public policy, comparative foreign policy, and other thematic studies.

At the graduate level the book provides a useful core text for courses on West European politics or comparative political behavior. My intent was to summarize the existing knowledge in the field, as well as introduce the controversies at present dividing researchers. I hope the instructor will find that the materials covered here facilitate discussion of the readings from primary research materials. Even senior scholars will find familiar data interpreted in new and thought-provoking ways.

A central theme of this book is the controversy between supporters and critics of the "quality" of citizen politics. The critical eye of scientific researchers has frequently exaggerated the political limits of the average citizen, providing the basis for normative statements condoning an elitist version of democracy. To borrow a phrase from a recent book: The good news is, the bad news is wrong. Citizens are not as uninvolved, uninformed, and undemocratic as their critics would have us believe, and the nature of citizen politics is changing in ways that should strengthen the democratic process—if political systems respond to these trends. Some readers may disagree with my interpretation of the data, but I hope every reader will agree that the issues are central to understanding the changes now affecting these political systems. Thinking about these issues provides students with an excellent introduction to the nature and ideals of democratic politics.

Acknowledgments

This study is more than an individual effort at summarizing the field of comparative political behavior. More than my own efforts, this book reflects the insights I have gained from working with other scholars. These experiences broadened my understanding of political behavior in advanced industrial societies and made it possible to write an extensive comparative study of the changing nature of citizen politics.

First, I am indebted to Kendall Baker and Kai Hildebrandt, with whom I authored a study of West German political behavior entitled *Germany Transformed*. This is an in-depth study of the tremendous social changes occurring in West Europe and the political consequences of these changes. Many of the themes we first explored in *Germany Transformed* appear in more comparative terms in these pages.

Second, I was fortunate to work with an exceptional team of scholars on the *Political Action* project. Samuel Barnes, Max Kaase, Hans Klingemann, Ronald Inglehart, M. Kent Jennings, and the other members of the study sensitized me to the problems and rewards of comparative political research. The chapters on political participation in this book draw heavily on these experiences.

Third, co-authoring a recent book, *Electoral Change in Advanced Industrial Democracies,* provided an opportunity to discuss changes in party politics and voting behavior with a gifted group of political scientists. I am indebted to my co-authors in this project, especially Paul Beck and Scott Flanagan, for expanding my understanding of this aspect of citizen politics.

I have borrowed liberally from these experiences in writing this book and owe these individuals a great debt. I consider these colleagues as silent co-authors to this volume.

During the writing of this book many others helped with advice, survey data, or moral support. Paul Abramson, Paul Beck, Scott Flanagan, Ronald Inglehart, Manfred Kuechler, and Michael Lewis-Beck commented on early drafts of the manuscript. A paper drawing on several chapters was presented at the Sixth New England Workshop on German Politics; I would like to thank

Jim Wright, Richard Hamilton, and the other members of the workshop for their critiques. Samuel Barnes, Adam Clymer, Wolfgang Gibowski, Steve Harding, Max Kaase, Hans Klingemann, William Macridis, and Jacques-Rene Rabier provided me with access to data that ensured a truly comparative analysis. Throughout the writing, Edward Artinian provided the patience and support that denotes a good publisher.

The initial phases of this work were financed by a Developing Scholar grant from the Florida State University Foundation. The latter stages of the project were completed with the support of a National Science Foundation award (SES 85-10989).

This book has a bold objective: to provide an overview of the nature of citizen politics in Western democracies. The task is clearly beyond the means of any one individual; but with a little help from these friends, the resulting product can begin to outline the political changes, and political choices, facing citizens in these societies.

Citizen Politics in Western Democracies

1. Introduction

This is a book about people—as citizens, voters, protesters, campaign workers, community activists, party members, and political spectators they are the driving force of the democratic process. Who could observe the spectacle of an American party convention, the intensity of a French farmers' protest, the commitment of an Easter peace march in Britain, the community spirit of a New England town meeting, or the dedication of a West German environmental group and not be impressed with the democratic process? Granting power to the people, even if that process is incomplete, is a radical development shared by less than a third of the world's nations.

This volume presents a populist view of the democratic process, emphasizing the attitudes and behaviors of the average citizen. The analyses are therefore incomplete; we do not study the role of elites, interest groups, and other political actors. This approach does not presume that the public is all-knowing or all-powerful. Indeed, there are many examples of the public's ignorance or error on policy issues (as there are examples of elite errors), or instances when the public's will was disregarded by policymakers. The democratic process, like all human activities, is imperfect, but its strength lies in the premise that people are the best judges of their own destiny. The success of democracy is largely measured by the public's participation in the process and the responsiveness of the system to popular demands.

One factor limiting the study of citizen political behavior in democracies is the complexity of the topic. It is difficult to make accurate generalizations about public opinion and political behavior because the public is not homogeneous. It consists of millions of individuals, each with his or her own view of the world and the citizen's role in politics. Individuals differ in the attention they devote to politics, the experiences they bring to the political process, and the views they hold. Although a few individuals are full-time politicos, most citizens possess modest political interests and ambitions. Some citizens are liberal, some moderate; some are conservative, socialist, reactionary, communist, or none of the above. The study of public opinion underscores the diversity of the public.

The public's involvement in the policy process is another variable factor. On some issues a broad spectrum of society may become involved; other issues are greeted with widespread apathy. The public's views generally define the acceptable bounds of politics, within which political elites can resolve the remaining controversies. When elites exceed these bounds, or when the issues immediately affect people's lives, the potential for political action is substantial. The difficulty is to understand and predict which course of action the public will take.

In short, as social scientists we deal with the most complex problem in nature: to understand and predict human behavior. Yet this is not a hopeless task. The development of scientific public opinion surveys in the early 1950s provides a valuable tool for researchers. With a sample of a few thousand precisely selected individuals, one can make reliable statements about the distribution of attitudes and opinions (Weisberg and Bowen, 1977). Not only can we observe behavior, but with the survey interview we can inquire into the motivations and expectations that guide behavior. Furthermore, a survey can be divided into subgroups to examine the diversity in individual opinions.

Drawing on an extensive collection of opinion surveys, this volume examines the nature of public opinion in several Western democracies.[1] I describe how individuals view politics, how they participate in the process, what opinions they hold, and how they choose their leaders through competitive elections. These findings should lead to a better understanding of citizen politics and thereby the working of the political process in contemporary democracies.

The Comparative Study of Public Opinion

This is an explicitly comparative study, exploring the nature of public opinion and political behavior in several Western democracies. Our goal is to strike a balance between attention to national detail and the general characteristics of mass politics that transcend national boundaries. There are several advantages to the comparative approach.

A common historical and cultural tradition unites Europe and North America. While these nations differ in the specifics of their government and party systems, they also share broad similarities in the basic functioning of the democratic process and the role of the citizen in the process. A comparative approach thus provides a basis for studying those aspects of political behavior that should be valid across nations. General theories of why people participate in democratic politics should apply to citizens regardless of their nationality. Other theories to explain party preferences should hold for Americans and Europeans because they are derived from basic views about human nature. Yet most of the major studies of public opinion focus only on one nation (Baker et al., 1981; Butler and Stokes, 1974; Campbell et al., 1960; Michelat and Simon, 1977a; Nie et al., 1979; Saarlvik and Crewe, 1983).

A comparative study of several nations provides a broader based assessment of general theories of citizen political behavior. In most instances we expect similar patterns of behavior in different democracies. Even if these theories do not function in the same manner across nations, however, we learn a great deal. Science often progresses by finding exceptions to general theory, which necessitate further theoretical work. The same applies to social science.

Comparative analysis also allows us to examine the effects of other political characteristics on citizen political behavior. For example, in what nations is class voting stronger than the average, and why? Or, does the nature of a nation's electoral system affect the public's voting behavior? Each nation produces another "natural experiment" where general theories can be tested in a different political context.

Finally, even if we are interested only in a single nation, comparative research is a useful approach. An old Hebrew riddle expresses this idea: "*Question*: Who first discovered water? *Answer*: I don't know, but it wasn't a fish." By immersing oneself in a single environment, the characteristics of the environment are unobtrusive and unnoticed. It is difficult to understand what is unique and distinctive about American political behavior, for example, by studying only American politics. Indeed, many students of American politics may be surprised to learn that the United States is often the atypical case in cross-national comparisons. American public opinion is unique in many ways, but this is understood only by rising above the waters.

In order to balance our needs for comparison and attention to national differences, this study focuses on public opinion in four nations: the United States, Britain, West Germany, and France.[2] The choice of these nations is guided by several criteria. By most standards these are the major powers among the Western democracies. Their population, size, economy, military strength, and political influence earn them leadership positions in international circles. The actions of any one of these nations can have significant consequences for all others.

These nations also were chosen because they highlight many of the important variations in the structure of democratic politics. Table 1.1 summarizes some of the most important differences. For example, Britain is a pure parliamentary system of government, with a fusion of legislative and executive power. American government is based on a presidential system, with extensive checks and balances to maintain a separation of legislative and executive power. French politics functions within a modified presidential system; West Germany has a modified parliamentary system.

TABLE 1.1

A COMPARISON OF POLITICAL SYSTEMS

	United States	Great Britain	West Germany	France
Population (in millions)	240	56	61	55
Gross domestic product/capita	$11,706	$7,627	$9,590	$9,268
Political regime established	1789	17th century	1949	1958
State form	Republic	Constitutional monarchy	Republic	Republic
Government structure	Presidential	Parliamentary	Modified parliamentary	Modified presidential
Chief Executive	President	Prime minister	Chancellor	President
Method of selection	Direct election	Elected by Parliament	Elected by Parliament	Direct election
Legislature	Bicameral	Bicameral	Bicameral	Bicameral
Lower house	House of Representatives	House of Commons	Bundestag	National Assembly
Upper house	Senate	House of Lords	Bundesrat	Senate
Power of upper house	Equal	Subordinate	Equal on state issues	Subordinate
Electoral system				
Lower house	Single-member districts	Single-member districts	PR and Single-member districts	Single-member districts
Upper house	Statewide elections	Hereditary and appointment	Appointed by states	Appointed by communes
Major parties	Democrats Republicans	Labour Social Democrats Liberals Conservatives	Greens Social Democrats Free Democrats Christian Democrats/ Christian Social Union (CDU/CSU)	Communists Socialists Ecologists UDF Gaullist (RPR) National Front

Electoral systems are equally diverse. Britain and the United States select the members of the national legislature from single-member districts, and a plurality is sufficient for election. West Germany uses a hybrid system, which combines proportional representation (PR) and single-member districts. In order to share in the proportional distribution of party seats, a party must gain at least 5 percent of the national vote. The French electoral system is based on single-member districts with a second ballot *(tour)* if no candidate receives a majority on the first ballot.

The party systems in these four nations are also varied. Party competition in the United States is limited to the Democratic and Republican parties. Both are broad "catchall" parties that combine diverse political groups into weakly structured electoral coalitions. In contrast, most European political parties are hierarchically organized and firmly controlled by the party leadership. Candidates are elected primarily because of their party label and not because of their personal attributes; in the legislature most party members vote as a bloc. Party options are also more diverse in Europe. Britons can select from at least three major party groups; West Germans have four major parties in the Bundestag. French party politics is synonymous with diversity and political polarization. Jacques Fauvet described French politics in the following terms:

> France contains two fundamental temperaments—that of the left and right; three principal tendencies, if one adds the center; six spiritual families; ten parties, large or small, traversed by multiple currents; fourteen parliamentary groups without much discipline; and forty million opinions. (Ehrmann, 1983, p. 211).

Although Fauvet was describing French politics in the late 1950s, much of his description still applies today. France, a nation of "perpetual political effervescence," provides the spice of comparative politics.

As this brief outline suggests, these four nations provide a rich mix of sociopolitical conditions to study mass political behavior. Subsequent chapters occasionally include survey data from other nations to highlight a specific point or place these four nations in a broader comparative context. In general, however, the bulk of the study focuses on the political behavior of American, British, West German, and French publics.

A New Style of Citizen Politics

The reader will quickly realize that the theme of this volume is the changing nature of citizen political behavior. I suggest that these changes derive from the socioeconomic transformation of these four nations over the past generation and the political consequences of this development. Western democracies are developing a set of characteristics that collectively represent a new form of "advanced industrial" or "postindustrial" society (Bell, 1973; Inglehart, 1977).

The most dramatic changes involve economic conditions. An unprecedented expansion of economic well-being has occurred since World War II. Economies in Western Europe and North America grew at phenomenal rates. In France, for example, the economic expansion between 1950 and the mid-1960s exceeded the total growth of all the years of the Third Republic (1875 to 1940). The astonishing expansion of the West German economy is described as the *Wirtschaftswunder* (Economic Miracle). Income levels in our four nations are two to four times greater than at any time in prewar history. By almost any economic standard, the four nations of this study rank among the most affluent nations of the world.

Western democracies also changed in the degree of the government's involvement in society. Two world wars and the Great Depression expanded the government's role in economic and social activities. Western publics now hold the government responsible for protecting and managing society. Governments increased their control of their national economy, and government programs became the guarantor of social needs. Many European societies developed the characteristics of a welfare state, where an extensive network of generous social programs protect the individual against economic or medical hardship (Heidenheimer and Flora, 1981). Unemployment, illness, and similar problems still cause hardships, but the consequences under the welfare state are less dire than during earlier periods. Western publics consequently enjoy both a high level of affluence and relative security.

Along with increasing affluence has come a restructuring of the labor force. The size of the agricultural workforce has decreased dramatically in most Western nations, and the industrial sector has remained stable or declined. Advanced industrial societies are characterized by a marked shift in the labor force to the service sector. In addition, because of the expansion of national and local governments, public employment now constitutes a significant share of the labor force. Several of the nations in this volume already have passed Daniel Bell's (1973) threshold for postindustrialism: half of the labor force employed in the service or governmental sector.

Advanced industrialism is associated not only with changes in the relative size of the three principal employment sectors but also with changes in the context of the workplace and the residential neighborhood (Dahl and Tufte, 1974; Verba et al., 1978). The continuing decline of rural populations and the expanding size of metropolitan centers stimulate changes in life expectations and life styles. Urbanization means a growing separation of the home from the workplace, a greater diversity of occupations and interests, an expanded

6

range of career opportunities, and more geographic and social mobility. With these trends come changes in the forms of social organization and interaction. Communal forms of organization are replaced by voluntary associations, which in turn become less institutionalized and more spontaneous in organization. These changes reflect the fact that communities are less bounded, that individuals are involved in increasingly complex and competing social networks that divide their loyalties, and that interpersonal and institutional loyalties are becoming more fluid.

Educational opportunities also expanded rapidly in the postwar period. European societies historically applied an elitist model to public education; university education was restricted to a privileged few, and the vast majority received only minimal education (often only four years). In the late 1930s the proportion of university students among 20 to 24 year olds was only 1 percent in England, 1 percent in Germany, and 3 percent in France (Flora, 1983, pp. 553ff). Education received a higher value following World War II. Minimal education standards were increased, and university enrollments skyrocketed. By 1975 the proportion of university students among college-age youth was 7 percent in Britain, 14 percent in West Germany, and 20 percent in France (Flora, 1983). Even the United States, with initially higher university enrollments, experienced a tremendous growth in its university population, to 40 percent of the 18 to 24 year-olds. This expansion of educational opportunities has fundamentally changed the educational composition of contemporary mass publics.

These increases in education were accompanied by parallel increases in information resources. The growth of the electronic media, especially television, has been exceptional. Other information sources, such as books and magazines, also are increasing. Even more revolutionary is the growth of electronic information processing: computers, information and retrieval systems, word processing, and related technologies. Information is no longer a scarce commodity. The contemporary information problem is how to manage an ever-growing volume of complex and sophisticated knowledge.

The transformation of Western democracies is thus more than simply the politics of affluence. Changes in the occupational and social structure are altering life conditions and life styles. Expanded educational opportunities represent an enduring trait of modern societies. The information revolution is continuing. And even though growth rates have slowed in recent years, the living standards of advanced industrial societies are still far better than a generation ago.

As the socioeconomic characteristics of these nations have changed, so too have the characteristics of the public. More educational opportunities mean a growth in political skills and resources, producing the most sophisticated publics in the history of democracies. Changing economic conditions redefine the issues of concern to the public. The weakening of social networks and institutional loyalties is associated with the decline of traditional values and social norms. Recent studies of mass political behavior thus echo this theme of change: *The Changing American Voter, Political Change in Britain, Germany Transformed, Electoral Change in Advanced Industrial Democracies.*

What emerges from these studies is the image of a new style of citizen politics. The elements of this new style are not always, or necessarily, linked together. Some elements may be transitory; others may be coincidental. Nevertheless, several traits coexist for the present, defining a new pattern of citizen political behavior. The goal of this volume is to present a systematic study of public opinion that also explores this new style of citizen politics.

One area of change affects the public's involvement in politics (chapters 2-4). Greater public participation in economic and political decision making has become an important social goal. This development is closely tied to the spread of protest, citizen action groups, and unconventional political participation; but it involves more. Citizens are less likely to be passive subjects and are more likely to demand a say in the decisions affecting their lives. The new style of citizen politics includes a more active participation in the democratic process.

Another broad area of change involves the values and attitudes of the public (chapters 5-6). Industrial societies aimed at providing affluence and economic security. The success of advanced industrialism fulfills many basic economic needs for a sizable sector of society. Thus, concerns are shifting to new political goals (Inglehart, 1977). Several of these new issues are common to advanced industrial democracies: social equality, environmental protection, the dangers of nuclear energy, sexual equality, and human rights. In some instances historical conditions focus these general concerns on specific national problems; for example, racial equality in the United States, regional conflicts in Britain, or center-periphery differences in France. Many of these issues are now loosely integrated into an alternative political agenda that constitutes another element of the new style of citizen politics.

The nature of partisan politics is also changing (chapters 7-10). Until recently, the prevailing theme in comparative party research was the stability of democratic party systems. This situation has changed dramatically in the last decade. Stable party alignments are weakening, producing increased fragmentation and fractionalization in most Western party systems. Declining class differences in voting behavior reflect the general erosion in the social bases of voting. Studies in the United States and Britain document a decline in the public's identification with political parties and growing disenchantment with par-

8

ties in general. In another place (Dalton et al., 1984, chap. 15) we describe these patterns as the *decomposition* of established party alignments.

These trends are at least partially the result of the addition of new issues to the political agenda and the difficulties the established parties have had in responding to these issues. New parties have arisen across the face of Europe — from the Greens in West Germany to the Social Democrats in Britain — and new political movements seek access to the Democratic and Republican parties in the United States. Increased party volatility is also caused by the changing characteristics of contemporary publics. Unsophisticated voters once relied on social-group cues and party leaders as a basis for making political decisions. Because of the dramatic spread of education and information sources, more citizens are now able to deal with the complexities of politics and make their own political decisions. Consequently, issues are becoming a more important basis of voting behavior as the influence of traditional party and group allegiances wanes. The new style of citizen politics includes a more sophisticated and issue-oriented public.

Finally, discussions of a crisis of confidence facing political institutions and political leaders are now commonplace (chapter 11). Evidence from several nations indicates a decline in trust of political elites and institutions. The conflict over new issues and new participation patterns may be a partial explanation of these trends. In addition, emerging value priorities that stress individualism and political participation produce skepticism of elite-controlled hierarchical organizations (such as bureaucracies, political parties, and large interest groups). Some observers therefore suggest that a more demanding and assertive mass public will be a continuing feature of the democratic process in advanced industrial societies.

The development of this new style of citizen politics places new strains on democratic systems. Protests, social movements, partisan volatility, and political distrust are disrupting the traditional political order. Adjustment to new issue concerns and new patterns of citizen participation may be a difficult process. But instead of a crisis of democracy, these are signs of growth. More people now take democratic ideals seriously, and they expect political systems to live up to these ideals. The new style of citizen politics is a sign of vitality and an opportunity for Western societies to make further progress toward their democratic goals.

Notes

1. Most of the data analyzed in this volume were acquired from the Inter-university Consortium for Political and Social Research in Ann Arbor. Additional data were made available by the ESRC Archive, University of Essex, England; the Zentralarchiv fuer empirische Sozialforschung, University of Cologne, West Germany; and the Banque de Donnees Socio-Politiques, University of Grenoble, France. See the appendix for additional information on the major data sources. Neither these archives nor the original collectors of the data bear responsibility for the analyses presented here.

2. For a brief review of these nations, see Almond and Powell (1988) and Jacobs et al. (1983). More detailed national studies can be found in Rose (1986) for Britain, Dalton (1988) and Conradt (1986) for West Germany, and Ehrmann (1983) for France.

PART ONE

Politics and
the Public

2. The Nature of Mass Beliefs

Any discussion of citizen politics is ultimately grounded on basic assumptions about the political abilities of the electorate — the public's level of knowledge, understanding, and interest in political matters. For voters to make meaningful decisions, they must understand the options on which they are voting. Citizens must know the workings of the political system if they intend to influence and control the actions of their representatives. In short, for citizen politics to be meaningful, the electorate must possess at least a basic level of political sophistication.

Another reason for examining the sophistication of voters is to improve our understanding of the public opinion data presented in this volume. With what depth of understanding and conviction are opinions held? Do survey responses largely represent reasoned assessments of the issues or the snap judgments of individuals faced by an interviewer on their doorstep? It is common to see the public labeled as uninformed (especially when public opinion conflicts with the speaker's own views). Conversely, the electorate cannot be wiser than when it supports one's own position. Can we judge the merits of either position based on public opinion surveys?

Despite several decades of public opinion polling, analysts still disagree in their evaluations of the public's political sophistication. The fundamental source of controversy involves differing views of how sophisticated the public should be in order for democracies to fulfill their political ideals. These different perspectives are based on political theory, historical evidence, and normative assumptions about democratic politics.

The Supercitizen

Historically, many theorists maintained that democracy was workable only when the public possessed a high degree of political information and sophistication. Mill, Locke, Tocqueville, and other writers saw these public traits as essential requirements for a successful democratic system. Moreover, most theorists claimed that the citizenry should be supportive of the political system and share a deep commitment to democratic ideals such as pluralism, free expression, and minority rights (see chapter 11). Otherwise, an uninformed and unsophisticated electorate might be manipulated to distort the democratic process. Democracies required an ever-attentive public. In a sense, some democratic theorists posited a supercitizen model: The public must be a paragon of civic virtue in order for democracy to survive.

This model of the ideal democratic citizen was often discussed in reference to the American electorate.[1] A popular lore grew up about the sophistication of the American public. Alexis de Tocqueville praised the social and community involvement of Americans when he described the United States in the nineteenth century. Voters in early America supposedly yearned for the stimulating political debates of election campaigns and flocked to political rallies in great numbers. The New England town hall meetings became a legendary example of the American political spirit. Even on the frontier, it was claimed, conversations around the general store's cracker barrel displayed a deep interest and concern with political matters.

While these democratic norms were initially of European origins, the historical experience of many European nations painted a less positive picture of the average citizen. The vote came much later to the mass of Western European citizens, often delayed until the beginning of the twentieth century. The aristocratic institutions and deferential traditions of British politics limited citizen participation beyond the act of voting and severely restricted the size of the eligible electorate. In France, the excesses of the French Revolution undercut public support for the principle of mass participation. In addition, the instability of the political system supposedly produced a sense of *incivism*, and people avoided political discussions and political involvement.

Germany presented the most graphic example of what might follow when democratic norms fail to develop among the public. Democracy in West Germany is a development of the post-World War II period; previously, the Germans simply lacked strong democratic traditions. Authoritarian governments ruled during the Wilhelmine Empire (1871-1918); under this regime, citizens were taught to be seen and not heard. The democratic Weimar Republic (1919-32) was but a brief, and turbulent, interlude in Germany's nondemocratic history. The frailties of popular democratic norms during the Weimar Republic contributed to the system's demise and the rise of National Socialism. One of the major topics preoccupying social science for the next several decades was the question of why Germans allowed democracy to fail and be replaced by the horrors of Hitler's Third Reich. These historical experiences strengthened the belief that a sophisticated, involved, and democratic public was a necessary requirement for democracy to succeed.

The Unsophisticated Citizen

The advent of scientific survey sampling in the 1940s and 1950s provided the first opportunity to move beyond the insights of political theorists and social commentators and to study public opinion directly. The lofty images of the democratic citizen could be tested against reality. The public itself was directly consulted.

In contrast to the classic image of the democratic citizen in political theory, these early surveys painted an unflattering picture of the average citizen. The political sophistication of mass publics fell far short of the supercitizen model of classic democratic theory. For most citizens, political interest and involvement barely extended beyond casting an occasional vote in national or state elections. Furthermore, citizens apparently brought very little understanding to their participation in politics. It was not clear that voting decisions were based on rational evaluations of candidates and their issue positions; voting was conditioned by group loyalties and personalistic considerations. The seminal work in the area succinctly summarized the findings:

> Our data reveal that certain requirements commonly assumed for the successful operation of democracy are not met by the behavior of the "average" citizen. . . . Many vote without real involvement in the election. . . . The citizen is not highly informed on the details of the campaign. . . . In any rigorous or narrow sense the voters are not highly rational. (Berelson et al., 1954, pp. 307-10)

These early findings were substantiated by the landmark study, *The American Voter* (Campbell et al., 1960). Campbell and his colleagues documented a lack of ideological awareness or understanding by the American electorate. Criticism of the public's political sophistication focused on three points. First, public opinion apparently lacked a general ideological structure. Most individuals did not evaluate political phenomena in terms of a broad ideological framework, such as liberalism versus conservatism or capitalism versus socialism. Second, there seemed to be only a weak relationship between issues that presumably were connected. Many people expressed unrelated or inconsistent opinions on specific issue questions. For example, voters who felt taxes were too high nevertheless favored increases in spending for many specific government programs. Third, issue beliefs were not very stable over time. An analysis of the same group of individuals interviewed in 1956, 1958, and 1960 found that the opinions of many citizens seemed to fluctuate capriciously (Converse, 1964). The lack of structure, consistency, and stability led Converse to conclude that public opinion researchers were often studying "nonattitudes" (Converse, 1970). On numerous issues of long-standing political concern, many voters apparently lacked informed opinions or *any* opinions. *The American Voter* concluded that the electorate "is almost completely unable to judge the rationality of government actions; knowing little of the particular policies and what has led to them, the mass electorate is not able either to appraise its goals or the appropriateness of the means chosen to secure these goals" (Campbell et al., 1960, p. 543). This research was soon followed by a series of surveys indicating that many citizens could not name their elected representatives, were unfamiliar with the institutions of government, and did not understand the mechanics of the political process. The image of the American voter had fallen to a new low.

This view of the unsophisticated citizen was generalized to Western European voters (Margolis, 1979, chap. 4). Once one moved beyond election turnout, political involvement in Europe was frequently lower than in the United States. Converse and Dupeux (1962) found that the level of political interest in France was lower than in the United States, despite the tumultuous and polarized nature of the French party system. French voters also lacked well-formed opinions on the pressing issues of the day (Converse, 1975b). Similar evidence emerged from surveys of the British public (Butler and Stokes, 1969). Sixty percent of Britons did not recognize the terms *Left* and *Right* as they applied to politics. There were again the telltale signs of nonattitudes—weak linkages between opinions on seemingly related issues and excessive opinion instability over time.

An influential survey by Gabriel Almond and Sidney Verba (1963) provided a comparison of public opinion in five nations—the United States, Britain, West Germany, Italy, and Mexico—during the late 1950s. Although the levels of political involvement and understanding generally were highest in the United States, the overall results spoke negatively about Western publics. Only a minority in each nation discussed politics frequently, and few citizens even followed news accounts of politics and government affairs on a regular basis.

Having found that most citizens failed to meet the requirements of classic democratic theory, this new generation of political scientists faced a paradox. Most individuals were not "good" democratic citizens, and yet democracies such as the United States and Great Britain had existed for generations. Gradually, an *elitist theory of democracy* developed as scholars attempted to interpret these survey findings in a positive light (Berelson et al., 1954, pp. 313-23; Almond and Verba, 1963, chap. 15). The new theory contended that democratic politics might prove unworkable if every citizen was active on every issue at all times. Images of the centrifugal forces destroying the Weimar Republic were fresh in many minds and generated concerns about the possible effects of excessive citizen participation. Consequently, they suggested that the model citizen "is not the active citizen; he is the potentially active citizen" (Almond and Verba, 1963,

p. 347). Citizens must believe that they can influence the government, and must be willing to make the effort if the issue is sufficiently important. But few citizens will realize this potential. This balance between action and potential presumably assured that political elites had enough freedom to make necessary decisions and that these decisions were made with the public in mind.

Another element of the new theory stressed the heterogeneity of the public. "Some people are and should be highly interested in politics, but not everyone is or needs to be" (Berelson et al., 1954, p. 315). From this perspective, the responsiveness of the political system was assured by a small core of active citizens, leaving the rest of the public blissfully uninformed and uninvolved. This mix between involved and indifferent voters reportedly assured the stability and flexibility of democratic systems.

The elitist theory of democracy was drawn from the realities of political life — or at least from the hard evidence of survey research. It is, however, a very undemocratic theory of democracy (Pateman, 1980; Barber, 1984). The theory maintains that "the democratic citizen . . . must be active, yet passive; involved, yet not too involved; influential, yet deferential" (Almond and Verba, 1963, pp. 478-79). The values and goals of democracy were at least partially obscured by a mountain of survey data.

Accepting this new creed, some analysts used this evidence to justify an extreme elitist model of the democratic process (Dye and Zeigler, 1970; Crozier et al., 1975; Brittan, 1975; Huntington, 1981). These critics of the public implied that citizen activism is undemocratic and politically destabilizing. Thomas Dye and Harmon Zeigler (1970) bluntly claimed:

> The survival of democracy depends upon the commitment of elites to democratic ideals rather than upon broad support for democracy by the masses. Political apathy and nonparticipation among the masses contribute to the survival of democracy. Fortunately for democracy, the antidemocratic masses are generally more apathetic than elites. (p. 328)

In other words, if a supportive and quiescent public ensures a smoothly functioning political system, then it is virtually the duty of the average citizen to remain unconcerned about politics. When citizens began to challenge political elites during the turbulent 1960s, these political scientists cautioned that democracy required that the public should follow and should not question political elites too extensively. Too much democracy, it was argued, could threaten the democratic process.

This theory of unsophisticated voters and elitist democracy has been challenged on both normative and empirical grounds in recent years (Wright, 1976; Almond and Verba, 1980). Certainly, modern electorates are not comprised of full-time politicos; but at the same time, the picture is not nearly as bleak as that painted by early survey research. More than a quarter century has passed since the stereotype of the unsophisticated citizen was established. A reassessment is necessary.

Political Sophistication Reconsidered

Our challenge to conventional descriptions of a generally unsophisticated electorate is based on several points. Western societies have undergone profound social and political changes in the postwar period that have increased the public's political abilities. In addition, we now have a more refined knowledge of the methodological strengths and weaknesses of survey research. Finally, and most important, past research has enriched our understanding of how voters conceptualize political matters. Each point deserves detailed attention.

A PROCESS OF COGNITIVE MOBILIZATION

During the past thirty years a dramatic transformation in the characteristics of Western mass publics has occurred. The political skills and resources of contemporary electorates—traits such as education, media exposure, and political awareness—are vastly improved over the levels of the 1950s. These trends have contributed to a growth in the public's overall level of political sophistication, or what is described as a process of *cognitive mobilization* (Inglehart, 1977, chaps. 10-12; Dalton, 1984a). Cognitive mobilization means that citizens possess the level of political skills and resources necessary to become self-sufficient in politics. Instead of depending on elites and reference groups (external mobilization), citizens are now better able to deal with the complexities of politics and make their own political decisions.

The most visible change involves the educational levels of Western mass publics. Advanced industrial societies require a more educated and technically sophisticated electorate, and postwar affluence has provided the funding for an expanded educational system (see chapter 1). University enrollments grew during the 1950s and then exploded upward in the 1960s. Between 1950 and 1975, university enrollments increased by 347 percent in the United States, 472 percent in Britain, 503 percent in West Germany, and 586 percent in France— far outstripping population growth rates. These trends gradually are producing a fundamental change in the educational level of contemporary electorates. Older, less-educated generations slowly are leaving the electorate and are being replaced by better-educated young people. For instance, almost half of the electorate eligible for the 1948 American election was composed of people with a primary education or less. At that time, the number of Americans with only grade school education outnumbered those with some college by about three to one. By 1984 the college-educated portion of the electorate grew to outnumber the voters with only primary education by a three-to-one ratio, and the college educated made up about 40 percent of the total electorate. Parallel changes are transforming European mass publics. In postwar West Germany the number of citizens with only primary schooling exceeded those with a secondary school diploma (*Mittlere Reife*) by approximately five to one; today, the better-educated group is nearly two times larger than the lesser educated.

There is not a direct one-to-one relationship between years of schooling and political sophistication. Nevertheless, the evidence from survey research is virtually unanimous in indicating that education is strongly linked to a citizen's level of political knowledge, interest, and involvement. A doubling of the public's educational level may not necessarily double the level of political sophistication, but some increase should occur. Contemporary electorates are clearly the most educated in the long history of democracies — and this should contribute toward making a more sophisticated electorate and a new style of citizen politics.

At the same time that the cognitive skills of Western mass publics have improved, so too have the publics' political resources. The expansion of the mass media, especially television, greatly increases access to political information. The average citizen once might have suffered from a lack of information; today, there is a nearly unlimited supply and variety of political news. The growth of the mass media is a well-known fact, but it is easy to forget how much has changed in the past few decades.

Thirty years ago, it took a substantial effort for an individual to remain informed about politics. One could read newspapers or magazines; this was a time-consuming task, however, especially for an electorate with limited education. Particularly in Britain and West Germany, the printed press is of uneven quality, and many mass newspapers are little more than scandal sheets. Radio expanded access to political information, but the major change came with the advent of television.

Television is a ubiquitous part of contemporary life, although in the early 1950s it was still a novelty to most Americans and a luxury to most Europeans. At that time, about half of American homes had a television set, less than 10 percent in Britain and France, and less than 5 percent in West Germany. The expansion of television ownership over the next two decades was closely paralleled by the public's increasing reliance on television as a source of political information (figure 2.1). In the 1952 American election 51 percent of the electorate utilized television news; by 1960, this had risen to a plateau of about 90 percent. In 1961 only 50 percent of the West German public depended on

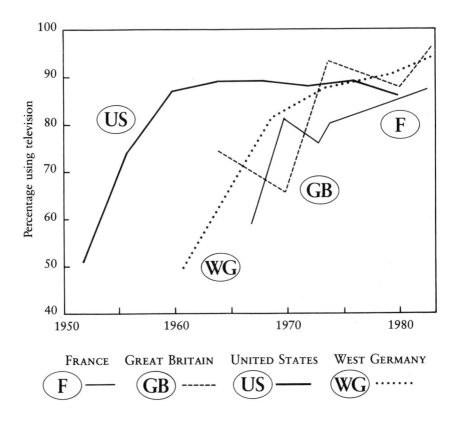

FIGURE 2.1

THE GROWTH OF TELEVISION AS A SOURCE OF POLITICAL INFORMATION

sources: *United States,* SRC/CPS Election Studies; *Great Britain,* 1963-74, British Election Studies; 1980-83, Eurobarometers; *West Germany,* 1961-69, West German Election Studies; 1974, Baker and Norpoth (forthcoming); 1980-83, Eurobarometers; *France,* 1965-74, Gallup (1976b); 1980-83, Eurobarometers.

television for political information; by 1974, the 90 percent plateau also had been reached. The available data from Britain and France present a similar pattern.

As television viewership has increased, so too has the amount of political information provided by the medium. The now-standard American nightly half-hour national news program was inaugurated only in 1963. Since then, technology and viewer interest have increased the scope of network programming devoted to news and political affairs. Today, news reporting is instantaneous and done on a worldwide scale. Many Americans now have access to news on a 24-hour-a-day basis through cable and satellite television. European television contains an even larger proportion of news and political information because the government supervises national networks (BBC in Britain, ZDF and ARD in West Germany, TF1/A2/FR3 in France). The time devoted to news, politics, and current events constitutes about a third of all television programming in France and West Germany, and about a quarter in Britain. European television is partially constrained by government oversight and the small number of available channels; but these factors are also changing. Government limits on television have gradually weakened in all three European countries. For example, before the 1964 election, the BBC was prohibited from carrying election news during the campaign period; now television coverage is a central part of British campaigns. The reorganization of French national television in 1974 expanded the autonomy of the French media, and the Mitterrand government encouraged even greater press freedom. Moreover, cable and satellite television are being introduced in Western Europe. A further expansion in television usage and greater diversity in television programming thus lie ahead.

As a consequence of these trends, television now plays a primary role in informing and educating the public in most Western democracies (table 2.1). Television is uniformly cited as the most frequently used information source, even though slightly different questions were asked in the four nations.[2] It should also be noted, however, that the high ranking for television does not mean that other media are necessarily used less often. With the exception of radio, public usage of most media apparently has remained stable or increased over the past

TABLE 2.1

MOST IMPORTANT SOURCE OF POLITICAL INFORMATION

(IN PERCENT)

	United States 1980	Great Britain 1983	West Germany 1980	France 1974
Television	62	63	51	63
Papers/magazines	27	29	22	13
Personal conversation	— [a]	3	16	8
Radio	11	4	6	10
Other/no opinion	0	1	5	6
TOTAL	100%	100%	100%	100%

SOURCES: *United States,* CPS Election Study; *Great Britain,* Dunleavy and Husbands (1985, p. 111); *West Germany,* Noelle-Neumann (1981); *France,* Cayrol (1980, p. 148).

a. Response was not available.

twenty years (Baker et al., 1981, chap. 3; Asher, 1985). Opinion surveys routinely find that large majorities of the public regularly watch television, read news in the papers and magazines, and hear news on the radio. Contemporary publics thus have access to a rich array of media sources that would have been unimaginable a generation ago. These increases in the quantity and quality of political information provided by the media should encourage an improved public awareness of political affairs.

A final trend affecting the political sophistication of the public is the growing politicization of Western societies. During the past thirty years governments have assumed increasing influence over the everyday lives of their citizens. In simple economic terms, between 1950 and 1980 the government's share of the gross domestic product (GDP) increased significantly in all four of the nations under study (Heidenheimer et al., 1983, chap. 5). In 1980 public expenditures accounted for over a third of the GDP in the United States and almost half in Britain, West Germany, and France. Similarly, governments now take a more activist policymaking role in a wide variety of areas from traditional economic policy matters to family and social programs to new energy and environmental policies.

Public opinion data suggest that citizens recognize the increasing impact of politics on their daily lives. Western publics now feel that the resolution of most social problems is the responsibility of government (Heidenheimer et al., 1983, chap. 12). A longitudinal study of the personal hopes and fears of Americans finds that politically relevant concerns increased between the late 1950s and early 1970s (Nie et al., 1979, p. 108).

The growing relevance of politics to the individual citizen should stimulate greater attention to politics and government affairs. Figure 2.2 presents several measures of general political interest tracked over time.[3] Interest and participation in specific elections may vary widely from campaign to campaign, but these data suggest a secular trend of increasing interest in politics by Western publics. General political interest has grown most steadily in West Germany, partially for the reasons cited above and partially because of the nation's resocialization to democracy. Yet there are similar trends of expanding political interest in the United States, Britain, and France. The available evidence is often incomplete, and different survey questions are used in each nation, but the trend of increasing political interest is unmistakable.

In sum, contemporary electorates are substantially more educated, have easier access to more political information, and are more interested in politics than the electorates of a generation ago. The consequences of this process of cognitive mobilization can be seen in several areas. The debate over the electorate's sophistication has focused on the public's ideological awareness, deter-

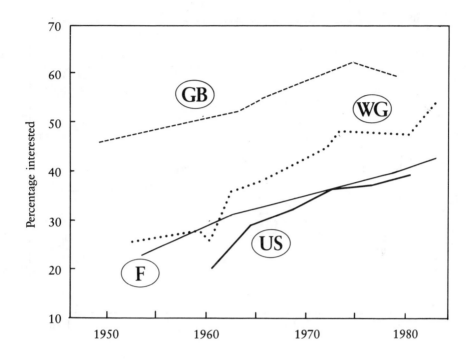

FIGURE 2.2

INTEREST IN POLITICS

SOURCES: *United States,* SRC/CPS Election Studies; *Great Britain,* 1949, Gallup (1976a); 1963-79, British Election Studies; *West Germany,* 1952-83, Noelle-Neumann and Piel (1984); Conradt (1980); *France,* 1953 and 1978, Charlot (1980); 1962, Gallup (1976b); 1983, Eurobarometer 19.

mined by whether citizens use ideological concepts in evaluating political parties (Converse, 1964). Time-series data from the United States and West Germany indicate an increase in this highest level of ideological sophistication (figure 2.3). In 1956, at the time *The American Voter* was written, only 12 percent of the American public actively used ideological concepts in evaluating the Republican and Democratic parties. This group of "ideologues" increased to 27 percent during the tumultuous years of the mid-1960s, and in the 1980s stands at nearly double the 1950s level. The shorter German trend is also moving upward, and suggestive evidence from Great Britain indicates growing ideological sophistication among the British public (Klingemann, 1979, p. 233). We see shortly that this definition of ideologues may significantly underestimate the sophistication of contemporary electorates.

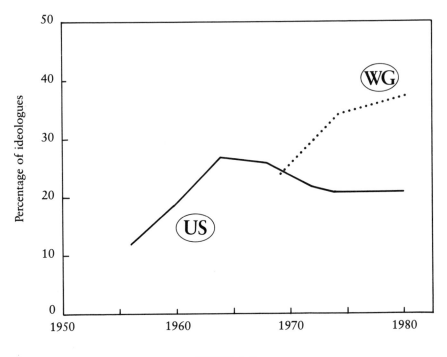

FIGURE 2.3

PERCENTAGE OF POLITICAL IDEOLOGUES

SOURCES: *United States,* 1956-80, Pierce et al. (1982); *West Germany,* 1969-74, Klingemann (1979); 1980, Klingemann, personal communication.

Indications of a changing electorate also are apparent in other aspects of mass politics. The present level of issue voting is generally higher than during earlier periods (see chapter 9). Cognitive mobilization is also expanding political participation to include more demanding forms of political activity. Many of these specific trends are examined much more closely in the following chapters, but it is clear that the stereotype of an unsophisticated voter is much less applicable today than it was during the 1950s.

PROBLEMS OF MEASUREMENT

The description of the public as unsophisticated also has been challenged on a variety of methodological grounds. In the simplest case, the issue is whether the appropriate questions are being asked. For instance, early surveys found that few voters could recall the name of their congressman — an apparent indication of a poorly informed public. When the task is name recognition rather

TABLE 2.2

LEVELS OF IDEOLOGICAL AWARENESS

(IN PERCENT)

	Active use of Ideology	Recognition/ Understanding Left and Right	Left/Right Placement
West Germany	34	56	92
Netherlands	36	48	90
Great Britain	21	23	82
France	— a	— a	81
Switzerland	9	39	79
Austria	19	39	75
Italy	55	54	74
United States	21	34	67

SOURCES: *France*, Eurobarometer 12; *other nations*, Political Action Survey, 1974-75.

a. Data were not available.

than recall, however, most electors (over 70 percent) can identify their representative (Mann, 1978). Mann argues that the necessary level of political knowledge is more realistically measured by the name-recognition question, and thus conclusions about the public's political sophistication are dramatically altered. This same argument could be made for most measures of political (and nonpolitical) knowledge.

Question format also has a dramatic affect on assessments of the public's overall ideological sophistication. The first column in table 2.2 presents the proportion of the public in several nations who actively use ideological concepts in evaluating political parties (similar to figure 2.3). These data suggest that the active use of ideological thinking is still limited in most Western democracies. Nevertheless, if citizens are presented with the ideological labels *Left* and *Right,* a much higher percentage of the public can recognize these concepts and explain them in ideological terms. A third definition of ideology merely requires that voters can locate themselves on a Left/Right scale, without having to articulate the meaning of the scale. By this standard, the vast majority of Western publics can be described as ideological.

The data in table 2.2 also highlight the importance of context when measuring public opinion. The percent of the public displaying an active use of ideological thinking ranges from 9 percent in Switzerland to 55 percent in Italy. These patterns probably do not signify intrinsic differences in the conceptual abilities of these publics; the nature of political competition in each nation is a more likely explanation.[4] For instance, the polarized nature of Italian politics (including a large Communist party) yields high levels of ideological usage and recognition, even though Italians have less education and political interest than most of the other nationalities in the table. Conversely, the moderate climate of American politics leads to a low level of ideological sophistication on this measure, when compared to most other nations. This low ranking for the United States is ironic, since the American electorate has been the primary basis of research on citizen political sophistication.

Another measurement controversy involves the concept of issue consistency. During the 1970s researchers found evidence of substantial increases in the relationship between the opinions held by the American electorate (Nie with Andersen, 1974; Nie and Rabjohn, 1979). Opinions on various issues were becoming more strongly interrelated. Subsequent analyses indicated that a major portion of the increased constraint was caused by improvements in question wording and format (Sullivan et al., 1978; Bishop et al., 1978). Critics of citizen sophistication therefore argued that political sophistication was not growing as rapidly as others claimed. In the ensuing debate the major lesson of these data was often overlooked. The effects of question format meant that early researchers had significantly *underestimated* the issue consistency of the electorate.

Debates over question wording and format highlight a more fundamental concern of opinion researchers. By most standards, survey research is a fairly blunt tool for measuring public opinion. Complex beliefs must be simplified to categories such as *agree* or *disagree,* and the dividing line between response categories often is imprecise. What exactly is the difference between following politics *sometimes* versus *now and then*? It is easy to imagine how a person may give different responses to the same question even if his or her interest in politics remains essentially constant. Faced with unclear or insufficient question options, the public's responses to survey questions may appear as inconsistent or unstable. The imprecision of the survey instrument (measurement error) thus contributes to perceptions of an unsophisticated electorate.

The magnitude of the measurement problem can be substantial. Campbell, Converse, and Rodgers (1979, p. 185), for example, find a .71 correlation between two identical questions measuring satisfaction with housing asked thirty minutes apart in a survey. Clearly, most people know whether they are satisfied with their own homes, and little should change in such a short time. These researchers therefore attribute instability largely to the imprecision of the housing-satisfaction question. This instability is not much different from the correlations of some political opinions over a two-year period, which Converse (1964; Converse and Markus, 1979) interprets as evidence of a lack of political attitudes.

Social psychologists and survey methodologists are well aware of the consequences of measurement error, and advanced statistical techniques can compensate for these measurement problems. When measurement error is taken into account, the stability of political opinions is much higher than previously recognized (Judd et al., 1981; cf. Converse, 1980). In addition, the relationships between opinions in different policy areas is much stronger (Judd and Milburn, 1980). We now realize that opinion instability and limited issue constraint are at least partially a product of imprecise measurement.

The methodological evidence thus points in the same direction. As our expertise in survey research methods has improved, so too has our evaluation of the public's political sophistication.

SOPHISTICATION VERSUS SATISFICING

It probably was inevitable that early empirical studies would reach negative conclusions about the public's political sophistication. Citizens were judged against the lofty ideals of classic democratic theory, and reality fell short of the theoretical ideals. When this occurred, analysts stressed the shortfall. A more balanced view of the topic is needed; stripping away the idealized standards of classic democratic theory and the rationalizations of elitist democracy theory, and looking at politics from the perspective of the voter. Several decades of survey research yield a better understanding of how citizens actually deal with the complexities of politics.

Politics is only one part of people's lives. Given the pressing needs of a family and career, the time that can be devoted to politics is limited. The typical American, British, West German, or French citizen cannot afford to keep informed on all political issues — few political elites or political scientists attempt this task. Similarly, participation in politics must be balanced against other time commitments. Citing these factors, the elitist democracy theorists argue that many (or most) citizens are overwhelmed and become political dropouts, and democracy is better for it. While politics is complex, it also is an activity that has important effects on one's life. Most citizens do not drop out of politics altogether. Instead, they find a means of balancing the costs and benefits of political activity. Between the extremes of full-time political activity and dropping out there is a realistic middle course.

In order to manage the demands of politics, most people seek ways to lessen the costs of political involvement. One method is to focus one's political interests. Instead of following all issues, citizens appear to concentrate their attention on a few topics of direct personal relevance or interest. The total electorate thus is divided into a number of partially overlapping *issue publics* (Converse, 1964). Simply expressing an opinion is not sufficient to establish membership in an issue public, since many people will state an opinion when confronted by an interviewer even if they have given little prior thought to the topic.

An issue public implies that citizens have devoted prior attention to the issue and possess firm beliefs. Many farmers, for example, closely monitor government agricultural policy while paying scant attention to urban renewal programs. Parents with school-age children may display considerable interest in educational policies, while the elderly may show a special concern for social security. The largest issue publics generally exist for topics of broad public concern, such as economic policy, taxes, and basic social programs. At the other extreme, only a small number of voters regularly follow issues relating to foreign aid, agriculture, or international trade. Very few citizens are interested in every issue, but most citizens are members of at least one issue public. To paraphrase Will Rogers, "Everybody is sophisticated, only on different subjects."

The concept of issue publics has basic implications for the study of political sophistication. When citizens are allowed to define politics in terms of their own interests, a surprising level of political sophistication often appears. Robert Lane's conversations with a group of working-class men finds coherent individual systems of political beliefs that sharply conflict with the findings of survey research (Lane, 1962). David RePass (1971) documents a high level of rational issue voting when citizens are able to identify their own issue interests. Opinion stability also is higher among members of the relevant issue public (Converse, 1964, pp. 244-45; Schuman and Presser, 1981, chap. 9). Thus, low issue constraint and low issue stability in public opinion surveys do not necessarily mean the electorate is unsophisticated; the alternative explanation is that not all citizens are interested in all issues.

Philip Converse views issue publics as a negative aspect of mass opinion because a proliferation of distinct issue groups works against policymaking based on a broad, coherent ideological framework. Converse's criticism may be overstated, however. If citizens limit their issue interests, this does not mean that they fail to evaluate these issues in terms of a broad political framework. Different clusters of issue interests still may emanate from a common underlying set of values. In addition, Lane (1973, 1962) points out the potential negative consequences of an overly structured and constrained belief system; for example, dogmatism and intolerance. In a slightly different context, analysts maintain that the existence of a large number of competing political groups, with overlapping and cross-cutting memberships and shifting political alignments, is an essential characteristic of pluralist democracy (Dahl, 1971). Issue publics may, therefore, be a positive aspect of citizen politics.

Another method of managing the complexity of politics is to rely on one or more reference standards to simplify political decisions. Social groups provide one common source of political cues. A large number of policy issues can be cast in terms of conflicts between class, religious, ethnic, or other social groupings. Membership in a social group, either formally or through psychological ties, can be a valuable guidepost in dealing with these policy questions. The French steelworker, for example, might prefer nationalizing industry because he feels it will benefit working-class interests; an avowed French Catholic presumably supports government aid for religious schools. These voters may not be able to explain their policy preferences in terms of sophisticated ideological arguments or specific legislative proposals, but they still are making reasonable political choices.

Early voting studies emphasized social groups as a source of voting cues. Lazarsfeld et al. (1948) constructed an *index of political predisposition* based on social class, religion, and rural/urban residence; this index was a potent predictor of American voting behavior. The highly stratified nature of Western European societies produces even stronger group differences in European voting patterns. Furthermore, studies of ideological sophistication find that group references are one of the most frequently used bases of party evaluation. For many less educated citizens, group references may reflect a broad political orientation that they have difficulty explaining in the terminology that would classify them as sophisticated ideologues. When the social conflicts in which a voter is involved are clear, and the parties take clear positions with regard to these conflicts, then social characteristics can provide sufficient cues for orienting oneself to politics.

An even more powerful source of political cues is partisanship. Many citizens develop a psychological bond to a specific political party that may persist through an entire lifetime (Campbell et al., 1960, chap. 6). This *party identification* often is based on emotional and nonrational criteria, such as strict inheritance of parental partisanship, and may serve as a surrogate for social-reference-group cues. But party attachments also contain a rational evaluative component which changes to incorporate new political experiences (Fiorina, 1981; Alt, 1984).

Although the usefulness of social-group cues is limited to topics directly related to group interests, party identification has broader applications (Miller, 1976). Parties are the central actors of democratic politics, so almost all political phenomena can be evaluated within a partisan framework. Party attachments obviously can simplify voting choices, since virtually all elections involve a choice between parties. In Western Europe, where parties act as cohesive units, party voting is an effective and efficient method of decision making. The heterogeneity of American parties lessens the policy value of party voting, but the complexity of American elections still makes party a valuable voting cue. Partisanship is also an important force in shaping evaluations of political leaders and new political issues (Baker et al., 1981, chap. 8; Niemi and Westholm, 1984;

Barnes and Pierce, 1971). If voters are unsure about an issue, party cues can suggest where their interests lie. An issue supported by one's party is more likely to benefit the individual, while the policies of the opposition are suspect. In sum, because of its ability to make sense of distant, complicated, and often arcane political phenomena, party identification frequently is viewed as the central thread connecting the citizen and the political process.

Finally, Left/Right orientations may serve as another source of political cues. Although most voters do not express sophisticated ideological views, they still can locate themselves in terms of a broad ideological family, or *tendance* (see table 2.2 on page 25). This Left/Right orientation summarizes the issue opinions of a citizen and provides a reference structure for evaluating political objects (Inglehart and Klingemann, 1976; Klingemann, 1979). In most nations partisanship and ideological orientations exist side by side and tend to have reinforcing effects. However, Left/Right orientations hold special importance in political systems where party cues are weak; for example, in France. The French party system is notoriously volatile, which undercuts the continuity and value of partisanship. Ideological tendance thus plays a larger role in guiding the political behavior of the French electorate (Percheron and Jennings, 1981). By evaluating politics in a Left/Right framework, the French voter can bring some order to an ever-changing political landscape.

The diverse political criteria that citizens utilize is suggested by the results in table 2.3. Citizens in several nations were asked to evaluate the good and

TABLE 2.3

BASES OF PARTY EVALUATIONS[a]

(IN PERCENT)

Criteria based on	United States	Great Britain	West Germany
Ideological concepts	21	21	34
Social groups	40	41	45
Party organization and competence	49	35	66
Policy concepts	45	46	53
Nature of the times	64	59	86
Political figures	40	18	38
Intrinsic values	46	65	49
No content	14	18	6
TOTAL	319[a]	303	377

SOURCE: Political Action Study, 1974-75.

a. Totals exceed 100% because multiple responses were possible.

bad points of two major political parties in their nation. In general, only a small number of citizens actively employ ideological concepts in evaluating the parties (see also table 2.2); this does not mean, however, that the remaining individuals are devoid of political judgments. Approximately 40 percent of the American, British, and West German electorates evaluated the parties according to social-group alignments. An even larger group of voters judged the parties in terms of their organization and political competency. Outright policy criteria were mentioned in nearly half of the survey responses. Even the broadest and most frequently used criteria—evaluating parties in terms of the nature of the times—provided a meaningful basis of decision making. In short, far from suggesting that citizens in Western democracies are uninformed and unsophisticated, these data indicate a diversity and complexity of public opinion that often is overlooked.

Politics and the Public

This chapter has focused on a set of changes affecting all advanced industrial democracies: the rise of political interest, cognitive skills, and information resources. There are, of course, important differences in these traits among our group of nations. Political interest and involvement apparently are more extensive in the United States than in Britain, West Germany, or France. Conversely, politics and public opinion generally are more ideological in Europe than in the United States. While subsequent chapters draw out these national differences in more detail, this chapter describes a broad pattern of increasing political sophistication that is common to publics in most Western democracies.

Even though the public's political sophistication has increased, democratic electorates will never match the political awareness and sophistication posited by classic democratic theory and displayed by political elites such as members of Congress or Parliament. It makes little sense to debate this point. Instead, the findings of survey research can be used more meaningfully to describe how citizens actually perceive and evaluate politics, and reach political decisions — how publics utilize the sophistication they now possess. The evidence of this chapter describes a pattern of public opinion that Kinder and Sears (1985) term the "pluralistic roots of political beliefs."

Citizens rely on various methods to manage the complexities of politics. Many voters focus their attention on a few issues of particular interest, rather than devote equal attention to all issues. Thus the electorate is composed of overlapping issue publics, each evaluating government action in terms of different policies. The bases of evaluation also vary within the electorate. Some citizens evaluate politics in terms of a broad ideological framework, but this constitutes only a minority of the public. Many more citizens depend on political cues, such as social-reference groups or party attachments, to guide their behavior. By limiting their issue interests and relying on political cues and other decision-making "shortcuts," the average voter is able to balance the costs and benefits of political involvement and still make reasonable political decisions.[5]

This pluralistic model has several implications for the study of public opinion that should guide the analyses in later chapters. Unstable or inconsistent issue opinions should not be interpreted as evidence that voters lack any attitudes. Survey questions are imprecise, the public's issue interests are specialized, and a complex mix of beliefs may be reflected in any single issue. In addition, we must be sensitive to the diversity and complexity of mass politics. Simple models of political behavior that assume a homogeneous electorate might be theoretically elegant and empirically parsimonious, but also unrealistic. Citizens function on the basis of diverse criteria and motivations. We should attempt to model this diversity, instead of adopting overly generalized theories of mass politics. Finally, we must not underestimate the potential for change. As this chapter has documented, the electorates of Western democracies have undergone a major transformation during the postwar period. Public opinion reflects a dynamic process, and static views of an unchanging (or unchangeable) public should be avoided.

We should not, of course, be guilty of overestimating the sophistication of Western publics. There will always be instances when the electorate holds ill-advised or ill-informed opinions; some citizens will remain ignorant of all political matters. Such is the imperfect nature of all human behavior. But, while few individuals deserve the rating of full ideologues, an equally small number are devoid of all bases of making meaningful political choices. The important lesson is not to ignore or belittle the varied criteria citizens rely on in dealing with politics.

The ultimate question, then, is not whether the public meets the maximum ideological standards of classic democratic theory but whether the public possesses a sufficient basis for rational political action. Phrased in these terms, and based on the evidence presented in this chapter, we can be more sanguine about the nature of belief systems in contemporary publics.

Notes

1. Other voices were more critical of the public's sophistication; notable was the work of Lippmann (1922).

2. The French question asked which source was most important in reaching a voting decision in 1974; in the other nations the question asked about information used more generally.

3. The British, West German, and French questions measure general interest in politics, although the question wording and response options are different in each nation. The American question asked whether respondents followed politics regularly, even between elections. Because of the differences in question wordings, the absolute levels of political interest should not be compared across nations; for such comparisons, see Barnes, Kaase et al. (1979), Almond and Verba (1963).

4. Similarly, figure 2.3 shows that the contextual influences on ideological sophistication also can change over time. The American public's ideological sophistication increases sharply during the polarized years of the mid-1960s and then declines in the 1970s as political conflict moderates.

5. The public's reliance on various decision-making shortcuts is similar to the pattern of "satisficing" behavior common to decision makers in business and government (Cyert and March, 1963). Only in dealing with the public, however, is such behavior denigrated.

3. Conventional Citizen Action

The new style of citizen politics extends beyond the call for an informed and concerned public. Citizen involvement in the political process is essential for democracy to be viable and meaningful. If political involvement is limited, then most analysts would agree that democracy is weak, because it is through discussion, popular interest, and participation in politics that societal goals should be defined and implemented in a democracy.

In recent history, authoritarian regimes temporarily have stripped away democratic rights in Western Europe; even some democratic leaders have resisted expansions of citizen input. A generally accepted belief within Western democracies maintains that public involvement in politics should be encouraged and maximized. When West Germans take the time to cast informed votes, British electors canvass their neighbors, or Americans write their president, the democratic process is at work.

Although the general objectives of participation may be similar for American, British, West German, and French citizens, the actual methods and contexts of citizen input often vary across nations. This chapter examines several methods of "conventional" citizen action. By this we mean voting, campaigns, group activities, and other methods normally associated with democratic politics. This does not mean that unconventional forms of participation (protests, demonstrations, etc.) are unimportant; they are, in fact, examined in the next chapter. Rather, the sources and motivations of conventional and unconventional participation are sufficiently important to deserve separate attention.

The Modes of Participation

Most discussions of citizen action equate the public's participation in politics with the act of voting. Although voting is the most visible and widespread form of citizen action, it certainly is not the only means of citizen input. The public's participation in politics is not limited to election periods, nor is voting necessarily the most effective means of influencing the political process. Moreover, for purposes of cross-national comparison, voting may be one of the least accurate measures of the public's overall involvement in the political process.

A rich set of cross-national studies has explored the different forms of conventional political action in which citizens might participate (Verba et al., 1971, 1978). These researchers find that various activities are not used interchangeably, as many early analysts assumed. Instead, people tend to specialize in activities that match their motivations and goals. Specific kinds of activities frequently cluster together; that is, a citizen who performs one act from a particular cluster is likely to perform other acts from the same cluster, but not necessarily activities from a different cluster. These clusters of activities are called *modes of democratic participation*, and several distinct modes of activity have been identified: voting, campaign activity, communal activity (working with a group in the community), and contacting officials on personal matters.[1]

Separate participation modes exist because political activities differ systematically in the requirements they place on the citizen and how the activities relate the individual to the government. Some activities are very demanding and may require a high level of political sophistication; other forms of political participation are fairly routine. Participation modes also differ in their goals. The public possesses considerable political power through its ability to select political leaders. Through primaries, caucuses, and elections, the public has its say in the choice of government leadership. Citizen action also may attempt to influence the policy decisions of political elites or inform the public and elites on pending policy issues. At other times, citizens may try to resolve specific administrative problems involving government agencies.

Verba and his colleagues categorize the differences between participation modes in terms of several criteria: (1) whether the influence exerted by the act conveys information about the individual's preferences and/or applies pressure for compliance; (2) whether the act is directed toward a broad social outcome or a particularized interest; (3) the potential degree of conflict involved in the activity; (4) the amount of effort and initiative required; and (5) the amount of cooperation with others required by the act (table 3.1).

Voting, for example, is a high-pressure activity because it determines control of the government, but its information content is limited because numerous issues are involved in an election. Voting also is a reasonably simple act that requires little initiative or cooperation with others. In contrast, participation in community groups requires considerably more effort by the individual and produces a qualitatively different form of citizen input. Thus, our discussion of citizen action in Western political systems focuses on the three most common modes of conventional participation: voting, campaign activity, and communal activity.[2]

TABLE 3.1
DIMENSIONS OF POLITICAL ACTIVITY AND MODES OF ACTIVITY

Mode of activity	Type of influence	Scope of outcome	Conflict	Initiative required	Cooperate with others
Voting	High pressure/low information	Collective	Conflictual	Little	Little
Campaign activity	High pressure/low to high information	Collective	Conflictual	Some	Some or much
Communal activity	Low to high pressure/ high information	Collective	Maybe yes/ maybe no	Some or much	Some or much
Contacting officials on personal matters	Low pressure/high information	Particular	Nonconflictual	Much	Little
Protest	High pressure/ high information	Collective	Very conflictual	Some or much	Some or much

SOURCE: Verba et al. (1978, p. 55) with modifications.

VOTING

The history of modern democracies has followed a pattern of almost ever-expanding citizen involvement in elections (Rokkan, 1970). The voting franchise in most nations initially was restricted to property owners, and long residency requirements existed. The United States was one of the first nations to begin liberalizing suffrage laws. By 1850 virtually the entire white adult male population in the United States was enfranchised. The extension of voting rights proceeded more slowly in Western Europe. These societies lacked the populist tradition that existed in the United States. In addition, social cleavages were polarized more sharply than in America; many European conservatives were hesitant to enfranchise a working class that might vote them out of office. An emerging socialist movement pressed for the political equality of the working class, but mass suffrage often was delayed until war or revolution disrupted the conservative political order. Voting rights were granted to French adult males with the formation of the Third Republic in 1870. Britain limited election rolls until early in the twentieth century by placing significant residency and financial restrictions on voting, and by allowing multiple votes for business owners and university graduates. Electoral reforms followed World War 1 and granted the vote to virtually all British males. Germany, too, had limited the franchise and allowed for multiple votes during the Wilhelmine Empire. True democratic elections with mass suffrage began with creation of the Weimar Republic in 1919.

During the twentieth century, suffrage rights were gradually extended to the rest of the adult population. The right of women to vote was acknowledged first in Britain (1918), and this was quickly followed in Germany (1919) and the United States (1920). French society lagged behind most of Western Europe in this instance; French women were enfranchised only in 1944. The Voting Rights Act of 1965 removed most of the remaining formal restrictions on the voting participation of American blacks. Finally, in the 1970s the voting age was uniformly lowered to 18 years of age in all four nations.

In contemporary democracies the right to vote now extends to virtually the entire adult population. There are, however, distinct national differences in the rate at which citizens actually turn out to vote. Figure 3.1 presents the turnout rates in recent national elections for our four nations. Voting rates are consistently higher in European elections, especially in West Germany where about 90 percent of the electorate casts a ballot in Bundestag elections. Voting turnout ranges between 70 and 80 percent in most British House of Commons and French National Assembly elections. In contrast, barely half of the eligible American electorate exercises its franchise in presidential elections and even less in congressional elections. Furthermore, American turnout rates have been declining almost steadily for the past two decades.

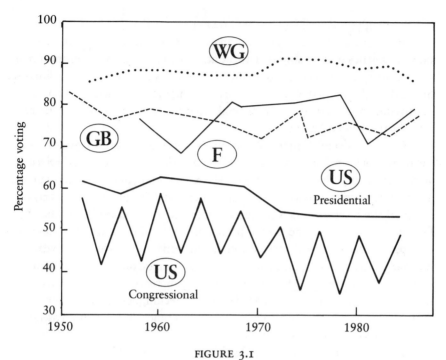

FIGURE 3.1

TURNOUT IN NATIONAL ELECTIONS

   The low American rates of voting often are cited as evidence of the electorate's limited political involvement. But a more complex set of factors is at work
(Powell, 1980, 1986; Crewe, 1981; Verba et al., 1978, chap. 4). Voter registration systems and other electoral procedures are a major influence on transatlan-
tic differences in turnout. Most European citizens are automatically included
on the roster of eligible voters, and these electoral registers are updated by the
government. Thus a larger percentage of the European public is eligible to participate in elections. In contrast, most Americans must make an initial application to vote, which dissuades many potential voters. By most estimates, participation in American elections would increase by at least ten percentage points
if the European system of electoral registers was adopted. Turnout also is encouraged by the scheduling of West German and French elections on weekends,
when more voters can find the time to visit the polls. In addition, the West
German electoral system and many others in Europe are based on proportional
representation (PR) rather than plurality-based single-member districts, as in
the United States and Britain. Proportional representation is generally believed
to stimulate turnout because any party, large or small, can increase its representation in the legislature as a direct function of its share of the popular vote.

G. Bingham Powell (1980, 1986) demonstrates that political competition is another strong influence on turnout rates. Sharp social or ideological cleavages between parties tend to stimulate turnout. The more polarized European party systems generally encourage higher voting rates than in the United States. Similarly, regional patterns of one-party dominance and the decreasing competitiveness of American congressional elections contribute to lower turnout rates in the United States.

While the overall pattern of turnout in national elections is well known, the participation mode of voting includes a broader range of electoral activities: voting for other political offices, primaries, referendums, and initiatives. In most Western democracies this total "amount of electing" is quite limited. Only one house of the bicameral national legislature is directly elected in Britain, West Germany, and France; the French president is one of the few directly elected European heads of state. Local, regional, and even national elections in Europe normally consist of casting a single ballot for a single office; the extensive list of elected offices and long ballots common to American elections are unknown in Western Europe. Finally, direct democracy techniques such as the referendum and initiative are used only sparingly in France and Britain, and not at all in West German national politics.

When the United States is judged by these same criteria, the amount of electing is quite high:

> No country can approach the United States in the frequency and variety of elections, and thus in the amount of electoral participation to which its citizens have a right. No other country elects its lower house as often as every two years, or its president as frequently as every four years. No other country popularly elects its state governors and town mayors; no other has as wide a variety of nonrepresentative offices (judges, sheriffs, attorneys general, city treasurers, and so on) subject to election. Only one other country (Switzerland) can compete in the number and variety of local referendums; only two (Belgium and Turkey) hold party "primaries" in most parts of the country. The average American is entitled to do far more electing — probably by a factor of three or four — than the citizen of any other democracy. (Crewe, 1981, p. 232)

A simple comparison of the electoral experiences of a typical European and American voter highlights this difference in the amount of voting. For example, between 1975 and 1980 a resident of Cambridge, England, could have voted about 4 times; a resident of Tallahassee, Florida, could have cast 165 votes in the same period.[3] Even if differences in turnout rates are taken into account, American citizens do not necessarily vote less often than other nationalities; most probably, they participate more often in one or more of the activities of this participation mode (Crewe, 1981, p. 262).

Turnout rates in national elections thus provide a very poor indicator of the overall political involvement of the public. More important than the quantity of voting is the quality of this participation mode. Verba et al. (1978, chap. 3) describe voting as an activity of high pressure because leaders are being chosen, but little policy information or influence is involved. The infrequent opportunity of most Europeans to cast a single vote for a prepackaged party is a very limited tool of political influence. This influence may increase when elections extend to a wide range of political offices and include referendums, as in the United States. Still, it is difficult for elections to be treated as policy mandates because they assess relative support for broad political programs and not specific policies. Even a sophisticated policy-oriented electorate cannot be assured that important policy options are represented in an election, nor that these policies will be followed in the period between elections. Consequently, research indicates that many people vote because of a sense of civic duty, involvement in a campaign, or as an expression of political or partisan support, rather than as an instrumental attempt to influence policy (Verba and Nie, 1972; Conway, 1985).

The limits of voting have led some critics to claim that by focusing mass participation on voting, parties and political elites are seeking to protect their privileged position in the policy process and actually limit citizen influence (Burnham, 1980). Even if this skepticism is deserved, voting will remain an important aspect of democratic politics, as much for its symbolic value as for its instrumental influence on policy. Voting is the one activity that binds the individual to the political system and legitimizes the rest of the democratic process.

CAMPAIGN ACTIVITY

Participation in campaign activities represents an extension of electoral participation beyond the act of voting. This mode includes a variety of political acts: working for a party or candidate, attending campaign meetings, persuading others how to vote, membership in a party or political organization, and other forms of party activity during and between elections. Fewer citizens are routinely active in campaigns because this participation mode is more demanding than merely casting a vote. Campaign activities require more initiative, and there is greater need to coordinate participation with others (see table 3.1). As a result of the additional effort, this participation mode provides more political influence to the individual citizen and conveys more information than voting. Campaign activities are important to parties and the candidates, and candidates generally are more sensitive to, and aware of, the policy interests of activists (Verba and Nie, 1972, chaps. 17-19).

TABLE 3.2
CAMPAIGN ACTIVITY IN THE UNITED STATES, 1952–84
(IN PERCENT)

Activity	1952	1956	1960	1964	1968	1972	1976	1980	1984
Belong to a club or political organization	2	3	3	4	3	—[a]	—[a]	3	—[a]
Work for a party or candidate	3	3	6	5	6	5	4	4	4
Go to meetings	7	7	8	8	9	9	6	8	8
Give money	4	10	12	11	9	10	16	8	12
Wear a button or have bumper sticker	—[a]	16	21	17	15	14	8	7	9
Persuade others how to vote	28	28	34	31	33	32	37	36	32

SOURCE: SRC/CPS American Election Studies.

a. Data were not available.

The pattern of campaign activities can take many forms, depending on the context of electioneering in the nation. In the United States, for example, campaigns are now largely media events. Popular involvement in organized campaign activities is limited. Table 3.2 indicates that few Americans attend party meetings, work for a party or candidate, or belong to a party or political club. The most frequent campaign activities are individualistic forms of political involvement: contributing money to a campaign or trying to persuade others. Financial contributions have increased in frequency, probably as a result of the burgeoning of direct-mail solicitations by political groups. Personal involvement in campaign discussions has held steady or even increased slightly over the past thirty years.

The structure of British campaigns differs in important ways from American elections. British elections do not follow a regular time schedule; the prime minister may dissolve Parliament and call for new elections at almost any time during a legislative term. Therefore, elections are often quickly organized and brief, averaging little more than a month. In addition, British parties depend on a large pool of formal party members for the bulk of campaign work. Party members attend political rallies, canvass the constituency during the campaign, and go door-to-door contacting potential voters on election day. Beyond the core of party members, popular participation in most campaign activities is limited (table 3.3). Moreover, along with declines in the percentage of party members has come a general decrease in organized campaign activities.

West Germany's development of a democratic political system during the past thirty years has increased citizen involvement in campaigns and most other aspects of the political process (Dalton, 1988, chap. 6). Membership in political parties has remained stable or even increased, and participation in campaign activities has grown. For example, 11 percent of the public attended a campaign meeting in the 1961 election; by 1976 this figure had nearly doubled (20 percent). Similarly, beginning in the 1970s, popular displays of party support became a more visible aspect of campaigns. Citizen action groups formed to display electoral support independent of the party-run campaigns, so campaign activity now extends beyond formal party members to include a significant proportion of the general public. In 1976, for instance, 36 percent of the public claimed that they openly showed their party support in some manner. Although popular participation in campaigns is still limited, past stereotypes of an unconcerned and uninvolved West German electorate no longer apply.

The available evidence on party and campaign activity in France is less extensive. Formal party membership has generally increased during the Fifth Republic, first as a consequence of the consolidation of a Gaullist majority and more recently because of Mitterrand's revitalization of the socialist Left

TABLE 3.3

CAMPAIGN ACTIVITY IN GREAT BRITAIN, 1964-83

(IN PERCENT)

Activity	1964	1966	1970	February 1974	October 1974	1979	1983
Canvass	3	2	1	2	2	2	3
Work for party or candidate	8	2	2	2	3	2	—ᵃ
Attend meeting (indoors)	8	7	5	5	6	4 ⎫	4
Attend meeting (outdoors)	8	3	6	4	3	2 ⎭	
Display poster	—ᵃ	—ᵃ	10	9	11	8	11
Party member	14	—ᵃ	10	—ᵃ	8	—ᵃ	7
Read electoral address	46	49	53	51	43	56	—ᵃ

SOURCES: 1964-75, Gallup (1976a); 1979-83, and party membership data from British Election Studies.

a. Data not available.

(Wilson, 1979). At the same time, however, attendance at campaign meetings, public displays of party support, and other campaign activities probably have decreased during the past two decades.

It is difficult to abstract a general pattern of campaign activity from these diverse national experiences. Overall levels of campaign activity apparently are increasing in West Germany, holding steady in the United States, and declining in Britain and France. Nevertheless, several common trends are at work in each nation. The expanding electoral role of the mass media is lessening the importance of campaign activities designed to inform the public: campaign rallies, canvassing, and formal party meetings. The media's growing importance has also encouraged the spread of American-style electioneering to Western Europe. British candidates orchestrate "walkabouts" to generate stories for the evening television news, campaigns focus more attention on candidate personalities than in the past, and televised preelection debates are the norm in Germany and France.

In addition to these institutional changes, the public's increasing sophistication and interest in politics generally spurs involvement in politics. Many individuals are still drawn to the excitement and competition of elections, but now campaign participation tends to be more individualistic—such as a display of party support or discussing the elections with friends. The level of campaign activity may be changing less than the nature of the public's involvement.

COMMUNAL ACTIVITY

Communal activity constitutes a third participation mode. Most communal activities involve group efforts to deal with social or community problems, although direct citizen contact with elites on such problems also is included (Verba and Nie, 1972, chap. 4). This mode is distinct from campaign activity because communal participation takes place largely outside the electoral setting and lacks a partisan focus.

Because the parameters of participation are not defined by elections, a relatively high level of political sophistication and initiative is required of communal activists (table 3.1). Citizens define their own issue agenda, the methods of influencing policymakers, and the timing of influence. The issues might be as broad as nuclear disarmament or as narrow as the policies of the local school district—citizens, not elites, decide. This control over the framework of participation means that communal activities can convey more information and exert more political pressure than the public's circumscribed participation in campaigns. In short, the communal mode shifts control of participation to the public and thereby increases citizen influence in the political process.

The relatively unstructured nature of communal activities makes it difficult either to measure accurately the extent of the public's participation or to compare participation levels across nations. Still, general impressions of national differences exist. Americans have always been noted for their group-based approach to political participation. This trait has been embedded in the American political culture as far back as the nineteenth century, when Tocqueville commented on the American proclivity to form groups to address community problems:

> The political activity that pervades the United States must be seen to be understood. No sooner do you set foot upon American ground than you are stunned by a kind of tumult; . . . here the people of one quarter of a town are met to decide upon the building of a church; there the election of a representative is going on; a little farther, the delegates of a district are hastening to the town in order to consult upon some local improvements; in another place, the laborers of a village quit their plows to deliberate upon a project of a road or a public school. . . . To take a hand in the regulation of society and to discuss it is (the) biggest concern and, so to speak, the only pleasure an American knows. (Tocqueville, 1966, pp. 249-50)

Recent studies still find that many Americans favor organized groups as a method of dealing with political problems (Almond and Verba, 1963; Verba et al., 1978).

Communal activities are also common in Britain and West Germany, but usage is probably less extensive than in the United States. European political norms traditionally have placed less emphasis on group activities (Almond and Verba, 1963, chap. 7), and the structure of European political systems does not encourage direct citizen contact with elected representatives. For instance, Almond and Verba (1963, chap. 11) find a relatively high level of membership in various social organizations in Britain and West Germany, but these groups are less often involved in political affairs.

By most accounts, communal activity is even more limited in France. For example, Tocqueville contrasted American social cooperation with the individualism of the French political culture. The French tradition of individualism continues to the present. The average French citizen is somewhat hesitant to cooperate with others and thereby subsume individual interests to those of the group. As a result, France presumably possesses the characteristics of a "mass society," where citizens are politically isolated and group activity is limited (Kornhauser, 1959, pp. 84ff).

In recent years these national differences in communal participation probably have lessened as a result of a general increase in communal participation in most Western democracies (Rochon, 1983). In the United States a variety of new political movements and single-issue groups have become active: the environmental lobby, the women's movement, disarmament groups, moral/ religious groups, and other organizations. A similar proliferation has occurred in Western Europe. In the early 1970s individuals with similar issue concerns organized into citizen action groups (*Buergerinitiativen*) in West Germany (Helm, 1980). Membership in these groups now exceeds formal membership in the West German political parties. Philip Lowe and Jane Goyder (1983, p. 1) claim that the British environmental movement is now larger than any political party or trade union, and this is just one movement in a spectrum of new issue groups. France has experienced a similar growth in civic associations (Cerny, 1982). In sum, this form of political involvement is becoming a more common aspect of political action in contemporary democracies.

TABLE 3.4

CONVENTIONAL POLITICAL PARTICIPATION (IN PERCENT)

	United States	Great Britain	West Germany	France
Voting				
Voted in last election	68	73	90	81
Campaign activity[a]				
Convince others how to vote	19	9	22	—
Attend meeting/rally	18	9	22	—
Work for party/candidate	14	5	8	—
Communal activity[a]				
Work with group to solve community problem	37	17	14	—
Contact officials	27	11	11	—
Participation typology[b]				
Inactives	18	20	7	—
Voting specialists	27	50	55	—
Campaign activists	7	7	19	—
Communal activists	25	15	5	—
Complete activists	23	8	14	—
TOTAL	100	100	100	

SOURCE: Political Action Survey; French vote turnout percentages are from official statistics. Comparative French survey data are not available.

a. Table entries are the percentage participating frequently or sometimes.
b. Based on respondents age 21 or older.

A Participation Typology

A recent cross-national survey by Samuel Barnes, Max Kaase, and their colleagues (1979) provides an overview of participation patterns in the United States, Britain, and West Germany (table 3.4). Voting rates are high in all three nations, especially among the West German public. Fewer citizens participate in the more demanding forms of campaign activity or communal activity, although in several instances participants constitute a sizable proportion of the public. For example, about one of every three Americans works with a community group or sometimes contacts a political official.

The idea of participation modes assumes that citizens focus their political activity in one of these areas. In other words, people distinguish between activity in campaigns and participation in communal activities. This is because the various participation modes place different demands on the participants and have different consequences. How do citizens fit into these participation modes? The political activities in the first part of table 3.4 were used to classify citizens according to their primary pattern of participation.[4] This participation typology is presented in the last panel of the table. Only a minority of the public in each nation are "complete inactives"—not involved in any of the political acts listed. When citizens become active, the pattern of participation varies cross-nationally (cf. Verba et al., 1978, app. A).

The American public contains the largest proportion of "complete activists," those who participate in all three modes. Americans also display a tendency to participate in communal activities—25 percent are communal activists. The majority of West Germans are politically active only as "voting specialists," but many are also involved as campaign activists. The surprising finding from these data is the generally low level of British participation in all three modes of political activity. Britain is, after all, the birthplace of modern democracy, and Britons traditionally have displayed high levels of political participation in cross-national comparisons. The British have the smallest number of complete activists and the largest number of inactives. Nearly three-quarters of the British public is not active beyond voting. This pattern probably reflects the general decline in British political involvement that has occurred over the past two decades (Marsh, 1977, pp. 66-68). Based on evidence from other surveys, we would expect French citizens to display relatively low levels of campaign and communal activity.[5] In the absence of comparable French data, however, these conclusions must remain speculative.

The Predictors of Participation

The question of who participates in politics is as important as the question of how many citizens participate (Wolfinger and Rosenstone, 1980; Conway, 1985). First, the characteristics of participants help us to interpret the meaning of political activism. For example, policy dissatisfaction conceivably may either increase or decrease the likelihood of political action. These two alternatives cast a much different light on the significance of participation; it might be an indicator of disapproval or popular support. Second, if citizen participation influences policy outcomes, then the pattern of participation suggests which citizens are making their voices heard by policymakers—and which interests are not represented. Finally, comparing the correlates of participation across nations and participation modes provides insights into the political process in each nation and the distinct aspects of each mode.

The most common explanation of political activism stresses the role of social status as a stimulant to participation. Politics can be a demanding activity in terms of the time required to stay informed and the conceptual abilities needed to understand complex political issues; social status reflects the necessary resources. Higher-status citizens are more likely to have the time, the money, the access to political information, the knowledge, and the ability to become politically involved. So widespread is this notion that Verba and Nie refer to social status as the "standard model" of political participation (Verba and Nie, 1972, chap. 8; Verba et al., 1978). So, social status is the first variable that should be added to our inventory of the potential causes of participation.

Another explanation of political activism is based on the concept of a political life cycle (Nie et al., 1974). For many young people, politics is a remote and irrelevant activity. As individuals age, however, they take on social responsibilities that increase their motivations to develop political interests. Citizens become taxpayers and homeowners, their children enter public schools, and they may begin to draw benefits from government programs. Most studies find that political involvement increases with age.

Gender is also an important social determinant of political activism. Men are more politically active than women in virtually all Western democracies (M. Inglehart, 1981). Part of this gap is because of differences in political resources (e.g., education, income, and employment patterns), which place women at a disadvantage in dealing with the world of politics. In addition, early life socialization often portrays politics as inappropriate to the female role; this undoubtedly restrains the motivation of women to participate and the willingness of the male world to accept female participation. In an age of changing sex roles, we can determine whether gender is still an important predictor of participation.

In addition to these expected differences between social groups, several political attitudes also may affect participation levels. Because campaigns and elections are largely partisan contests, party attachments are often a potent pre-dictor of participation (Verba et al., 1978, chap. 6). Many people develop a strong psychological identification with their preferred party (see chapter 9). This sense of party identification motivates individuals to vote or participate in campaigns as a display of party support; they are concerned that their party wins. Conversely, citizens with weak or nonexistent party bonds are less concerned with election outcomes and less likely to participate. Therefore, the strength of party identifications may be an important influence on participation patterns.

Political participation is also encouraged by civic attitudes that convince the individual that citizens should participate in politics and that participation makes a difference (Nie et al., 1969). This latter belief is described as a sense of *political efficacy*, the feeling that one's political action can affect the political process (Abramson, 1983, chap. 8).[6] Perceptions of political efficacy might be at odds with reality, but these perceptions are what guide individual behavior. A feeling of political efficacy motivates individuals to become active in politics, while the absence of efficacy evokes political apathy and withdrawal. If one cannot affect the political process, why bother to try?

Policy dissatisfaction is another political attitude that might influence participation patterns (Farah et al., 1979). The causal role of policy dissatisfaction is a point of debate. On the one hand, some people argue that dissatisfaction stimulates participation in an attempt to change policy. From this perspective, high turnout rates indicate widespread public dissatisfaction with the government. On the other hand, some observers maintain that policy satisfaction increases support for the political process and thereby political participation. In these terms, high turnout rates indicate the public's basic support of the government. While researchers may disagree on the causal direction of policy dissatisfaction, this clearly is regarded as an important motivation affecting participation levels.

Among the many factors possibly influencing a citizen's decision to participate, our inventory includes the major ones identified by prior research:

- ☐ Socioeconomic status
- ☐ Age
- ☐ Gender
- ☐ Strength of party identification
- ☐ Political efficacy
- ☐ Policy dissatisfaction

It also should be clear that the effects of these variables tend to overlap. Age, for example, should have an independent influence on participation rates; but

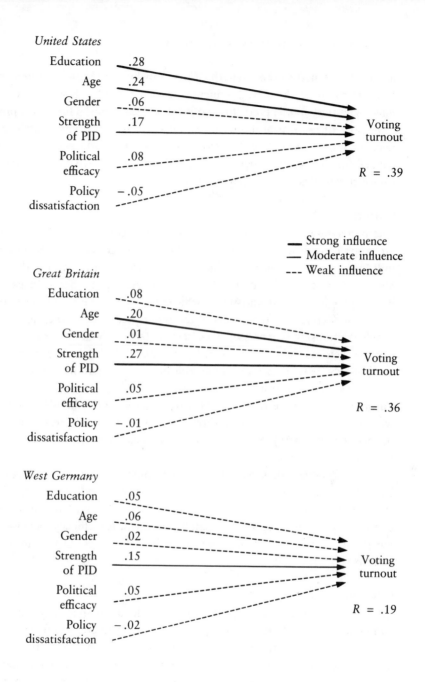

FIGURE 3.2

PREDICTORS OF VOTING TURNOUT

SOURCE: Political Action Study, 1974-75.

NOTE: Figure entries are standardized regression coefficients that measure the independent impact of each predictor while controlling for the effects of the other predictors in the model.

age is also related to the strength of partisanship and socioeconomic status. In order to assess the actual influence of each variable, they were combined into a summary model predicting political participation.[7] This model provides a measure of the causal importance of each factor on political activism, independent of the effects of the other variables. The model was separately calculated for voting, campaign activity, and communal activity to compare the causal patterns across participation modes.

VOTING

The correlates of voting turnout in the three nations with comparable data are graphically displayed in figure 3.2. The arrows connecting age and voting indicate that turnout increases significantly with age, especially in the United States (b^* = .24) and Britain (b^* = .20). These causal effects are expressed in the figure in terms of statistical coefficients, where the effects of age are estimated independent of the effects of the other predictors in the model. If the simple relationship is expressed in percentage terms, about 80 percent of Americans in their 50s claim to have voted, compared to less than 60 percent among 20-year-olds. Voting turnout follows this life-cycle pattern in all three nations.

The second major influence on turnout rates is the strength of party identifications. Because elections are partisan contests, those who identify strongly with a party are more likely to show up at the polls (and presumably cast a ballot for their party). Strong party attachments heighten the motivation to participate in elections.

The other variables in the model exert some influence on voting turnout, but their effects are fairly weak. Generally, there is a modest positive relationship between the social-status variable, educational level, and voting. Males consistently vote at a higher rate than females. Political efficacy increases turnout slightly, and policy dissatisfaction slightly depresses turnout in all three nations.

CAMPAIGN ACTIVITY

Participation in election campaigns is a more demanding activity than simply voting, and so a different pattern of causal factors emerges in figure 3.3. The strength of party identification is even more important in explaining campaign activism than voting turnout because campaign work is a more intensely partisan activity. In percentage terms, for example, 52 percent of the strong partisans in the United States participate in at least one campaign activity, compared to only 20 percent among nonpartisans.

The greater initiative required by campaign activity also means that a sense of political efficacy is a significant predictor of whether citizens commit them-

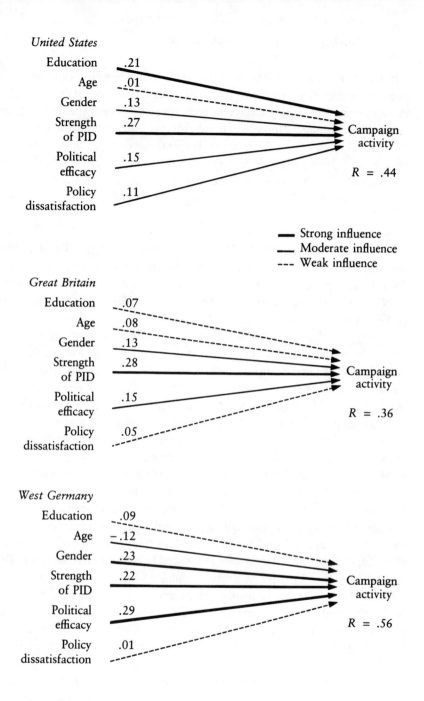

FIGURE 3.3

PREDICTORS OF CAMPAIGN ACTIVITY

SOURCE: Political Action Study, 1974-75. For note on figure entries, see figure 3.2.

selves to campaign work. People must feel that participation can have an impact before they invest the effort to work for a party or candidate. In addition, in every nation there is a clear tendency for men to be more active in campaigns than women. Moreover, these strong gender differences emerge from a statistical model that adjusts for male-female inequalities in education, political efficacy, and the other predictors in the model. Perhaps it is the higher visibility of campaign work that increases the impact of sex roles on this participation mode.

COMMUNAL ACTIVITY

The predictors of communal activity are presented in figure 3.4. This mode also requires a great deal of initiative and sophistication from the participant. As a result, the politically efficacious and better educated are more likely to participate in communal activities. Sex roles also influence communal participation, with men being substantially more active than women.

This participation mode is distinct from voting and campaign activity because communal participation is generally not a partisan activity. In fact, in many instances participants are drawn to political groups because they lack strict party allegiances. Consequently, the figures show that party ties have the least impact on communal participation from among the three modes.

The causal relationships for all three participation modes are fairly uniform across nations. Two national deviations deserve attention, however. In West Germany the young participate more than the old in campaign and communal activities—a direct reversal of the normal life-cycle pattern. This age relationship reflects German historical conditions. In a stable democratic system (such as the United States or Britain), experience in a democratic participatory role steadily accumulates through life, and political involvement consequently increases with age. Older West Germans lack this continuous democratic experience; their political norms were influenced by the authoritarian Third Reich or the Wilhelmine Empire. As a result, younger West Germans, who have been raised exclusively under the democratic procedures of the Federal Republic, are more integrated into the democratic process and actually participate more than older citizens. With the eventual passage of the older generations, the normal life-cycle pattern probably will emerge in future West German participation rates.

A second national difference involves the social-status variable, education. For all three participation modes, social status has a much stronger influence on political activity in the United States than in the other two nations. American social-status differences in voting ($b^* = .27$), for instance, are far greater than in Britain ($b^* = .08$) or West Germany ($b^* = .05$). Some differences in

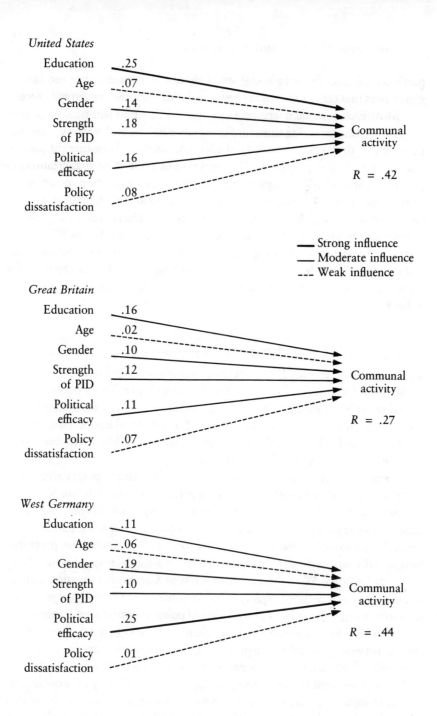

United States

Education	.25
Age	.07
Gender	.14
Strength of PID	.18
Political efficacy	.16
Policy dissatisfaction	.08

Communal activity

$R = .42$

— Strong influence
— Moderate influence
--- Weak influence

Great Britain

Education	.16
Age	.02
Gender	.10
Strength of PID	.12
Political efficacy	.11
Policy dissatisfaction	.07

Communal activity

$R = .27$

West Germany

Education	.11
Age	−.06
Gender	.19
Strength of PID	.10
Political efficacy	.25
Policy dissatisfaction	.01

Communal activity

$R = .44$

FIGURE 3.4
PREDICTORS OF COMMUNAL ACTIVITY

SOURCE: Political Action Study, 1974-75. For note on figure entries, see figure 3.2.

participation rates between social strata should be expected, but too large a gap implies that certain groups are being excluded from the democratic process.

Most European democracies have avoided this problem of large social-status differences in voting turnout. Strong labor unions and working-class parties mobilize the working class and the less educated, and equalize the participation rates of all social strata. The weakness of these same organizations in the United States, when coupled with the restrictive registration requirements of the American electoral system, has created a serious participation gap between social groups. Walter Dean Burnham (1980) maintains that this problem is worsened by the absence of meaningful party choices in America. The consequence, he argues, is a growing alienation of many Americans from the political process. At the least, this large participation gap indicates the need for some method of maximizing the involvement of all social groups in American politics.

Changing Publics and Political Participation

This chapter has provided an overview of conventional political participation in the United States, Britain, West Germany, and France. These publics are involved in politics. Voting turnout is high in almost all Western democracies, averaging better than 70 percent in most electorates. In addition, a sizable proportion of the public is involved in more demanding political activities, such as campaigns or communal participation.

These findings generally support the belief that contemporary electorates are fairly sophisticated about politics. Yet a paradox remains. Measures of political information, interest, and sophistication in chapter 2 display a sharp increase over the past few decades. In general terms, conventional participation levels do not exhibit these same dramatic increases; in some areas participation actually has declined. Voting turnout rates have decreased in the United States and Britain. With the exception of West Germany, campaign activity has held steady or declined slightly. Why are some aspects of political participation decreasing, if the public's general level of political involvement is increasing?

These conflicting trends can be explained by looking more closely at the linkage between political sophistication and participation patterns. Increasing political sophistication does not necessarily imply a growth in the the level of all forms of political activism; rising sophistication levels may be more important in changing the *nature* of participation. Voting, for example, is an area where elites and political organizations traditionally were able to mobilize even disinterested citizens to turn out at the polls. High turnout levels often reflect the organizational skills of political groups rather than the public's concern about the election. Moreover, citizen input through this participation mode is limited by the institutionalized structure of elections, which narrows (and blurs) the choice of policy options and limits the frequency of public input. A French environmental group bluntly stated its disdain for elections with a slogan borrowed from the May Revolts of 1968: *Elections — piege a cons* (Elections — trap for idiots). An increasingly sophisticated and cognitively mobilized electorate is not likely to rely on voting and campaign activity as the primary means of expanding its involvement in politics (Dalton, 1984a).

The growing political skills and resources of contemporary electorates have had a more noticeable impact on increasing participation in areas where activity is citizen initiated, less structured, and more policy oriented. Thus, referendums are preferred over elections, and communal activity over campaign work. The use of referendums has, in fact, increased dramatically in Western democracies in recent years (Butler and Ranney, 1981). Similarly, the activity of citizen lobbies, single-issue groups, and citizen action movements is increasing in nearly all Western democracies. Even the electoral arena might be reinvigorated in Europe by expanding the public's decision-making responsibilities to include primaries, preference-ranking mechanisms for party-list voting, or candidate ranking within party lists. Why have the electoral opportunities of European citizens not kept pace with the general expansion of democratic politics?

The new style of citizen politics thus seeks to place more control over political activity in the hands of the citizenry. These changes in the nature of participation make greater demands on the participants. At the same time, however, these activities can increase public pressure on political elites. Citizen participation is becoming more closely linked to citizen influence.

Notes

1. A study of Buffalo residents by Milbrath and Goel (1977) identifies these same four modes and two additional ones: communication and protest. Their communication mode is a residual category that encompasses the additional items Milbrath and Goel added to their participation list, and the protest mode is studied in the next chapter.

2. Verba and Nie (1972) found only 4 percent of the American public is active primarily through contacting officials on personal matters. These individuals tend to be sophisticated, but also unconcerned with broad political issues. Because of the very small size of this group, we will not study this fourth participation mode.

3. The British votes include local council, county, the Common Market referendum, and the 1979 House of Common election. The American votes include both primary and general elections: 13 votes for city offices, 49 for county offices, 40 for state offices, 13 for federal offices, and 50 referendums.

4. Complete activists participate in at least one activity from each of the three participation modes. Communal activists participate in at least one activity from this mode. Campaign activists have voted in the last election and performed at least one campaign activity. Voting specialists have limited their participation to voting. Inactives did not take part in any of the listed activities.

5. For instance, the 1981 European Values study found fairly equivalent levels of political interest for British, French, and West German publics. But the French consistently were less likely to be members of a variety of sociopolitical groups (charities, education-arts, political parties, human rights, and environmental organizations).

6. The Political Action study measured political efficacy by combining three questions: (1) Do people like the respondent have a say in government; (2) is voting the only way to influence the government; and (3) is politics too complex to understand?

7. The analyses in figures 3.2, 3.3, and 3.4 are based on multiple regression; figure entries are standardized regression coefficients. Campaign and communal activity were measured by the average participation score for items listed within the mode in table 3.4.

4. Protest Politics

Citizen action is not limited to voting, campaign activity, and communal activity. Citizen participation occasionally bursts beyond the bounds of conventional politics to include demonstrations, protests, and other forms of unconventional political action.

Protest activity differs from conventional politics in several ways. Protest is a direct-action technique of confronting political elites, instead of participating within a framework defined by elites. Protest can be focused on specific issues or policy goals and can convey a high level of political information with substantial political force (see table 3.1). The timing and location of protest activities are also controlled by the public. Sustained and effective protest is thus a demanding participation mode that requires initiative and cooperation with others. The advocates of protest have argued that the public can substantially strengthen its influence on policymakers by adopting a strategy of direct action.

Protest is certainly not a new component of politics in Western democracies (Tilly, 1969). The history of the United States is repeatedly punctuated by political conflict (Garner, 1977; Graham and Gurr, 1969). The colonial period was marked by frequent agrarian revolts against taxation, property restrictions, and other government policies. When rural elements allied themselves with the urban poor and bourgeoisie, an American revolution against British control became inevitable. After independence, political conflict continued with the growth of workers' movements and agrarian/populist movements in the 1800s. Large scale, nonviolent protests and demonstrations were used by abolitionists, suffragettes, and other political groups throughout the past century. The early half of this century was a period of often intense and violent industrial conflict.

A revolutionary tradition is perhaps even more deeply ingrained in the French political culture (Cerny, 1982). To many French liberals, the foundations of French democracy are traced to the revolutions of 1789, 1830, and 1848, as well as the Paris Commune of 1871. Between these dramatic political events, French society displayed a high level of protest and collective violence for most of the past century (Tilly et al., 1975, chap. 2). Food riots and similar conflicts were widespread in the mid-1800s, and the second half of the century and the early 1900s were marked by industrial conflict. A call to the barricades stirs the hearts of many Frenchmen, contributing to historically high levels of unconventional political activity. In the words of one expert, protest in France is a national way of life.

Although the available historical evidence indicates that political protest and collective action occurred on a more limited scale in Germany and Britain, these forms of political conflict were not totally unknown. An incipient democratic revolution was crushed by the German government in 1848, and intense political conflict eventually consumed the Weimar Republic (Tilly et al., 1975, chap. 4). Conflicts over industrial policy during the Wilhelmine Empire and Weimar Republic often manifested themselves in mass protests. Even Britain, with its tradition of gradual political change, has a history of violence and political conflict that is often overlooked by political scientists (Marsh, 1977, chap. 2).

The history of Western democracies is thus marked by repeated episodes of protest and vigorous political dissent by the citizenry. This record has persisted to the present. For example, the civil rights movement and ghetto riots of the 1960s were a divisive and violent period in America. Similarly, peasant protests—pouring milk onto highways, blocking traffic, or symbolic animal slaughters—are nearly an established part of contemporary French politics. The 1980s in virtually all Western democracies have seen widespread protests over environmental protection and disarmament. And these nations continue to experience at least modest levels of protest over industrial issues.

Despite the historical roots of unconventional political participation, many observers expected protest politics to fade with the spreading affluence of contemporary societies. Yet the frequency of protest and other unconventional political activities apparently has increased in recent years (Barnes, Kaase, et al., 1979). Cross-national comparisons also find that protest levels are higher in more affluent nations (Powell, 1982, pp. 129-32). These trends have led some analysts to argue that a new style of protest is becoming a regular form of political action in advanced industrial societies.

In historical terms, protest and collective action were often the last desperate acts of citizens, arising from feelings of frustration and deprivation. Protest was concentrated among the socially disadvantaged, repressed minorities, or groups that were alienated from the established political order. Unconventional political action was an outlet for groups that lacked access to politics through conventional participation channels. More recently, however, the use of protest has broadened from the disadvantaged to include a wider spectrum of political groups. A wave of student protests swept through Western societies in the late 1960s, and protest has become an accepted form of political action by the better educated. Political protest is now common among the middle class and the politically sophisticated. Protest is shifting from ghettos and slums to the Ivy League, Oxbridge, and the Grand Ecoles.

Along with the changing locus of protest came a shift in the focus of unconventional political action. Protest historically was an extreme political act. Protests and demonstrations frequently were indicators of revolutionary ferment and often challenged the basic legitimacy of political institutions. Food riots, tax revolts, and socialist worker uprisings are examples of this antigovernment activity. The new forms of protest in advanced industrial societies are seldom directed at overthrowing the established political order—the affluent and well-educated participants often are some of the primary beneficiaries of this order. Revolutionary fervor has been replaced by reformism.

Finally, prior to modern times, collective political action was often a spontaneous event, such as an unorganized crowd attacking a tax collector or staging a food riot. Modern protest behavior has become a planned and organized activity (Tilly, 1969, pp. 28-37). Political groups consciously plan protests when these activities will benefit their cause. Modern protests are often orchestrated events, with participants arriving in chartered buses to preplanned staging areas complete with demonstration coordinators and facilities for the media. Protest is seen as simply another political resource for mobilizing public opinion and influencing policymakers (Tilly, 1975).

There are numerous examples of the new style of protest politics. One of the earliest examples was Britain's Campaign for Nuclear Disarmament (CND) in the early 1960s (Parkin, 1968). Tens of thousands of largely middle-class citizens marched and protested in opposition to nuclear weapons. Protest did not spontaneously arise out of frustration and alienation from the political system. The CND's decision to rely on unconventional political action was based on pragmatic grounds; it was thought that nonviolent protest could mobilize public opposition to government policy.

In the late 1960s there was a flowering of protest movements throughout Western societies. In Bonn, London, Paris, and Washington, students took to the streets. Opposition to the Vietnam war and American foreign policy was an initial stimulus in many cases. But soon student protest spread to challenge virtually all the traditional social values (Keniston, 1968; Allerbeck and Rosenmayr, 1971; Citrin and Elkins, 1975).

The May Revolts in France highlighted and dramatized this pattern (Brown, 1974). The *Events* in 1968 began as a student protest against university regulations (including dormitory visitation guidelines) at the small university of Nanterre. When university administrators were unable to handle the situation, they closed the university and thereby turned several thousand students into the streets. The spark of protest rapidly spread to the student quarter around the Sorbonne in Paris. Students and many of their middle-class supporters began to question the general goals of the government and the bureaucratized structure of society. Wall posters proclaimed the search for new alternatives:

The dream is reality.
To be free is to participate.
Beauty is in the streets.
Imagination to power.
I participate, you participate, they profit.
I have something to say, but I don't know what.

Pitched street battles between students and government forces appeared on the nightly news and stirred popular dissatisfaction with the political and economic systems. Many industrial workers and government employees also went on strike, and France was brought to the verge of collapse. France's spirit of revolutionary protest had been rekindled, not by the poor and deprived, but by the future leaders of French society—the university educated.

New waves of protest have spread through Western democracies in recent years. One source was the growth of the environmental movement (Nelkin and Pollack, 1981; Lowe and Goyder, 1983). Environmental groups in the United States and Western Europe mobilized in opposition to nuclear power and in support of environmental protection. American environmentalists staged repeated demonstrations and blockades at target facilities such as Seabrook (New Hampshire), Barnwell (South Carolina), and Diablo Canyon (California). Residents near nuclear power plants across the rest of the country took an active interest in the nuclear controversy, producing a series of local political actions.

This pattern was repeated in Western Europe. Environmentalists organized protests in opposition to nuclear facilities at Wyhl, Grohnde, and Brokdorf in West Germany, Creys-Malville and Plogoff in France, and Windscale in Britain. Massive demonstrations at Creys-Malville and Brokdorf led to armed clashes between the police and protesters, including two deaths. The nuclear plant accident at Chernobyl added even more fuel to the anti-nuclear movement. Environmental groups also oppose other large development projects that might threaten the environment, such as the Frankfurt airport expansion, the English Channel tunnel, and completion of the Rhine-Danube canal. Moreover, numerous small groups exist at the local level to deal with the environmental problems of their own community.

Another series of protest groups demonstrated in favor of nuclear disarmament and nuclear freeze proposals. By several accounts, over 3 million West

Germans participated in demonstrations against new NATO nuclear missiles during a single week in 1983 (*Aktion Woche*). Hundreds of thousands also marched in Britain. Several million Americans signed nuclear freeze petitions, and nuclear freeze referendums were held in a number of states and hundreds of cities.

The recent examples of protest activity mark a change in the style of contemporary political action. Even more significant than these activities is the development of an infrastructure for continued protest activities for other issues. The creation of citizen lobbies, environmental groups, and the like provides a basis for organizing future protests. The existence of these new opposition groups may be crucial in permanently changing the style of citizen politics.

Protest is still a political resource of minorities and repressed groups, and demonstrations by racial minorities (foreign workers in Europe), the economically disadvantaged, and similar groups will continue. In addition, the use of protest has spread; first to students, and now to a broader spectrum of society. Gray Panthers protest for senior-citizen rights, consumers are active monitors of industry, environmentalists call attention to ecological problems, and action groups of all kinds are proliferating. Clearly, these are not revolutionary groups. This participation mode is used whether the issue is a relatively mundane one, such as zoning regulations, or a fundamental issue, such as nuclear war (Marsh, 1974; cf. Miller et al., 1982). Protest has become less unconventional; it is a continuation of conventional political participation by other means.

Many people claim that this period of protest is passing; just the opposite is true. As protest becomes less unconventional, it also becomes less noticeable and newsworthy. The growing use of protests in European societies and the spread of single-issue groups in the United States should convince us that protest politics will continue.

Measuring Protest

Although protest and other forms of collective action have been a regular feature of Western societies, this participation mode was absent from early empirical studies of political participation. This partially reflected the relatively low level of protest that existed in the 1950s and early 1960s, as well as the unconventional label applied to protest activities. The growing wave of protest in the last decade stimulated several studies that focused on this void in our knowledge of citizen politics (Muller, 1972, 1979; Marsh, 1974, 1977; Barnes, Kaase, et al., 1979).

The first task was to measure participation in unconventional political activities. To guide this effort, Muller (1972) and Marsh (1974) developed a con-

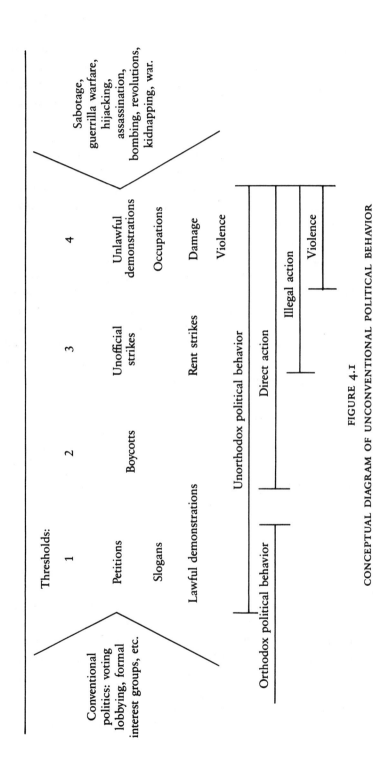

FIGURE 4.1

CONCEPTUAL DIAGRAM OF UNCONVENTIONAL POLITICAL BEHAVIOR

SOURCE: Marsh (1977, p. 42), with modifications.

ceptual model of this participation mode. The various unconventional forms of participation are ordered along a single continuum from least to most extreme. This continuum is marked by several thresholds (figure 4.1). The first threshold indicates the transition from conventional to unconventional politics. Signing petitions and participating in lawful demonstrations are unorthodox political activities but still within the bounds of accepted democratic norms. The second threshold represents the shift to direct-action techniques, such as boycotts. A third level of political activities involves illegal, but nonviolent, acts. Unofficial strikes or a peaceful occupation of a building typify this step. Finally, a fourth threshold includes violent activities such as personal injury or physical damage. Research has shown that unconventional political action is cumulative. Individuals active at any one threshold also generally participate in milder forms of protest.

This schema has been used by several cross-national studies to measure unconventional political participation in Western democracies. Table 4.1 presents the levels of protest activity in our four nations, drawn from surveys in 1974 and 1981. On the whole, most citizens participate in some form of unconventional political participation, even if only in the most mild forms. The levels of participation in moderate forms of unconventional politics rival activity in conventional participation modes (see table 3.4).

TABLE 4.1

UNCONVENTIONAL POLITICAL PARTICIPATION (IN PERCENT)

	United States 1974	United States 1981	Great Britain 1974	Great Britain 1981	West Germany 1974	West Germany 1981	France 1981
Sign petitions	58	61	22	63	30	46	44
Participate in lawful demonstration	11	12	6	10	9	14	26
Join in boycott	14	14	5	7	4	7	11
Participate in unofficial strike	2	3	5	7	1	2	10
Occupy building	2	2	1	2	*	1	7
Damage property	1	1	1	2	*	1	1
Personal violence	1	2	*	1	*	1	1
N	(1719)	(2325)	(1483)	(1231)	(2307)	(1305)	(1200)

SOURCES: 1974 Political Action Study; 1981 European Values Survey; 1981 CARA Values Survey.
NOTE: Table entries are the percentages who say they have done the activity.
* Less than 1 percent.

The dark side of unconventional politics occurs when citizens pass the fourth threshold and engage in violent behavior. The abortion-clinic bombers or the terrorist activities of the West German Red Army Faktion go far beyond the tolerable bounds of politics; these actions are fundamentally different from the protest behavior of most citizens. Even though protest politics is widely accepted, the number of participants in violent activities is minimal. For example, 44 percent of the French public have signed a petition, but only 1 percent have damaged property or engaged in personal violence. Citizens want to protest the actions of the democratic political process, not destroy it.

Interesting cross-national and cross-temporal patterns are also present in these data. The level of unconventional activity is generally highest in France and the United States. In the former case, this verifies our earlier description of France as a volatile political system, where conventional politics is disdained and protest is accepted (Hoffmann, 1974). In a much earlier work, Kornhauser (1959) argued that the very weakness of social groups and conventional participation channels in France encourages support for protest. In just the single year following the 1981 French survey there were large-scale national protest actions by medical students, truck drivers, farmers, and manual workers. French protest knows no social bounds. The high levels of protest in the United States probably reflect the activist orientation of Americans; citizen action extends across all participation modes.

Longitudinal comparisons are also available for American, British, and West German publics. In every nation, unconventional political activities are more common in 1981 than in 1974. The growth of protest probably results from a general increase in small demonstrations over highways, schools, neighborhood issues, and other specific concerns, rather than a few large-scale movements. Protest is becoming a common political activity in advanced industrial democracies.

Predictors of Protest

Why do citizens protest? Every protester has an individual explanation for participation. For some, it may be an intense commitment to an issue or ideology. Other protesters are motivated by a general opposition to the government and political system, and search for opportunities to display their feelings. Still others are caught up in the excitement and sense of comradeship that protests produce, or simply accompany a friend to be where the action is. Social scientists have attempted to systematize these individual motivations in order to explain the general sources of protest activity. A number of general theories have been suggested (see Palmer and Thompson, 1978, chap. 7; Muller, 1979, chap. 2).

The *deprivation approach* maintains that protest is primarily based on feelings of frustration and political alienation. Analysts since Aristotle have seen personal dissatisfaction and the striving for better conditions as the root cause of political violence. For Aristotle, the principal causes of revolution were the aspirations for economic or political equality on the part of the common people who lack it, or the aspirations of oligarchs for greater inequality than they have. Much later, Tocqueville linked the violence of the 1789 French Revolution to unfulfilled aspirations expanding more rapidly than objective conditions, thereby increasing dissatisfaction and the pressure for change. Karl Marx similarly posited personal dissatisfaction and the competition between the haves and have-nots as the driving force of history and the ultimate source of political revolt.

These themes have been echoed and quantified by modern social scientists. The theory has a psychological base: Frustration leads to aggression; therefore, dissatisfaction with society and politics can lead to political violence. The seminal study in the area is the work of Ted Robert Gurr (1970). Gurr states:

> The primary causal sequence in political violence is first the development of discontent, second the politicization of discontent, and finally its actualization in violent political action against political objects and actors. (1970, pp. 12-13)

Gurr's conclusions are largely based on analyses of cross-national levels of political violence. Recent analyses of public opinion data also show that policy dissatisfaction increases the likelihood of participation in protest activities (Farah et al., 1979; Muller, 1979).

The basic implication of this model is that political dissatisfaction and alienation should be major predictors of protest. Indirectly, this theory suggests that unconventional political activity should be more common among lower-status individuals, minorities, and other groups who have reasons to feel deprived or dissatisfied.

A second explanation of protest is termed a *resource model* (Tilly, 1975; Lipsky, 1968). This model does not view protest and collective action as an emotional outburst by a frustrated public. Rather, protest is another political resource (like voting, campaign activity, or communal activity) that a group may use in pursuing its goals. Unconventional political behavior is not an irrational deviant act, as implied by the deprivation model; protest is seen as a normal part of the political process as competing groups vie for political power. Excluding voting, protest is one of the commonest forms of mass political participation.

The resource model provides some guidance in predicting who should resort to protest behavior. For example, a belief that protest will be effective should significantly increase the likelihood the individuals will participate. Indeed, one of the most interesting studies of protest found that participants in the American ghetto riots in the 1960s were actually more efficacious than nonparticipants (Aberbach and Walker, 1970). The resource model also implies that protest should be viewed as simply another participation mode. Consequently, protest activity should be higher among politically sophisticated individuals, even though these individuals may not be frustrated or politically alienated.

The six predictors of conventional political participation from chapter 3 — education, age, gender, strength of party ties, political efficacy, and policy dissatisfaction — were used to predict protest behavior. Figure 4.2 presents the results of this model for the United States, Britain, and West Germany.[1] The impact of policy dissatisfaction on protest behavior is stronger than its influence on any conventional participation mode (see figures 3.2 to 3.4). Yet dissatisfied citizens are only slightly more likely to protest than citizens who are satisfied with government policy performance. Furthermore, the causal patterns of other variables tends to undercut the dissatisfaction model. For example, protest is more common among males and the better educated than among women and the less educated. More directly, protest is higher among the politically efficacious.

Similar analyses of French protest behavior were conducted with the 1981 European Values Survey.[2] Personal dissatisfaction replaced the measure of policy dissatisfaction, and political efficacy was not measured; otherwise, the predictors are comparable to those in figure 4.2. Figure 4.3 indicates that the predictors of protest in France generally parallel our findings in the other three nations. Participation in protest activities is more dependent on education and gender than on dissatisfaction.

In short, protest is not simply an outlet for the alienated and deprived; often, just the opposite appears. Policy dissatisfaction is a motivation to protest, but protest is more accurately described by the resource model. Protesters are individuals who possess the abilities to organize and participate in political activities of all forms, including protest.

In one important area, however, the correlates of protest distinguish it from conventional political activity. Conventional political participation routinely increases with age, as family and social responsibilities heighten the relevance of politics. In contrast, protest is the domain of the young. In the United States, for example, two-thirds of the 20-year-olds have participated in at least one protest activity, compared to less than half of the 60-year-olds. Age is the strongest single predictor of protest activity in each of the four nations.

Political scientists differ in their interpretations of this age relationship. On the one hand, this relationship may reflect life-cycle differences in protest

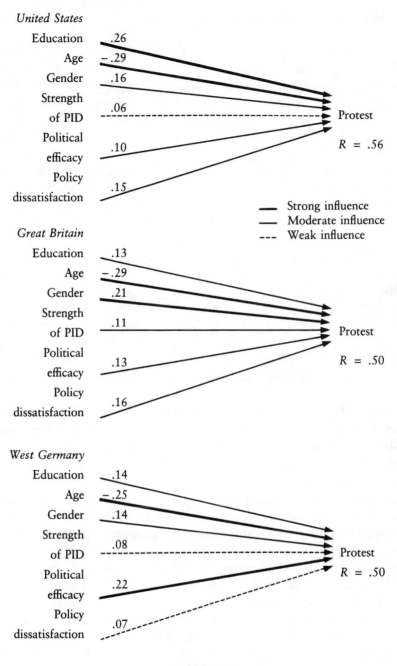

FIGURE 4.2
PREDICTORS OF PROTEST

SOURCE: 1974 Political Action Study.

NOTE: Figure entries are standardized regression coefficients that measure the independent impact of each predictor while controlling for the effects of the other predictors in the model.

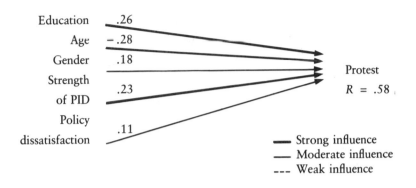

FIGURE 4.3

PREDICTORS OF PROTEST IN FRANCE

SOURCE: 1981 European Values Survey. For note on figure entries, see figure 4.2

activity. Youth is a period of enthusiasm and rebellion, which may encourage participation in protests. Young people also may be more accessible to protest because of their free time and concentration in university settings. This explanation would predict that an individual's protest activity should decline with age.

On the other hand, age differences in protest may represent a generational pattern of changing participation styles. That is, today's young people protest, not because of their youth, but because their generation has adopted a new style of political participation. The increasing educational levels, political sophistication, and participation norms among younger generations are producing support for direct-action techniques. If this is true, age differences in protest represent a historical change in participation patterns. Thus, youthful protesters should gradually mature into middle-age activists and not fade with the passage of time.

The observed age differences in protest probably represent a combination of life-cycle and generational effects. But attempts to assess the relative importance of either explanation stress the primacy of generational effects (Barnes, Kaase, et al., 1979, p. 524). Protest levels among the younger generations may decrease as these individuals move through the life cycle; but younger generations probably will remain more active than their elders. Moreover, this pattern of progressive generational change should continue among subsequent generations. In the long run this process implies an inevitable increase in citizen action in advanced industrial societies and a broadening of participation to include unconventional political activities.

Participation and Contemporary Democracies

The nature of political participation in advanced industrial societies is changing. Participation in citizen-initiated and policy-oriented forms of political activity is increasing. The last chapter discussed the growth of citizen action groups, communal participation, and direct democracy methods. This chapter documents the expansion of protest politics.

Increases in these participation modes are especially significant because these activities place greater control over the locus and focus of participation in the hands of the citizenry. Political input is not limited to the issues and institutionalized channels determined by elites. A single individual, or a group of citizens, can organize around a specific issue and select the timing and the method of influencing policymakers. These direct-action techniques are high-information and high-pressure activities. They therefore match some of the participation demands of an increasingly educated and politically sophisticated public far more than conventional participation in voting and campaign activities.

A major goal of democratic societies is to expand citizen participation in the political process and thereby increase popular control of political elites. Therefore, increases in communal participation, protest, and other citizen-initiated activities are generally welcomed. This changing pattern of political participation constitutes an important element of the new style of citizen politics in advanced industrial democracies.

At the same time, however, these changing participation patterns are creating some new problems for modern democracies. The growing complexity and technical nature of contemporary issues requires that citizens possess a high level of political sophistication in order to cope with the world of politics. In addition, participation in citizen-initiated activities is more demanding on the individual than voting or campaign activity. Electoral participation of the less sophisticated is often mobilized by political groups (unions, religious/ethic associations, etc.); communal activity requires greater personal initiative. Consequently, involvement in politics is becoming even more dependent on the skills and resources represented by social status.

This situation may increase the participation gap between lower-status groups and higher-status individuals. As the better educated expand their political influence through the use of direct-action methods, less-educated citizens might be unable to compete on the same terms. The politically active may become even more influential, while the less active see their influence wane. Ironically, overall increases in political involvement may mask a growing social-status bias in citizen participation and influence, which runs counter to democratic ideals.

Some evidence of this problem can be seen in the strong relationship of educational level with communal participation and protest. The solution to this problem is to raise the participation levels of lower-status groups, not limit the activity of the better educated. Political leaders must facilitate participation by a broader spectrum of the public and lower the remaining barriers to participation. The dictum of "maximum feasible citizen participation" needs to be followed more closely.[3]

Direct-action methods pose another challenge to contemporary democracies. By their very nature, direct-action techniques disrupt the status quo. These participation forms occasionally challenge the established institutions and procedures of contemporary democracies. This has led some critics to question whether rapidly expanding citizen participation, especially in protest activities, is placing too many demands on already overburdened political systems (Huntington, 1974, 1981; Crozier et al., 1975). Policy cannot be made in the streets, they argue. Efficient and effective policymaking must be based on a deliberative process, where political elites have some latitude in their decisions. A politicized public with intense policy minorities lobbying for their special interests would strain the political consensus that is a requisite of democratic politics.

In short, these analysts argue that it is possible to get too much of a good thing—political participation. Citizen activism must be balanced against the needs for government efficiency and rational policy planning. Hence, they believe that the expansion of participation in recent years may have upset this balance, leading to problems of governability in Western democracies. Samuel Huntington (1981) has taken these arguments to their illogical extreme by claiming that the problem of democracies is that the public takes the democratic creed too literally.

I return to these themes in chapter 11, but these cautions about the excess of participation display at least some disregard for the democratic goals they profess to defend. These writers implicitly assume that the level of citizen involvement during the relatively tranquil 1950s represents the ideal balance between activism and political acquiescence. Hence, increases in citizen participation are considered to be detrimental to the political system. Certainly, Gabriel Almond, Sidney Verba, and the other early survey researchers never intended their work to advocate the limitation of citizen participation; but some have interpreted their findings this way. Extreme levels of politicization and polarized political conflict would threaten the consensual aspects of democratic politics; Weimar Germany is always cited as an example. But contemporary democracies show little in common with the Weimar example. Protest today is generally not antidemocratic behavior; indeed, it is often an attempt by ordinary citizens to pressure the political system to become more democratic. More often than not, the protesters are pressing political elites to open up the political process and be responsive to new issue interests. Furthermore, very few citizens subscribe to the extreme forms of violent political action that actually might threaten the political system.

It is clear that contemporary democracies face new challenges, and their future depends on the nature of the response. But the response to this challenge must not be to push back the clock, to re-create the halcyon politics of a bygone age. Democracies must adapt to survive; maximizing the advantages of increasing citizen participation while minimizing the disadvantages. The experience of the past several years suggest that this is the course we are following. The excesses of politicization and polarization are being rejected, while institutions are changing to accommodate increased citizen participation (Wattenberg, 1985). Democracy is threatened when we fail to take the democratic creed literally and reject these challenges.

Notes

1. These analyses are based on the Political Action Survey (Barnes, Kaase, et al., 1979), which did not include a French sample. The protest measure is a simple additive scale of the respondent's willingness to participate in the seven protest activities of table 4.1. The analyses in figures 4.2 and 4.3 are based on multiple regression; figure entries are standardized regression coefficients.

2. The comparable British and German analyses are as follows:

	Britain	Germany
Education	.18	.18
Age	−.26	−.32
Gender	.19	.07
Strength of party	.12	.15
Personal dissatisfaction	.13	.07
R	.47	.45

3. This term is identified with the Great Society programs initiated by the Johnson administration to increase the participation of minorities and low-income groups. These institutionalized participation channels have been adopted by a range of citizen groups and governments in the United States and other democracies (Sharpe, 1979).

PART TWO

Political Orientations

5. Values in Change

The values of the mass public define the essence of democratic politics. Value priorities identify what are important to citizens—what are, or should be, the goals of society and the political system. The clash between alternative value systems underlies much of the political conflict and competition in Western democracies. Broad value orientations often are a strong influence on the more explicitly political attitudes and behaviors of the mass public.

Another element in the new style of citizen politics involves a fundamental change in the value priorities of many individuals. Even the most casual comparison of contemporary societies to those of a generation ago would uncover substantial evidence of changing social norms. Hierarchical relationships and deference toward authority are giving way to decentralization, quality circles, and participatory decision making (Toffler, 1980; Naisbitt, 1982). Citizens demand more control over the decisions affecting their lives. Previous chapters describe how these participatory norms stimulate greater political involvement, but the consequences of value change are much broader. The new values are affecting attitudes toward work, life styles, and the individual's role in society.

The definition of societal goals and the meaning of "success" are also changing. Until fairly recently, the mark of success for many Americans was measured almost solely in economic terms: a large house, two cars in the garage, and other signs of affluence. In Europe the threshold for economic success might have been lower, but material concerns were equally important. Once affluence became widespread, many people realized that bigger is not necessarily better, and that small is beautiful (Schumacher, 1973). The consensus in favor of economic growth was also tempered by a strong concern for environmental quality. Attention to the quality of life in advanced industrial societies is now as important as the quantity of life.

Social relations and acceptance of diversity are another example of values in change. Progress on racial, sexual, ethnic, and religious equality are transforming American and European societies. Moreover, social norms involving sex, social relations, and the choice of life styles have changed dramatically in a few short decades. Evidence of value change is all around us, if we look.

We think in the present, and so the magnitude of these changes is not always appreciated. But compare, if you will, the diversity of contemporary American life styles to the images of American life depicted on vintage TV reruns from the 1950s. Series such as "Ozzie and Harriet," "Father Knows Best," and "Leave It to Beaver" reflect many values of a bygone era. How well would the Nelsons or the Cleavers adjust to a world with women's liberation, the new morality, racial desegregation, punk rock, and alternative life styles?

A similar process of value change is affecting Western Europe. The clearest evidence of these changes can be seen in the attitudes and behaviors of the young. Student movements proliferated throughout Europe in the late 1960s. What often began as criticisms of specific government policies frequently led to deeper questions about the basic goals and procedures of the social and political systems. These views contributed to the protests and citizen action groups described in the last chapter. An alternative cultural movement gradually developed from these new value orientations. Many large European cities contain distinct counterculture districts where natural food stores, cooperative businesses, child-care centers, and youth-oriented restaurants and cafes offer a life style attuned to the new values. These communities place less emphasis on profit and stress self-management and social service. The influence of these alternative centers is gradually spreading into the rest of society. Many older Europeans view these developments with shock or dismay, especially when they equate the alternative scene only with punk hairdos, heavy metal, and unconventional life styles. But clearly the rivers of change run much deeper (and broader) than fashions and fads. Basic value priorities are being transformed in America and Western Europe.

The Nature of Value Change

Values are important to study because they provide the standards that guide the attitudes and behaviors of the public. Values signify a preference for certain personal and social goals, as well as the methods to obtain these goals. One individual may place a high priority on freedom, equality, and social harmony, and favor policies that strengthen these values; another citizen may stress independence, social recognition, and ambition in guiding their actions.

Values are so central to human actions that many personal and political decisions involve a choice between several valued goals. One situation may force a choice between behaving independently and obediently, or between behaving politely and sincerely. A national policy may present contrasts between the goals of world peace and national security, or between economic well-being and protection of nature. Citizens develop a general framework for making these decisions by organizing values into a value system, which ranks values in terms of their importance to the individual. Citizen behavior may indeed appear inconsistent and illogical (see chapter 2) unless the researcher considers the values of each individual and how these values are applied in specific situations. To one citizen, busing is an issue of social equality and civil rights; to another, it is an issue of freedom and providing for one's family. Both are correct, and attitudes toward busing are determined by how the individual weighs these conflicting values.

Value systems, by definition, are all-encompassing; they should include all of the salient goals that guide human behavior. Milton Rokeach (1973) developed an inventory of eighteen instrumental values focusing on the methods of achieving desired goals and eighteen terminal values defining preferred end-state goals. A complete list of important human goals should be much longer, and a complete list would be necessary to explain fully the pattern of citizen action. This chapter focuses on areas in which the value systems of Western publics are apparently changing.

The theme of value change became a center of research attention as the societal evidence of change became more obvious. In reaction to the individualization of society, David Riesman and others stress the shift from group-solidarity and other-directed values, to self-actualizing and inner-directed goals (Riesman, 1968; Huntington, 1974). Several authors noted the general decline in concern for economic security as Western societies initially entered an age of affluence (Bell, 1973; Lane, 1965). Moreover, the process of value change is broader than just economic interests; it involves declines in values such as respect for authority, conformity, religiosity, and the work ethic (Flanagan, 1982).

The most systematic attempt to describe and explain these value changes in a comprehensive fashion is the work of Ronald Inglehart (1977, 1979a, 1981, 1984a). His explanation of value change is based on two premises. First, he suggests that the public's basic value priorities are determined by a scarcity hypothesis: Individuals "place the greatest value on those things that are in relatively short supply" (Inglehart, 1981, p. 881). That is, when some valued object is difficult to obtain, its worth is magnified. But if the supply increases to match the demand, the object is taken for granted and attention shifts to other objects still in short supply. For example, water is a precious commodity during a drought, but when the rains return to normal, the concern over water evaporates. Conversely, the recent concern for clear water arose when pollution became widespread and the availability of clean water became uncertain. This general argument can be applied to other items valued by society.

The second component of Inglehart's theory is a socialization hypothesis. This hypothesis states that "to a large extent, one's value priorities reflect the conditions that prevailed during one's preadult years" (Inglehart, 1981, p. 881). These formative conditions include both the immediate situation in one's own family and the broader political and economic conditions of society.

The combination of both hypotheses—scarcity and socialization—produces a general model of value change. An individual's basic value priorities are initially formed early in life in reaction to the socioeconomic conditions of this formative period. Once basic value priorities develop, they tend to endure in the face of subsequent changes in social conditions.

The introductory chapter describes the development of advanced industrial societies in Western Europe and North America. These societies are characterized by unprecedented affluence, greatly increased educational levels, expanding information opportunities, an extensive social welfare system, and other related characteristics. Western societies have experienced dramatic changes in these areas over a relatively brief time period. We have linked these social trends to the growing sophistication, cognitive mobilization, and participation of modern electorates. In addition, Inglehart maintains that these social forces are important in changing the public's basic value priorities because these trends have substantially altered the socioeconomic structure of these nations. Hence the relative scarcity of valued goals has changed.

In order to generalize the scarcity hypothesis into a broader theoretical model, Inglehart draws on the work of Abraham Maslow (1954). Maslow suggests that there is a hierarchical order to human goals. Individuals first seek to fulfill basic subsistence needs: water, food, and shelter. When these needs are met, the search continues until enough material goods are acquired to attain a comfortable margin of economic security. Having accomplished this, individuals may turn to higher-order postmaterial needs, such as the need for belonging, self-esteem, participation, self-actualization, and the fulfillment of aesthetic and intellectual potential. Thus, goal seeking can be predicted in terms of this hierarchical ordering of values.

The logic of Maslow's value hierarchy has been applied to political issues as well (figure 5.1). Many political issues, such as economic security, law and order, and national defense, tap underlying sustenance and safety needs. Inglehart describes these goals as "material" values. In a time of depression or civil unrest, for example, security and sustenance needs undoubtedly receive substantial attention. If a society can make significant progress in addressing these goals, then the public's attention can shift to higher-order values. These higher-order goals are reflected in the issues of individual freedom, self-expression, and participation. These goals are labeled as "postmaterial" values. Inglehart contends that this material/postmaterial continuum provides a general framework for understanding the primary value changes now occurring in advanced

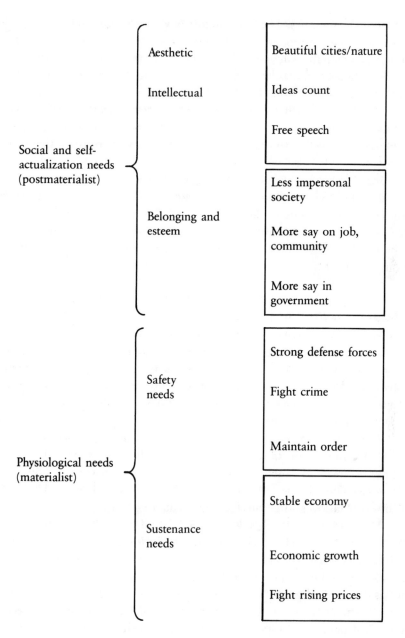

FIGURE 5.1

THE MASLOVIAN VALUE HIERARCHY

SOURCE: Inglehart (1977, p. 42).

industrial democracies. The broad nature of value change leads some researchers to describe the process as a transition from "Old Politics" values of economic growth, public order, national security, and traditional life styles to "New Politics" values of individual freedoms, social equality, and the quality of life (Miller and Levitin, 1979; Hildebrandt and Dalton, 1978). Other studies document the decline in adherence to strict moral codes in favor of greater personal autonomy (Harding, 1986). Regardless of how this process is conceptualized, there is general agreement that the public's basic value priorities are in a state of flux.

Many researchers foresee increasing support for postmaterial values in the decades ahead. Gradually, traditional material goals will be overtaken by new concerns for environmental quality, freedom of expression, participation in the decisions affecting one's life, social equality, and related themes. This chapter explores these value changes and some of their potential effects on advanced industrial democracies.

The Distribution of Values

Most individuals attach a positive worth to both material and postmaterial goals. The average individual prefers both economic growth and a clean environment, social stability and individual freedom. Politics, however, often involves a conflict between these valued goals. To understand fully the process of value change, it is important to identify which goals take priority in the public's mind.

The public's value priorities were assessed by asking survey respondents to rank the most important goals from a list of alternatives. Table 5.1 presents the top priorities of Americans and West Europeans across a set of twelve social goals. The selection of items included in each survey was guided by the theory of Maslow's value hierarchy, presented in figure 5.1.

Most citizens on both sides of the Atlantic still place material goals at the top of their value hierarchy. Americans give top priority to a stable economy, crime prevention, and a strong defense. Europeans most often stress the need for stable prices, law and order, and economic growth. Despite this emphasis on material goals, Europeans and Americans also give high rankings to the postmaterial goals of participating in job-related and political decision making. A significant proportion of these publics, albeit a small number, stress the other postmaterial goals.

A subset of the above items has been used to construct a single measure of material/postmaterial values (Inglehart, 1977). Survey respondents are asked the question:

There is a lot of talk these days about what the aims of the country should be for the next ten years. On this card are listed some of the goals which different people would give as top priority. Would you please say which of these you consider the most important? And which would be the next most important?

☐ Maintaining order in the nation
☐ Giving people more say in important government decisions
☐ Fighting rising prices
☐ Protecting freedom of speech

Individuals are classified into one of three value-priority groups on the basis of the choices made among these four items. Materialists select the first and third items, displaying an emphasis on personal and economic security. Post-

TABLE 5.1

THE DISTRIBUTION OF VALUES (IN PERCENT)

Value	United States	Great Britain	West Germany	France
Fighting rising prices (M)	29	25	25	33
Fighting crime (M)	43	32	23	22
Economic growth (M)	18	29	26	13
Maintaining a stable economy (M)	51	23	33	11
Maintaining order in the nation (M)	27	18	23	15
A friendlier, less impersonal society (PM)	6	9	11	31
Protecting freedom of speech (PM)	14	16	12	18
Giving people more say at work and in their community (PM)	25	12	8	21
Giving people more say in important government decisions (PM)	27	10	7	11
Maintaining strong defense forces (M)	39	11	5	3
A society where ideas count more than money (PM)	13	4	3	11
More beautiful cities	4	3	7	6

SOURCES: *United States,* Political Action Study, 1981; *other nations,* Eurobarometer 10.

NOTES: Table entries are the percentages ranking each goal as most important or second in importance from a list of twelve goals; in the United States the top three rankings are combined. Material goals are denoted by (M), postmaterial goals by (PM).

TABLE 5.2

THE TREND IN MATERIAL/POSTMATERIAL VALUES IN EUROPE
(IN PERCENT)

Country	1970	1973	1976	1979	1982	1984
Great Britain						
Material	36	32	36	25	25	24
Mixed	56	60	56	63	61	59
Postmaterial	8	8	8	11	14	17
	100	100	100	100	100	100
PDI[a]	28	24	28	15	11	7
West Germany						
Material	46	42	42	37	32	23
Mixed	44	50	47	52	54	58
Postmaterial	11	8	11	11	13	20
	100	100	100	100	100	100
PDI[a]	35	34	31	26	19	3
France						
Material	38	35	41	36	34	36
Mixed	51	53	47	49	55	51
Postmaterial	11	12	12	15	11	12
	100	100	100	100	100	100
PDI[a]	27	23	29	21	23	24

SOURCES: European Community Studies, 1970, 1973; Eurobarometers 6, 12, 18 and 20.

a. PDI (Percentage Difference Index) is the difference between the percent with material values and the percent with postmaterial values.

materialists choose the other two items, indicating their emphasis on self-expression and participation. Survey respondents who select one material and one postmaterial item are classified as having mixed value priorities. This four-item index is a very crude measure of the complex and extensive value systems we wish to study. Still, the simplicity of the index has led to its adoption in surveys of more than twenty nations (Inglehart, 1981).

The distribution of value groups is presented in tables 5.2 and 5.3. In all four nations the number of materialists exceeds the number of postmaterialists by a sizable margin. In the most recent French survey, for example, 36 percent of the public selected both material goals, while only 12 percent chose both postmaterial goals. This is not surprising; the conditions fostering value change

TABLE 5.3

THE TREND IN MATERIAL/POSTMATERIAL VALUES IN THE UNITED STATES
(IN PERCENT)

	1972	1976	1980	1984
Material	35	31	34	21
Mixed	55	59	56	63
Postmaterial	10	10	10	16
	100	100	100	100
PDI[a]	25	21	24	5

SOURCE: CPS Election Studies.

a. PDI (Percentage Difference Index) is the difference between the percent with material values and the percent with postmaterial values.

should take several generations to accumulate, and in historical perspective the development of advanced industrialism is a relatively recent phenomenon. At the same time, these data provide important support for the value-change thesis. Already less than half of these populations focus exclusively on material concerns. Even the relatively small number of "pure" postmaterialists—8 to 15 percent—should not be discounted. Other studies find that postmaterialists are disproportionately represented among political elites and those actively involved in politics (Inglehart, 1981).

Many critics of the value-change thesis maintain that these are transitory beliefs, nurtured by the affluence and domestic tranquillity of the 1950s and early 1960s. At the first sign of socioeconomic difficulties, it is argued, the public's priorities will revert to material goals. The data in these tables undermine this criticism. In the face of major economic recessions and domestic disorders during the last decade, the distribution of value priorities has held fairly constant. Once value priorities are socialized, they appear to be relatively resistant to subsequent changes in social conditions. There certainly has not been a resurgence of material values; if anything, these data describe a continuing decline in the percentage of materialists. Indeed, the most recent American time point displays a significant shift away from material concerns, and a similar trend is evident in Britain, West Germany, and most other Western democracies.[1]

If data for a longer time period were available, we would expect to find a very substantial decline in material values over the past several generations.[2] This is because the process of value change has been closely tied to generational change within Western democracies (Inglehart, 1977; Abramson and Inglehart, 1986). Older generations, reared in the years before World War II, grew up in a period of widespread uncertainty. These individuals suffered through the Great Depression in the 1930s, endured two world wars and the social and economic traumas that accompanied these events. Social conditions were especially severe in Germany; older generations had successively experienced World War I, economic collapse in the 1920s, the Great Depression in the 1930s, the consolidation of the authoritarian Nazi state, and then the massive destruction of World War II. Given these circumstances, it is understandable that older generations in all four nations became concerned with material goals: economic growth, economic security, domestic order, and social and military security.

In contrast, younger generations in Europe and North America were raised in a period of unprecedented affluence and security. Present-day living standards are often two or more times higher than most Western nations ever experienced before World War II. The rapid growth of the welfare state now protects most citizens from even major economic problems. Postwar generations also have a broader world view, reflecting their higher educational levels, greater exposure to political information, and more diverse cultural experiences. Furthermore, the past four decades are one of the longest periods of international peace in modern European history. Under these conditions, the material concerns that preoccupied prewar generations have diminished in urgency. Growing up in a period when material and security needs seem assured, postwar generations are apparently shifting their attention toward postmaterial goals.

The changing values of the young were most clearly evident in the 1960s and 1970s, when the clash between generations occasionally spilled over into the streets. In recent years, the popular media has emphasized a seemingly different trend among the young: The growth of the Yuppie phenomenon and patterns of conspicuous consumption by some young people. In fact, the Yuppies are an example of the social changes we are discussing; young, highly educated professionals now earn salaries in excess of their basic needs. The use of this disposable income necessarily creates a materialist image. The value-change thesis maintains, however, that wealth cannot always be equated with materialism. While some young people measure success by the standards of the Ewings, such traditional values are not as widespread as they once were. As one counterexample to the Yuppie image, in 1985 the director of the Peace Corps went on a TV talk show asking for 600 volunteers to work on African relief projects (at a salary of $250 a month). By the weekend, the Peace Corps headquarters was overwhelmed with over 10,000 inquiries. Clearly many young people are not preoccupied with their careers and buying a BMW. Events such as Band-Aid, Live-Aid, Farm-Aid, Sport-Aid, and Hands Across America tap the activism and social concern that exists among the young. With scientific survey evidence we can determine how far the process of generational change has actually progressed.

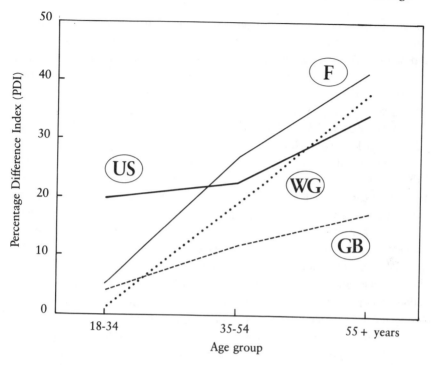

FIGURE 5.2

AGE DIFFERENCES IN VALUE PRIORITIES

SOURCES: *United States,* 1980 CPS American Election Study; *other nations,* Eurobarometer 18. The Percentage Difference Index shows the difference between the percentage with material values and the percentage with postmaterial values.

A sense of the generational pattern in value priorities can be gained by examining age differences in value orientations. Since values tend to be enduring beliefs, different age groups should retain the mark of their formative generational experiences.

Figure 5.2 displays the age differences in value priorities within each nation. Values are measured by the Percentage Difference Index (PDI), which is simply the percentage of materialists in each age group minus the percentage of postmaterialists. Positive numbers thus indicate a preponderance of materialists. Generally speaking, the younger cohorts socialized during affluent postwar years display greater attachment to postmaterial values, while the older cohorts reared in less affluent and secure periods retain a higher priority for material values.

The value difference between young and old also presents a cross-national pattern consistent with national historical conditions. Germany, for example, experienced tremendous socioeconomic change during the past few generations. Consequently, the value differences between the youngest (PDI = 1) and oldest West German cohorts (PDI = 38) are larger than for any other nation. In contrast, Britain's economic condition was already at a relatively high level early in this century and increased only gradually over the past fifty years. Thus, British cohorts display much smaller generational differences (youngest PDI = 5, oldest PDI = 18). In short, these data are quite consistent with a generational model of value change.

These age differences can, of course, also reflect life-cycle differences in value orientations. That is, it is possible that younger individuals show a greater preference for postmaterial values because they have, as yet, not experienced the demands of careers, mortgages, and other family responsibilities. Youth is a time when one is free to espouse new ideas and aesthetic values relatively unencumbered by practical economic realities. The life-cycle thesis holds that as these younger cohorts age, their value priorities should come to resemble those which older cohorts now display. Everyone knows of examples where radical young people became more conventional with age. Is this effect sufficient to explain all the age-group differences in figure 5.2?

The debate over the generational versus life-cycle interpretation of age differences in value priorities has been pursued at great length (Inglehart, 1977, 1984; Dalton, 1977; Flanagan, 1982; Boeltken and Jagodzinski, 1984). There is evidence to support both the generational and life-cycle theories; both processes are apparently influencing the public's value priorities to some extent. The weight of the evidence, however, suggests that generational change is the major explanation for the present value differences between young and old. This can be seen in figure 5.3, which tracks the value priorities of several European generations from 1970 until 1982.[3] The oldest cohort, age 65 to 85 in 1970, is clearly oriented toward material goals. The youngest cohort, age 15 to 24 in 1970, is almost evenly balanced between material and postmaterial values. More important, the broad generational differences in value orientations remain fairly constant over time, even though all cohorts are moving through the life cycle. The youngest cohort, for example, is approaching middle age by the end of the survey series, and yet its postmaterial value orientations do not lessen significantly. Life-cycle experiences can modify, but do not replace, the early learning of value priorities.

Another factor affecting value priorities is educational level. Obviously, the effects of education overlap with those of generation; the young are more likely to be better educated than the old. Educational level also is an indirect indicator of an individual's economic circumstances during adolescence, when value priorities were being formed. Educational level in the class-stratified Euro-

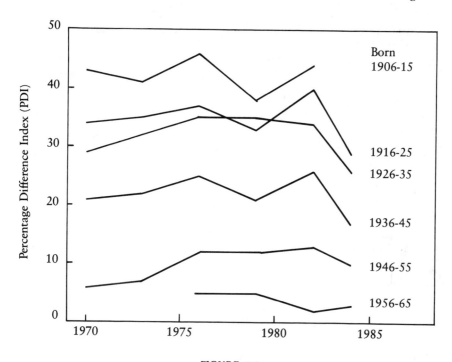

FIGURE 5.3

LONGITUDINAL COHORT DIFFERENCES IN VALUE PRIORITIES

SOURCES: European Community Studies, Eurobarometers; results are based on the combined samples of France, West Germany, Italy, Belgium, the Netherlands, and Luxembourg.

pean educational systems reflects the family's social status during an individual's youth. Education also may affect value priorities because of the content of instruction. Higher education generally places more stress on the values of participation, self-expression, intellectual understanding, and other postmaterial goals. Moreover, the diversity of the modern university milieu may encourage a broadening of social perspectives.

Differences in material/postmaterial values (PDI scores) by educational level are presented in figure 5.4. In every nation, individuals with only a primary education are oriented predominantly toward material goals. In France, for instance, this educational group was 50 percent materialist and only 3 percent postmaterialist, yielding a PDI score of 47. The proportion of materialists decreases fairly steadily with educational level. Among citizens with some college, postmaterialists actually outnumber materialists in all three European nations.

The concentration of these new values among the young and better educated gives added significance to these value orientations. If Inglehart's theory is

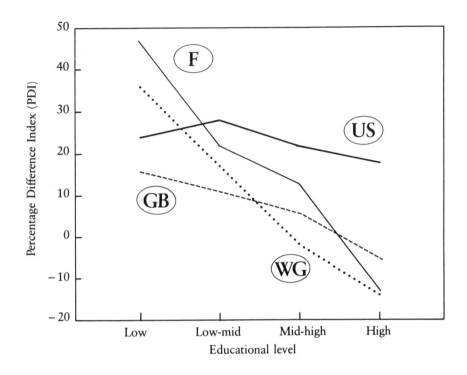

FIGURE 5.4

EDUCATION DIFFERENCES IN VALUE PRIORITIES

SOURCES: *United States,* 1980 CPS American Election Study; *other nations,* Eurobarometer 18.

correct, the percentage of postmaterialists should gradually increase over time, as older materialist cohorts are replaced by younger, more postmaterialist generations (Abramson and Inglehart, 1986). Similarly, if expanding educational opportunities continue to increase the public's educational level, support for postmaterial values should also grow. Value change has the appearance of an ongoing process.

The Consequences of Value Change

Even though postmaterialists now constitute only a small minority in most Western democracies, the impact of these values is already apparent, extending beyond politics to all aspects of society. At the workplace, for example, these new value orientations are fueling demands for a more flexible and individually oriented work environment. Rigid, hierarchical, assembly-line systems of production are being challenged by worker participation (codetermination), quality circles, and flexible working hours. Postmaterial values are linked to a shift from extrinsic occupational goals (security and a good salary) to intrinsic goals (a feeling of accomplishment and sense of responsibility) (Strumpel, 1976; Harding, 1986). Many business analysts bemoan the decline of the work ethic, but it is more accurate to say that the work ethic is becoming motivated by a new set of goals.

In more general terms, social relations are also changing in reaction to the public's new value orientations. Deference to authority of all forms is generally declining, as individuals are more willing to challenge elites. Bosses, army officers, university professors, and political leaders all decry the decline in deference to their authority. But the postmaterial credo is that authority is earned by an individual, not bestowed by a position. Similarly, many citizens are placing less reliance on social norms—from class, religion, or community—as a guide for behavior. The public's behavior in all aspects of social and political life is becoming more self-directed (Harding, 1986). This shows in the declining brand-name loyalty among consumers, and the decline of political party loyalty among voters. In short, contemporary life styles reflect a demand for greater freedom and individuality, which appears in fashions, consumer tastes, social behavior, and interpersonal relations. Two recent bestsellers, Alvin Toffler's *The Third Wave* (1980) and John Naisbitt's *Megatrends* (1982) discuss these and related phenomena in fascinating detail.

If we focus our attention on the realm of politics, postmaterial values have been linked to several elements of the new style of citizen politics. Postmaterialists have, for example, championed a new set of political issues—environmental quality, nuclear energy, women's rights, and consumerism—that often were overlooked by the political establishment. Debates in Washington about acid rain, toxic waste, and the safety of nuclear plants have close parallels in the capitals of Europe; and the proponents of these issues have similar characteristics. Many other issues—disarmament, codetermination, and social equality—have been revived by postmaterial groups and reintepreted in terms of new value perspectives. No longer are these transient "sunshine" issues, since the public's concern for these issues has persisted and grown through the 1970s and early 1980s. This new set of issues has been added to the political agenda of contemporary democracies.

Value change also affects the patterns of political participation examined in the two previous chapters. Postmaterial values stimulate direct participation in the decisions affecting one's life—whether at school, the workplace, or in the political process. Figure 5.5 documents the relationship between value priorities and general interest in politics. Postmaterialists are consistently more

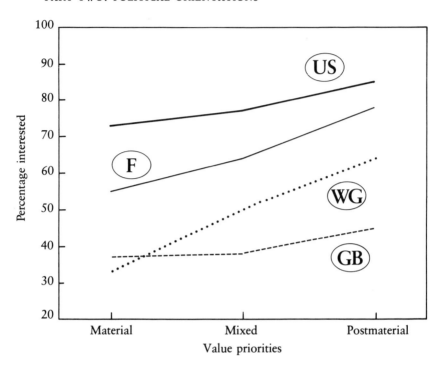

FIGURE 5.5

POLITICAL INTEREST BY VALUE PRIORITIES

SOURCES: *United States,* Political Action Study, 1974; *other nations,* 1981 European Values Study.

involved in politics than are materialists. The process of value change increases demands for greater citizen input. In addition, because postmaterialists are more active in politics, their political influence is greater than their small numbers imply. Indeed, among the group of future elites — university educated youth — postmaterial values predominate.[4] As these individuals succeed into positions of economic, social, and political leadership, the impact of changing values should strengthen (Szabo, 1983).

So far, at least, the participatory orientation of postmaterialists has not affected all participation modes equally (Inglehart, 1979b). Postmaterial values are not related to electoral participation, and in some instances voting turnout is actually lower among postmaterialists. This is partially because the establishment parties have been hesitant to respond to new issue demands. In addition, postmaterialists are generally skeptical of established hierarchical organizations, such as most political parties. Instead, postmaterial values have stimulated par-

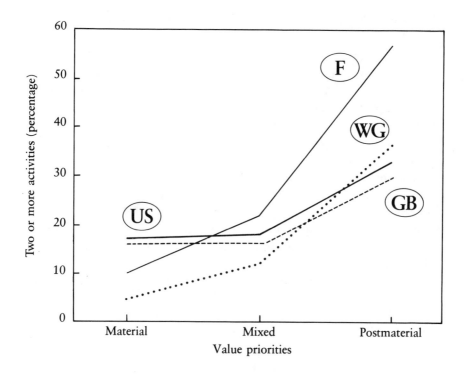

FIGURE 5.6

PROTEST PARTICIPATION BY VALUE PRIORITIES

SOURCES: *United States*, Political Action Study, 1974; *other nations*, 1981 European Values Survey.

ticipation in citizen initiatives, protests, and other forms of unconventional political activity. In the 1981 European Values Survey, for instance, postmaterialists are more than twice as likely as materialists to participate in protests (figure 5.6). These nonpartisan participation opportunities provide postmaterialists with a more direct influence on politics, which matches their value orientations. Most postmaterialists also possess the political skills to carry out these more demanding forms of political action. As an earlier chapter notes, along with increasing levels of citizen involvement has come a change in the form of political participation.

Value Change and Value Stability

This chapter has emphasized the changing values of Western publics, but a more accurate description would stress the increasing diversity of value priorities.

Most people still give primary attention to material goals and the socioeconomic issues deriving from these values will continue to dominate political debate for decades to come. The persistence of traditional values should not be overlooked. At the same time, a new type of postmaterial values is spreading within Western publics. For nearly every example of the persistence of traditional material value patterns, there is now a counterexample reflecting postmaterial values. For every Yuppie driving a BMW, someone is conscientiously volunteering time to work on some issue (often it is the same person). The diversity of values marks a major change in the nature of citizen politics.

The consequences of value change can be seen in the issues of contemporary political debate. Concerns for environmental protection, individual freedom, social equality, participation, and the quality of life have been *added* to the traditional political agenda of economic and security issues. For now, and the foreseeable future, democratic politics will be marked by a mix of material and postmaterial issues.

Inevitably, changes in the public's basic value priorities should carry over to the structures of the political process. Already there are signs of institutional change to accommodate these new political demands. For example, there has been a general increase in the use of referendums in Western democracies, at least partially in reaction to demands for more participatory democracy (Butler and Ranney, 1981). Even in West Germany, where Hitler's plebiscites in the 1930s discredited direct democracy methods, environmental and other postmaterial groups are calling for a revival of the referendum and initiative. Similarly, bureaucracies in most systems are being pressured to open the policy process to citizen advisory panels and planning groups (Foster, 1980; Kweit and Kweit, 1981).

Another question involves the impact of these new values on the political parties and citizen voting behavior. Most of the established political parties are still oriented to traditional social divisions, and if anything, they have resisted attempts to incorporate postmaterial issues into a partisan framework. Nevertheless, subsequent chapters show that postmaterial values and issue concerns are injecting new volatility into Western party systems, often leading to the fragmentation of the established parties or the creation of new parties.

Only a few skeptics still doubt that value priorities are changing among Western publics; the evidence of change is obvious. It is more difficult to anticipate all of the consequences of this process of value change. By monitoring these trends, however, we may get a preview of the future nature of citizen politics in advanced industrial democracies.

Notes

1. Even during this relatively brief time span, generational turnover contributed to a postmaterial trend (Abramson and Inglehart, 1986). For instance, in 1970 the pre-World War I generation constituted about 16 percent of the West German public; by 1982, this group constituted about 5 percent. In the place of these older citizens, young Germans, socialized in the affluent post-World War II era, had entered the electorate.

2. Arnold Heidenheimer and Donald Kommers (1975, p. 119) document a dramatic long-term reversal between 1949 and 1970 in the public's priority for two freedoms: freedom from want and freedom of speech.

3. Figure 5.3 is based on the combined results of samples from six nations: Britain, West Germany, France, Italy, Belgium, and the Netherlands. The nations were combined to produce age-group samples large enough to estimate values precisely. Data are available for additional years and display more temporal variation than the figure. For a full discussion of these data see Boeltken and Jagodzinski (1984), Inglehart (1984a).

4. Inglehart (1981) finds that European political elites (candidates for the European parliament) are nearly three times more postmaterialist than the general public. Postmaterialists are also more common among younger elites.

6. Issues and Ideological Orientations

Issues are the currency of politics. The public's issue opinions identify their priorities for government action and their expectations for the political process. Parties are largely defined by their issue positions, and elections provide the public with a means of selecting between competing issue programs offered by the candidates and parties. Moreover, as citizens become more sophisticated and involved in the political process, issue beliefs are an increasingly important influence on voting and other political behaviors.

Issue beliefs fulfill a valuable linkage role between broad value orientations and everyday political concerns. Issue opinions are partially determined by the value orientations examined in the last chapter, but issues also reflect the influence of political factors external to the individual: the cues provided by political elites, the flow of political events, and the application of abstract values to specific situations. For example, a citizen may favor the principle of equal rights for all citizens; but attitudes toward voting rights, job discrimination, school busing, open housing, and other civil rights legislation represent mixes of different value orientations and practical concerns. Consequently, issue opinions tend to be more changeable than broad value orientations.

Another important characteristic of issues is that citizens tend to specialize their political interests by focusing attention on a few areas — to become members of one or more *issue publics* (see chapter 2). Some citizens may be especially concerned with education policy; others are more interested in the arms race, civil rights, environmental protection, or another issue. In general, only a minority of the public is normally interested and informed on any specific issue, but most citizens are members of at least one issue public. Members of each issue public are relatively well informed about the issue at stake, and follow the actions of political leaders and the political parties. The salient issues for members of an issue public are also likely to have a strong impact on their political behavior.

The size of issue publics is influenced by several factors. Citizens generally devote attention to the issues that have the most direct relevance for their everyday life. The economic and tax policies of the government therefore generate substantial public interest, while policies with a narrow scope are frequently less salient. Similarly, the issue publics for domestic policies generally are larger than for foreign policy, with the exception of the war-and-peace issue. In addition, a sophisticated study of the American public's changing issue interests indicates that the visibility of an issue in the media often affects popular interest in an issue (MacKuen, 1981). For instance, as political debate on the crime problem grows, so too does public interest in the crime issue.

Issue opinions should be viewed as a dynamic aspect of politics, and the theme of changing popular values can be carried over to the study of issue beliefs. In some areas, contemporary publics are obviously more liberal than their predecessors. The issues of women's rights, environmental protection, social equality, and individual life styles were unknown or highly divisive a generation ago; a growing consensus now exists on many of these issues. In other areas, citizens remain divided on the goals of government, and discussions of tax revolts, neoconservative revival, and supply-side economics suggest that conservative values have not lost their appeal for many citizens. This chapter describes the present issue beliefs of Western publics and highlights, where possible, the trends in these beliefs.

Domestic Policy Opinions

Domestic policy issues are the major topics of political debate in most Western democracies. Domestic policy was once synonymous with concern over economic matters, and economic issues still rank at the top of the public's political agenda for most elections. More recently, however, the number of salient domestic policy issues has proliferated. A growing number of citizens are concerned with noneconomic issues such as social equality, environmental protection, and citizen participation. No longer is political conflict based on a single set of issue concerns. This section provides an overview of the wide-ranging domestic policy concerns of Western publics.

SOCIOECONOMIC ISSUES AND THE STATE

For most of this century, the political conflicts that emerged from industrialization and the Great Depression dominated politics in Western party systems. A single dimension of political cleavage incorporated attitudes toward the size of government, socioeconomic conflict, and economic equality. A central topic in this area has been the government's role in society, especially the provision of basic social needs. Most Western democracies introduced some form of government-backed social insurance program early in the twentieth century, and comparable American programs flowed from Roosevelt's New Deal (Heidenheimer and Flora, 1981). These social insurance programs were designed to protect individual citizens against economic calamities caused by illness, unemployment, disability, or other hardship. Labor unions and working-class organizations favored the extension of government involvement as a way to improve the life chances of the average person; business leaders and members of the middle class opposed these same policies as an unnecessary government intrusion into private affairs. At stake was not only the question of government involvement in society but also the desirability of certain social goals and the distribution of political influence between labor and business. To a substantial extent, the terms *liberal* and *conservative* were synonymous with one's position on these questions. Attitudes toward these issues provided the major source of political competition in most Western democracies. Class-based opinions on socioeconomic issues were the major policy concerns of many voters.

The initial conflict concerned the government's implementation or expansion of basic social programs such as old-age security, unemployment compensation, sickness insurance, or health-care programs. Nearly all industrial democracies, with the exception of the United States, developed a full range of social programs that eventually were accepted by liberals and conservatives alike.

Following World War II, the political pressures of European socialist parties further expanded the government's role to include the ownership of a substantial portion of the industrial sector (Heidenheimer et al., 1983). In Britain, West Germany, and France the government owns a significant portion of the communication industry, railways, airlines, automobiles, steel, coal and other energy sources, and banking. The government's share of the national income has steadily grown over the past quarter century, reaching almost half of the gross domestic product (GDP) in most European nations and over a third in the United States.

The nearly steady expansion of government activity during the postwar period is often taken as evidence of growing public support for government action. Similarly, the more recent emergence of a tax revolt against big government and the electoral successes of Margaret Thatcher, Ronald Reagan, and Helmut Kohl under this banner are interpreted as evidence of a new conservative trend in public attitudes toward government. In actuality, public opinion is more complex than either description.

Survey evidence suggests that many citizens now believe that it is the government's role, or at least responsibility, to promote individual well-being and guarantee the quality of life for its citizens. Table 6.1 displays the percentage of citizens who think the government has an essential responsibility to deal with specific social problems. Britons and West Germans have uniformly high expectations of government: A majority think the government is responsible

TABLE 6.1

GOVERNMENT RESPONSIBILITY FOR DEALING WITH PROBLEMS
(IN PERCENT)

Problem area	United States	Great Britain	West Germany
Fighting pollution	56	69	73
Fighting crime	53	56	78
Providing good medical care	42	74	63
Providing good education	47	68	55
Looking after old people	41	58	51
Guaranteeing jobs	34	55	60
Providing adequate housing	25	60	39
Equal rights for minorities	33	24	20
Reducing income inequality	13	25	29
Equal rights for sexes	24	19	27
Average	37	51	49
N	(1719)	(1483)	(2307)

SOURCE: Political Action Study.

NOTE: Table entries are the percentages who think each problem is an essential government responsibility.

for correcting pollution, lessening unemployment, providing basic social services, fighting crime, and protecting the elderly. Support for government action to resolve social needs is a core element of the European political culture.

In contrast, Americans are much more reserved in their support for government action. Even in areas where the government is a primary actor, such as care of the elderly and civil rights, only a minority of Americans view these problems as essential government responsibilities. The United States is a major exception among Western democracies to the pattern of popular support for activist government (Heidenheimer et al., 1983, chap. 12). Public ownership of a significant portion of the economy was never attempted, and most Americans oppose nationalization on even a limited scale. Popular support for basic social programs remains underdeveloped by European standards. Data from the 1980 American election study indicate that the citizenry is evenly divided on the issue of a national health system—an established program in all of Western Europe. A more liberal proposal for government-guaranteed employment garners the support of barely a third of the American public. The conservative socioeconomic attitudes of Americans are often explained in terms of the individualist nature of American society and the absence of a socialist working-class party (Lipset, 1981a).

Not only do Americans generally place fewer demands on their government, but this support for government action has apparently lessened in recent

TABLE 6.2

BRITISH ATTITUDES TOWARD GOVERNMENT ACTIVITY (IN PERCENT)

Activity	1963	1964	1966	1970	February 1974	October 1974	1979	1983
Nationalization of industry								
Lot more	10	8	8	10	9	9	6	6
Few more	14	17	17	9	16	20	10	9
No more	36	45	42	40	40	41	40	35
Denationalize	22	18	19	29	21	20	37	37
No opinion	18	12	14	12	15	11	7	12
	100	100	100	100	100	100	100	100
Social services spending								
More	77	55	43	56	31	37	19	–
Same	20	41	44	36	32	38	26	–
Less	–a	–a	8	4	31	26	49	–
No opinion	3	4	5	4	5	6	6	–
	100	100	100	100	100	100	100	–

SOURCE: British Election Studies.

NOTE: The phrasing of the social spending question has changed over time; in 1963 and 1964 the spend-less option was not available; beginning in 1974, a new question format was used. The social services question was not asked in 1983.

a. Option was not available.

years. For instance, between 1964 and 1978, the number of Americans who believed that "government has gone too far in regulating business and interfering with the free enterprise system" rose from 42 to 58 percent. The American public also became more critical of taxation levels and the use of their tax money. Data from Gallup surveys show that in the 1950s less than half of the American public felt they were paying an unfair amount of taxes; by the late 1970s, over three-quarters believed their share of taxes was too high. Similarly, trend data from the University of Michigan election studies document an increase in the proportion believing that government "wastes a lot" of tax dollars, from 47 percent in 1964 to 64 percent in 1984. These sentiments fueled popular support for the tax revolt that spread across America in the late 1970s (Sears and Citrin, 1985).

Longitudinal data on British public opinion also depict a growing criticism of big government (table 6.2). The further nationalization of industry has received only minority support over the past two decades, and desires for denationalization of some industries has grown in recent years. Similarly, during the 1970s a rising number of Britons opposed further spending on social programs. In the early 1980s the West German public also displayed increasing disillusionment with the policies of the SPD-led government and their philosophy of big government, leading to a change in governing parties in 1982-83. Only France seemed to deviate from this general pattern by electing a socialist government in 1981 that was committed to further nationalization and expanding social programs. But the move toward greater government action is already being reversed by the conservative government elected in early 1986.

Yet, even as Americans and Europeans grow more critical about taxes and the overall size of government, support for increased spending on specific policy programs remains widespread. Table 6.3 displays the difference between the percentage of the American public who favor spending more in a policy area minus those who want the government to spend less. These data describe a decade-long consensus by Americans in favor of increased government spending on education, crime prevention, health care, and environmental protection. Only welfare, the space program, and foreign aid are consistently identified as candidates for budget cuts. Moreover, although specific spending priorities change over time, the average preference for increased government spending has varied very little across four administrations.

The public's spending priorities also respond to changes in the federal budget. For instance, the perceived military weakness of the Carter administration was reflected in calls for greater defense spending, especially in 1980 when 56 percent of Americans thought too little was being spent on defense. This attitude supported the large defense expenditures of the early Reagan adminis-

TABLE 6.3
BUDGET PRIORITIES OF THE AMERICAN PUBLIC (IN PERCENT)

Priority	1973	1974	1976	1978	1980	1982	1984	1986	1987
Halting rising crime rate	60	62	57	58	63	66	62	59	63
Improving and protecting nation's health	56	59	55	48	47	50	51	54	64
Dealing with drug addiction	59	53	51	46	52	48	57	52	60
Improving and protecting environment	53	51	45	43	32	38	54	54	60
Improving education system	40	42	41	41	42	47	59	56	56
Solving problems of big cities	36	39	23	20	19	23	31	27	25
Improving condition of blacks	11	11	2	1	0	8	19	18	20
The military, armaments, defense	−27	−14	−3	5	45	−1	−21	−24	−26
Welfare	−31	−20	−46	−45	−43	−29	−16	−18	−23
Space exploration program	−51	−47	−51	−37	−21	−28	−27	−30	−24
Foreign aid	−66	−72	−72	−63	−64	−67	−65	−64	−62
Average	13	15	9	11	16	14	19	17	19

SOURCE: NORC General Social Survey.

NOTE: Table entries are the percentages saying "too little" being spent on the problem minus the percentages saying "too much."

tration, but as examples of Pentagon waste became commonplace (accounts of $500 hammers and $7000 coffeepots) popular support for greater defense spending was replaced by endorsements of the status quo or even a cut in defense budgets. Similarly, limitations on social spending enacted by the Reagan administration exceeded the wishes of many Americans. Between 1980 and 1987, support increased for *more* spending in the areas of health care, drug addiction, environmental protection, education, urban problems, and minority aid.

Similar evidence from a recent European survey indicates that budgetary support for specific policy programs such as health care, environmental protection, education, housing, and social services is widespread (table 6.4). For most policy areas, the British are more likely than the West Germans to favor greater government spending; this probably is a reaction to Thatcher's cuts in British social spending. Indeed, support for social welfare spending has significantly increased since Thatcher took office in 1979.[1] Public opinion surveys from West Germany mirror this pattern; during the 1983 election, most voters were concerned about the large government deficits, but support for cuts in specific social programs was more restricted (Dalton and Baker, 1985).

These public opinion data present a picture of contemporary politics that is somewhat at odds with the recent electoral successes of Reagan, Thatcher,

TABLE 6.4

BUDGET PRIORITIES OF THE BRITISH AND WEST GERMANS (IN PERCENT)

Priority	Great Britain	West Germany
Health care	80	45
Environmental protection	42	72
Primary and secondary education	69	31
Housing	53	45
Social security	25	43
Higher education (universities)	46	10
Assist trade and industry	37	7
Transportation	49	−9
Technology development	33	4
Sports and recreation	13	18
Public security (police, etc.)	14	−12
Arts and culture	−17	−19
Aid developing countries	−18	−22
European Community policies	−37	−24
Defense	−28	−53
Average	24	9

SOURCE: Eurobarometer 21.
NOTE: Table entries are the percentages saying the government spends "too little" on the problem minus the percentages saying "too much."

Kohl, and other fiscal conservatives. For instance, the American public does not want to slash domestic spending in many of the areas targeted by the Reagan administration. In fact, the public's policy priorities have become steadily more liberal since Ronald Reagan's election in 1980, with more citizens favoring increased spending on social programs and less on defense. This paradox reflects a common contradiction in popular attitudes toward government. Many citizens are skeptical of government as a general principle, but endorse many of the specific goals of government activity. Lipset and Ladd (1980) describe this paradox as the combination of "ideological conservatism" and "programmatic liberalism." While Reagan's attacks on wasteful and insensitive big government strike a responsive chord with many voters, the proposed cuts in specific government programs often lack this same popular support. Thatcher and Kohl face similar difficulties in translating their electoral victories into specific budget cuts. The attitudes of Americans and Europeans remain an ambiguous mix of support and denial of government action.

The most accurate description of popular attitudes toward government might be that citizens are now critical of "big" government, but they also are accustomed to, and dependent on, the policies of the modern state (Lipset and Schneider, 1983). When Western publics are confronted with the choice between cutting taxes and maintaining government services, many surveys find that a plurality prefer the services option (Eurobarometer 4; Jowell and Witherspoon, 1985). Attitudes toward taxes have apparently become more conservative since 1975, but the basic message is that governments should grow no larger and neither should they shrink significantly.

SOCIAL EQUALITY

In recent years many citizens have developed more concern for issues of social equality. After generations of dormancy, the issues of civil rights and racial equality inflamed American politics in the mid-1960s. For most of the decade the civil rights issue preoccupied the attention of many Americans and was a major source of political conflict. Racial attitudes are often strongly held political beliefs, and their political impact has continued to the present (Carmines and Stimson, 1988). The success of the black civil rights movement encouraged similar activity among Latins, Asians, and other minorities.

European experience with ethnic and racial equality is more limited because most European nations have been fairly homogeneous in their ethnic composition. This situation began to change in the 1960s (Miller, 1981). Decolonialization in Britain and France was followed by a steady flow of black and brown immigrants from former colonies. Labor force shortages led the West Germans to invite "guestworkers" from less-developed Mediterranean

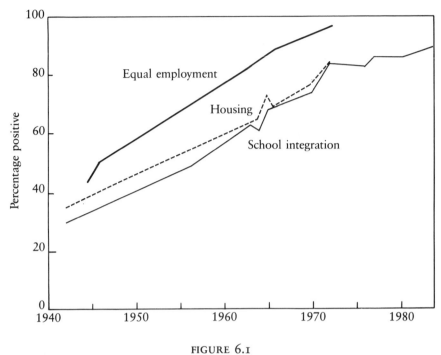

FIGURE 6.1
SUPPORT FOR RACIAL INTEGRATION IN AMERICA

SOURCE: Adapted from Smith and Sheatsley (1984).

countries to work in German factories. Nonwhites now account for approximately 5 percent of the population in these three nations, and as much as a quarter of the workforce in some cities. During the last decade European societies have experienced some of the same social divisions based on race and ethnic origin that plague American politics. Governments usually addressed these problems in a responsible manner, but a reaction against minorities frequently surfaces. For example, in the 1970 British election, Enoch Powell advocated a "white England" policy; tensions between French and North Africans often erupt into violence in southern France, and the new National Front party espouses antiforeigner policies; wall slogans of *Guestworkers Out* can be seen in West Germany.

The trends in racial attitudes over the past generation document a massive change in the beliefs of Americans. In the 1940s racial segregation of education, housing, transportation, and employment was endorsed by a majority of white Americans (figure 6.1). The values of freedom, equality, and justice that constitute the American creed did not apply to blacks. A phenomenal growth in racial tolerance occurred over the next four decades; the same issues that attracted only minority support in the 1940s are now endorsed by nearly everyone. Still, the American public remains divided on actions to redress racial inequality. Affirmative action policies such as school busing, preferential treatment, and racial quotas fail to attract much public support (Smith and Sheatsley, 1984). Americans seem to stress the equality of opportunity rather than policies that aim at the equality of results (Verba and Orren, 1985).

European attitudes toward racial issues are still evolving. The British elections studies indicate that since the early 1960s more than 80 percent of the British public has felt that too many immigrants were allowed into the country. Yet widespread opposition to immigration is not translated into equal hostility toward the minorities who live in Britain. The majority of Britons endorse legislation that bans racial discrimination, and only a minority of the public hold discriminatory attitudes toward minorities (Jowell and Airey, 1984).

West German attitudes toward guestworkers have been more restrained than the British (and the French) for several reasons. West Germans are still sensitive to the past and the horrors resulting from racist attitudes toward Jews during the Third Reich. In addition, the political context of the problem is different in West Germany because guestworkers lack a claim to the full rights of citizenship. Consequently, surveys indicate that while many West Germans are concerned with the problems involved with the presence of guestworkers, few citizens express or condone explicitly prejudicial views (Hoskin, 1982).

Although the climate of opinion now endorses racial equality, one must be cautious not to overlook the substantial racial problems that still exist. Support for the principle of equality coexists with the remnants of segregation in the United States; racial conflict can still flare up in Brixton, Liverpool, or Marseilles. Problems of housing segregation, unequal education, and job discrimination are real. Public opinion alone is not sufficient to resolve these problems, and undoubtedly some survey respondents overstate their racial tolerance. At the same time the shift of social norms in support of equality makes these problems more solvable than when discrimination was openly acclaimed.

Another dimension of social equality is the issue of equality between men and women. Gender roles were deeply entrenched on both sides of the Atlantic —American women faced limited career opportunities and German housewives were expected to devote their efforts to *Kinder, Kirche, und Kueche* ("children, church, and kitchen"). The women's movement grew most rapidly in the United States, but its presence also has been felt in Europe.

Most people now express belief in equal opportunities for men and women. The 1980 American election study found that only 19 percent of the public believe a woman's place is in the home; this percentage has decreased in each

TABLE 6.5

ATTITUDES TOWARD GENDER EQUALITY (IN PERCENT)

	United States	Great Britain	West Germany	France
Situation of women changed great deal	63	40	13	38
Women have equal job opportunities	48	38	31	37
General principle				
Women should obtain true equality in work and careers	–	81	77	86
Should be fewer differences between genders in society	–	58	63	74
Specific beliefs (men only)				
Man has more right to job if employment shortage	–	60	61	59
Women more responsible for housework	–	56	69	59
Prefer wife not to work	–	47	34	48
More confidence in male politician	–	26	45	28
Negative opinion of women's movement	–	55	40	35

SOURCES: First two questions from Gallup Human Needs and Satisfactions Study, 1974-75; other data are from Eurobarometer 19.

survey since it was first asked in 1972. Gallup surveys in 1983 and 1984 indicate that two-thirds of the American public still support the Equal Rights Amendment, even though ratification efforts failed. In addition, Gallup data show a striking increase in the number of people who say they would vote for a woman as president. In 1937 only 31 percent expressed this view; by 1983, this figure reached 80 percent.

Most Europeans support gender equality as a general principle (table 6.5). Nevertheless, the true measure of support for gender equality is when abstract principles are applied to specific instances. Recent evidence from European surveys indicates that most men feel that women are more responsible for housework and a man has more right to a job; a large proportion of males prefer that their wife does not work, have more confidence in male politicians, and have a negative opinion of the women's movement (table 6.5). Other survey data indicate that most European working women feel their situation is worse than men's regarding wages, promotion prospects, job opportunities, and job security (Eurobarometer 19). Traditional images of the role of women are still entrenched in the minds of many European males, but if comparable data were available, we might find that the picture is not significantly different in the

United States (Klein, 1987). Attitudes toward women are changing, but old stereotypes remain.

ENVIRONMENTAL PROTECTION

Slightly more than a decade ago, a new policy controversy—environmental protection—attracted the attention of Western publics. Environmental concerns were initially stimulated by a few very visible ecological crises, but environmental concerns have persisted and expanded. Separate issues have been linked together into environmental programs, and citizen groups have mobilized in support of environmental issues (Nelkin and Pollack, 1981; Lowe and Goyder, 1983). Environmental groups have become important, and contentious, new actors in the policy process of several Western democracies.

TABLE 6.6

ENVIRONMENTAL ATTITUDES (IN PERCENT)

	United States	Great Britain	West Germany	France
Issue salience				
Environmental protection is an important issue *(e)*	—	90	93	92
Condition of environment is a large problem *(a)*	76	81	91	—
Pollution is rising to serious levels *(a)*	70	79	91	—
Issue position				
Approve of strong environmental measures *(d)*	—	97	95	96
Environment more important than growth *(c)*	61	50	64	58
Environment more important than prices *(c)*	—	57	54	63
Positive opinion of environmental groups *(b)*	—	75	51	75
Oppose nuclear energy *(d)*	32	24	36	32

SOURCES: *(a)* Kessel and Tischler (1982), *(b)* Eurobarometer 17, *(c)* Eurobarometer 18, *(d)* Eurobarometer 19, *(e)* Eurobarometer 20. United States data on environment/growth item and nuclear energy from Gallup Index.

The broadest measure of environmentalism is the salience of environmental problems. A large number of Europeans are now interested in environmental issues (table 6.6), and longitudinal data from the Eurobarometer surveys indicate that interest has gradually grown over the past decade. Comparable data from the United States find high levels of environmental concern among the American public. Environmental policy has become a priority issue for many citizens.

Widespread interest in environmental policy also translates into public support for environmental protection (table 6.6). Western publics are nearly unanimous in agreeing that "stronger measures should be taken to protect the environment against pollution." Over 90 percent of the European samples endorse this position. Furthermore, even when citizens are asked to balance their environmental beliefs against the potential economic costs of environmental protection, a strong commitment to environmental protection remains in all four nations. For example, 61 percent of the American public favor protection of the environment even if it risks holding back economic growth; majorities in Europe also agree.

In most instances, environmental policy attracts the support of a majority of citizens, but there is one significant exception to this pattern — nuclear energy. Many individuals are concerned with the safety and storage problems associated with nuclear power, and few want to live in the vicinity of a nuclear installation. And yet the majority of citizens in 1983 agreed with the statement that "nuclear power should be developed to meet future energy needs." This issue has provided the battleground for some of the most intense conflicts over environmental policy (Nelkin and Pollack, 1981), but Western publics believe nuclear energy is necessary. It is still too early to know whether the fallout from Chernobyl will change these views.

Environmental attitudes are significant because they indicate how mass beliefs have broadened to include new issues interests, and especially issues that tap the noneconomic concerns typical of postmaterial values. In earlier periods, other social needs superseded concerns about the environment. As late as 1957, the West German Social Democrats explored an environmental issue as a campaign theme ("Blue skies over the Ruhr") and found public interest lacking. Today, a large number of citizens are willing to sacrifice some economic growth and lower prices for an improvement in the quality of the environment. Moreover, environmental groups have often spearheaded the New Politics challenge to the traditional political values of industrial societies.[2] Thus, Milbrath (1984) describes environmentalists as a vanguard for further social change.

SOCIAL ISSUES

A final set of domestic policy issues involves the conflicts emerging from the turbulent debate over social values and traditional lifestyles. Western societies have experienced a recurring battle over social norms and individual freedom that gradually has transformed social relations and life styles (Lipset, 1981b;

Harding, 1986). In the late 1960s and early 1970s another round of questioning began with symbolic statements, such as the use of drugs or the choice of hairstyles, clothing, and music.[3] The more fundamental issues tested the extent of individual freedom on matters such as abortion, divorce, homosexuality, and pornography.

These social issues differ from most other issues because of their moral content. The critic of abortion or homosexuality views the issue in terms of moral right and wrong; principles are at stake, unlike the negotiable monetary benefits of economic issues. Several consequences follow from the moral base of social issues. People find it is difficult to compromise on social issues because political views are intensely felt, and the issue public for social issues is often larger than might otherwise be expected. In addition, the active interest groups on social issues are religious organizations and Christian Democratic parties, not labor unions and business groups. Religious values are an important determinant of opinions on social issues.

TABLE 6.7

ATTITUDES ON SOCIAL ISSUES (IN PERCENT)

	United States	Great Britain	West Germany	France
Divorce sometimes justified	76	84	86	85
Sexual relations governed by moral rules	51	40	57	31
Extramarital sex sometimes justified	35	47	54	72
Homosexuality sometimes justified	33	54	58	51
Abortion sometimes justified	56	68	71	77
Approve of abortion				
When mother's health in danger	83	94	89	92
If child may be handicapped	53	78	82	88
When mother unmarried	23	32	24	34
Parents don't want child	23	32	37	48
Religious values				
Consider self religious	81	54	54	48
Believe in God	95	76	72	62
Believe in life after death	71	45	39	35
Importance of God in life[a]	8.21	5.72	5.67	4.72

SOURCE: 1981 European Values Study, 1981 CARA Values Study.

a. Importance of God in life measured on 10-point scale ranging from (1) not at all to (10) very important. Table presents mean score on this scale.

Table 6.7 presents public opinion on several social issues. Until fairly recently, traditional value orientations led many people to be highly critical of divorce.

Scandal, dishonor, and religious isolation often accompanied the divorce decree. During the 1970s, attitudes toward divorce became more tolerant; legislation removed the stigma of divorce and provisions discriminating against women. For instance, until new legislation in 1974, a West German husband could divorce his spouse if she took a job without his permission. The European Values Study indicates the scope of these changing attitudes—nearly all citizens now believe that divorce is sometimes justified.

Sexual relations is another area of social division. Western publics express diverse views on the issue of heterosexual relations. The French public holds distinctly liberal opinions toward extramarital sex and sexual relations generally; Americans are the most conservative. Attitudes toward homosexuality are surprisingly tolerant across all four nations. Approximately half of the public in each European nation feel that homosexuality is sometimes justified. The available longitudinal data for the United States and West Germany indicate a gradual liberalization of attitudes toward homosexuals over time (Noelle-Neumann and Piel, 1984; NORC General Social Surveys).

Abortion has been one of the most divisive social issues for contemporary politics. Proponents and opponents of the issue are intense in their issue beliefs and oriented toward political action. Furthermore, during the 1970s this issue became the subject of major legislative or judicial action in all four nations. Contemporary publics believe that abortion is sometimes justified, but additional questions indicate the limited range of this endorsement. Abortion is approved by a majority of these publics only when the health of the mother or the child is endangered. Many fewer individuals approve of abortion when the mother is unmarried or the parents just do not want a child. Some trend data indicate a slight increase in pro-abortion attitudes in recent years, but these attitudes seem to change very slowly.

Two further conclusions can be drawn from these findings. First, Americans are generally more conservative than Europeans on social issues (Harding, 1986). This pattern is likely the result of national differences in religious feelings, as seen in the last line of table 6.7. Despite the affluence, high mobility rates, and social diversity of Americans, the United States is probably the most religious of the advanced industrial societies (Dalton, forthcoming). Church attendance is among the highest in the world, religious feelings are widely held, and orthodox religious beliefs are extensive. Religion appears to be an integral part of the American culture (Lipset, 1981b).

Second, the moral basis of social issues also affects the variability of social attitudes. Although public opinion has generally become more tolerant on these issues, the pace of change is undoubtedly slowed because deep-seated moral values are involved. Attitudes toward abortion and other moral issues are more firmly rooted than socioeconomic opinions (Converse and Markus, 1979). So, social issues continue to divide Western publics into intensely differing groups.

Foreign Policy Opinions

In many instances, foreign policy is remote to the citizenry, something that neither touches their lives nor interests them. This situation often applies to the American public; the saliency of foreign policy is limited because the international dominance of the United States limits the impact of international activity on its citizens. International relations are more directly relevant to Europeans. More frequent exposure to foreign languages, foreign products, and foreign travel underscores the interrelatedness of nations. Moreover, membership in international organizations such as the North Atlantic Treaty Organization (NATO) and the European Communities (EC) is essential to the military and economic security of most Western European states. During the past decade, however, foreign policy issues have attracted more attention from publics on both sides of the Atlantic (Flynn and Rattinger, 1985), adding these issues to the already full political agenda of advanced industrial democracies.

NATIONAL IMAGES

Foreign policy is based on the action of nation-states, and national images therefore play an important role in structuring foreign policy attitudes. The most salient actors for Europeans are the two superpowers, and a relatively long time series tracks European images of the United States and the Soviet Union. Figure 6.2 presents the balance of positive versus negative opinions of both superpowers (Percentage Difference Index—PDI). In the 1950s most Europeans held sharply contrasting images of both nations. Opinions about the United States were generally positive because of the unifying experiences of the postwar period and the benevolence of *Pax Americana*. Somewhat surprisingly, the American image was more positive among West Germans than among the wartime allies of Britain and France. Images of the Soviet Union were distinctly negative in all three nations.

Popular images of the United States peaked in the early 1960s and then began a long downward slide with the beginning of the Vietnam war. European opposition to Vietnam was a major factor behind the erosion of the American image over the next decade. Disagreements over the general direction of American foreign policy has further weakened the American image in the 1980s. The American emphasis on defense buildup over detente was opposed by a strong peace movement in Western Europe, and American policy on a range of other issues—from Nicaragua to Cruise missiles—pushed Euro-

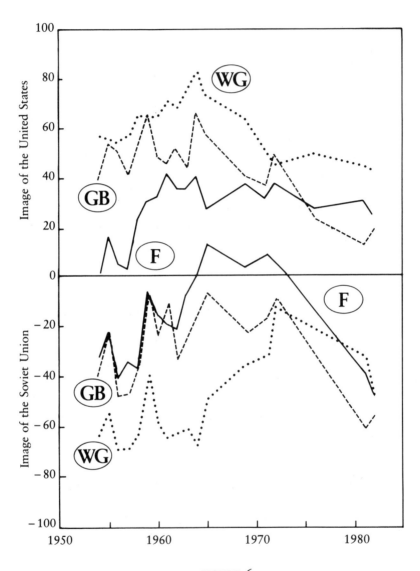

FIGURE 6.2

EUROPEAN IMAGES OF THE UNITED STATES AND THE SOVIET UNION

SOURCE: U.S. Information Agency polls. Note that when more than one survey was conducted during a year, the results have been averaged.

pean images of the United States to a new low in 1984. Europeans do not dislike the United States, but they have apparently lost confidence in American foreign policy leadership. A survey conducted by the U.S. Information Agency in 1982 found that half of the British and French, and more than a third of the West Germans, have little "confidence in the ability of the United States to deal responsibly with world problems." Longitudinal data from Britain track a fairly steady loss in confidence since the mid-1970s (Webb and Wybrow, 1983).

The decline in the American image should not be equated with a more positive view of the Soviet Union. The Soviet Union was almost uniformly disliked in the early postwar period; its image improved during the period of detente in the 1970s and then deteriorated again with the chilling of East-West relations in the 1980s. A 1982 Gallup survey showed that good opinions of the Soviet Union were held by only 14 percent of Britons, 20 percent of West Germans, and 13 percent of the French. Few Europeans hold positive illusions about the Soviet Union.

To some extent, American images of other nations parallel the European findings (figure 6.3). The American public was overwhelmingly critical of the Soviet Union for the first two decades following World War II. In the early 1970s the Soviet image benefited from the halo of detente pursued by Richard Nixon and Henry Kissinger; at one point in 1973, positive and negative opinions of the Soviet Union were almost evenly balanced. American antipathy toward the Soviets has grown over the past decade, especially after the invasion of Afghanistan. In 1982 only 21 percent of Americans expressed a favorable opinion of the Soviet Union.

American attitudes toward their European allies are more consistent over time. Since the early 1950s, Americans have shown a preponderance of favorable opinions toward the British, West Germans, and French. Furthermore, the available evidence indicates a gradual improvement in these attitudes through the late 1970s, at the same time Europeans were becoming more critical of the United States.

Europeans attitudes toward the United States are changing. No longer is America the shining model of affluence and freedom in a suffering postwar world. Images of World War II victory and the Marshall Plan are now tempered by the legacy of Vietnam, Iran, and other foreign policy failures. Europeans are also becoming more sensitive of their own policy needs independent of the United States. This may explain the contrasting national images among Western allies: increasing European skepticism of the United States, while Americans become more favorable toward Europeans. These data probably do not signify a serious weakness in the alliance—other questions shows strong support for future cooperation with the United States—but rather a European desire to

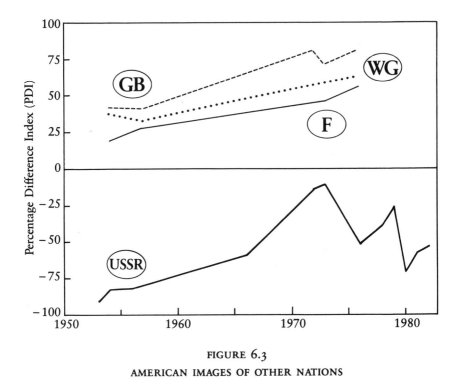

FIGURE 6.3

AMERICAN IMAGES OF OTHER NATIONS

SOURCE: Gallup Opinion Index. Note that when more than one survey was conducted during a year, the results have been averaged.

replace American leadership with partnership, and the need for greater American sensitivity to changing European foreign policy views.

WAR AND PEACE

Western publics entered the 1980s experiencing for the first time since the cold war a deep concern or even fear for the preservation of world peace. After decades of a stable truce between East and West leading to the detente of the 1970s, a series of events—Afghanistan, the Soviet buildup of SS-20 rockets in Europe, unrest in Poland, the American defense buildup, Nicaragua, NATO rockets—revived concerns about the possibility of war. In the spring of 1983, for example, large numbers of citizens in all four nations felt the threat of war was one of the most important issues facing their nation (see table 6.8).

While most citizens are concerned with the present state of international tensions, they are divided on the appropriate response to this situation. The traditional response to international threat is to strengthen one's national de-

TABLE 6.8

ATTITUDES ON FOREIGN POLICY ISSUES (IN PERCENT)

	United States	Great Britain	West Germany	France
Threat of war most important issue *(a)*	45	31	28	44
Cause of tensions *(a)*				
Soviet military capability	37	47	50	31
American military capability	19	37	41	20
Leader in military strength *(b/e)*				
Soviet Union	42	52	35	30
Equal	39	27	33	38
United States	11	11	18	16
How best to improve security *(b)*				
Strengthen NATO	–	31	21	18
Push arms control	–	40	35	50
Best method of ensuring security *(a)*				
Conciliatory policy	34	–	67	52
Policy of firmness	57	–	28	35
Approve of peace movement *(d)*	–	49	56	56
NATO essential to security *(b)*	–	79	88	44
Better to belong to NATO than be neutral *(b)*	–	67	67	45
Better to fight than submit to Russian domination *(a)*	83	75	74	57

SOURCES: *(a)* Atlantic Institute, *(b)* U.S. Information Agency, *(c)* Gallup Opinion Index, *(d)* Eurobarometer 17, *(e)* CBS/New York Times Survey.

fenses. This would seem appropriate now, since most Europeans and Americans see the Soviet Union as militarily stronger than the United States. But many citizens see military strength as the problem, not as a solution. A sizable proportion of Europeans say the cause of heightened international tensions is the increase in Soviet military capability *and* the increase in American military force.

Popular concerns about the arms race spawned an active peace movement in the early 1980s (Kaltefleiter and Pfaltzgraff, 1985). Millions of Americans signed petitions calling for a nuclear freeze, and many Europeans demonstrated against the stationing of new nuclear rockets in West Europe. These groups were only a minority of the population, but they represented a growing popular doubt that armaments were the road to national security. These sentiments can be clearly seen in several of the questions in table 6.8. For instance, in March 1981 a plurality of British (40 percent), West Germans (35 percent) and French (50 percent) feel that the best way to improve national security is through a program of arms control rather than a strengthening of NATO's defensive capabilities. Similarly, Europeans favor a policy of conciliation over a policy of firmness in dealing with the Soviet Union. At the same time that security is a major concern, only a small minority of Europeans endorse increased spending on national defense (see table 6.4). About half of the public in each nation also express approval of the peace movement in their country. In short, many Europeans feel that the cause of international tensions is competition between the superpowers, and would like to extricate Europe from this competition.

Despite these preferences for detente and disarmament, most Europeans continue to support the Atlantic Alliance and military cooperation with the United States. The British and West Germans clearly believe that military alliances such as NATO are essential and that it is better to belong to NATO than to be neutral. In March of 1982 citizens of all four nations said it is better to fight in defense of the homeland than to accept Russian domination.

On most of these questions the American public is more conservative than Europeans. While Europeans favor a policy of conciliation, more Americans prefer a policy of firmness. Support for increased defense spending is greater in the United States than in Europe; and Americans are more willing to resist the Soviet Union militarily. In contrast, French views on defense issues are generally more moderate than their European neighbors. The French express very modest support for NATO (in the late 1960s France withdrew from the military alliance and established its own defense force). The French public also tends to be less critical of the Soviet Union.

Perhaps the major lesson of these data is that the issues of war and peace have become politicized in Western democracies. The consensus on defense issues that existed for several decades has given way to questions about new policy alternatives. William Schneider (1985) describes American policy views as focusing on two seemingly inconsistent goals: peace and strength. The same description seems equally applicable to European policy opinions. Increasingly the tension between these two contrasting goals has become a source of partisan debate on both sides of the Atlantic, with no easy solution in sight.

The Left/Right Orientations of Citizens

The data in this chapter yield some evidence of how Western publics are changing their issues beliefs. Opinions on social-equality issues display dramatic changes over the past generation; prejudice toward racial minorities, women, and other minority groups are no longer condoned by most individuals. Tolerance of nonconformity is also more widespread, whether the objects of tolerance are political or social minorities (Nunn et al., 1978; Sullivan et al., 1982; Weill, 1979). Liberal attitudes toward new issues such as environmental quality and disarmament are also commonplace. Moreover, there is a broad consensus in support of the basic social programs provided by the modern state, although further growth is not endorsed; a generation ago, even these programs were a source of ideological conflict.

Still, it is difficult to use these issue questions to make sweeping generalizations about the changing political orientations of the public. Citizens are now interested in a wider range of issues than just socioeconomic concerns, and so a general assessment of overall political tendencies must weigh several different issues. The rate of social change across various issue interests also is uneven. Support for environmental protection has grown rapidly over the past decade, while attitudes on social issues have moved more slowly and unpredictably. Finally, the content of ongoing political controversies also changes over time. For instance, the racial issues that were intensely fought over in the 1960s — school desegregation, open housing, and public accommodations — now register overwhelmingly liberal responses; but new racial issues — busing and affirmative action programs — divide the American public. This represents progress in the development of racial tolerance, but racial issues remain politically contentious. One of the major points we have (re)learned from political trends of the past decade is that new issues of conflict inevitably replace old consensual issues.

One way to make a general statement about the overall political orientations of Western publics is to examine broad ideological orientations that extend beyond specific issue concerns. Political scientists frequently measure such broad orientations in terms of Left/Right attitudes (Inglehart and Klingemann, 1976; Klingemann, 1979). Discussions of issues in terms of Left/Right or liberal/ conservative philosophies is a basic aspect of politics. These labels help voters in interpreting and evaluating a range of political phenomena. The ability to think of oneself in Left/Right terms does not imply that citizens possess any sophisticated abstract framework or theoretical dogma. For many individuals, Left/Right attitudes are simply a kind of summary statement of their positions on the political issues of greatest concern. In this sense, Left/Right self-image measures a citizen's overall political orientation and perceptions of his or her position on the issues of current debate.

Hans Klingemann (1979) has shown that self-placement on a Left/Right "ideology" scale provides a robust measure of the public's overall political orientations. A very large proportion of the electorate in most industrial democracies can meaningfully place themselves along this scale (see table 2.2). The distribution of these Left/Right orientations in the 1981 Values Survey is presented in figure 6.4 on page 120.

In every nation, most citizens locate themselves near the center of the Left/ Right spectrum. Most individuals think of themselves as ideological moderates,

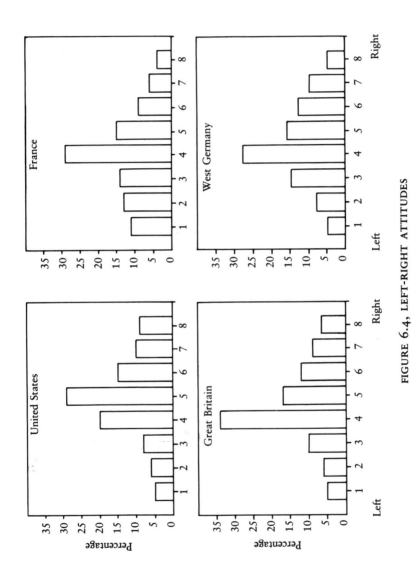

FIGURE 6.4, LEFT-RIGHT ATTITUDES

SOURCES: 1981 European Values Survey; 1981 CARA Values Survey.

which explains the centripetal tendencies of policymaking in these nations. Still, there are significant national deviations from this general pattern. The French electorate includes a large number of extreme Leftists, a cause and consequence of the large French Communist party. The British and West Germans are distributed fairly evenly around the center. The American public has a larger proportion of Rightists; a finding consistent with the conservative issue positions of Americans on economic, social, and foreign policy issues.

A better sense of the cross-national differences in overall Left/Right orientations can be obtained from figure 6.5. This figure plots the average Left/Right self-placement of electorates from over a dozen Western democracies. The United States is one of the most conservative nations in overall Left/Right terms; only Belgium, Ireland, and the Republic of South Africa are more Rightist. In contrast, the Mediterranean nations with significant Communist parties — France, Italy, and Spain — have the strongest Leftist tendencies.

The Left/Right scale cannot be used to track long-term trends in overall political orientations because the time series of relevant surveys is too brief. The evidence from generational comparisons normally indicates that the young are more liberal than their elders (e.g., Jennings et al., 1979). This generation gap suggests that Western publics are gradually becoming more liberal in their overall political orientations, but even these data tell only a partial story. Analyses of Left/Right attitudes indicate that the meaning of Left and Right varies across age cohorts. For older citizens, these terms are largely synonymous with attitudes on socioeconomic issues: *Left* means support for social programs, working-class interests, and the influence of labor unions; *Right* is identified with limited government, support for middle-class interests, and the influence of the business sector. Among younger Europeans, the New Politics issues of environmental protection, social equality, and life-style freedoms have been added to socioeconomic interests (Buerklin, 1985; Inglehart, 1984b). For the young, the term *Left* can mean opposition to nuclear energy, support for sexual equality, a preference for disarmament, or endorsement of social programs. The overall Left/Right placement of contemporary publics may differ from their elders, and the meaning of being *Left* is also changing.

Public Opinion and Political Change

One of the most significant features of contemporary issue opinions is that more people are interested in more issues. Whereas opinions on socioeconomic issues were once the predominate concern of voters and political elites, in recent years the number and nature of issues opinions has diversified. Socioeconomic matters still attract the attention of many individuals; but, in addition,

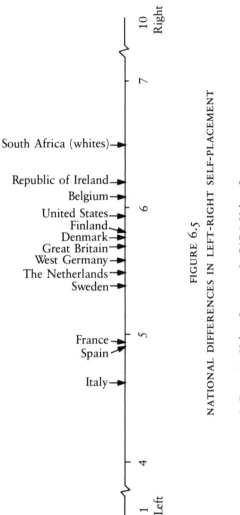

FIGURE 6.5

NATIONAL DIFFERENCES IN LEFT-RIGHT SELF-PLACEMENT

SOURCES: 1981 European Values Survey; 1981 CARA Values Survey.

issues of social equality, environmental protection, social morals, and foreign policy capture the interest of substantial numbers of citizens.

What can we say about the overall beliefs of Western publics? Social commentators frequently refer to a liberal or conservative mood sweeping a nation. The late 1960s and early 1970s were supposedly a time of radical change and liberal ascendance. Similarly, discussions of the new conservative mood in Western democracies is now commonplace, exemplified by the electoral strength of Reagan, Thatcher, Kohl, and Chirac. Tested against actual public opinion data, such generalizations are often difficult to substantiate. The counterculture movement of the 1970s was not as widespread as the media would suggest, and the conservative revival of the 1980s is equally overdrawn. Opinion change does not follow a simple predictable course, and the visible public actions of political groups can distort our images of the broader currents of public opinion.[4]

As a general rule, Western publics are becoming more tolerant of individual diversity and protective of individual rights. Similarly, support for big government is now tempered by demands for greater citizen input and decentralization. These trends are manifested in attitudes toward social equality, moral issues, and the quality of life. Although these trends can fluctuate over time, a growing time series of opinion surveys enables us to determine the general pattern of change. But it is difficult to interpret these trends in the traditional liberal/conservative framework of political competition because the meaning of these terms is also changing. For instance, when Ronald Reagan and the West German Greens both call for decentralizing political power to the local level, we must rethink our conventional use of liberal/conservative labels.

These developments complicate the study of politics. No longer is reference to the New Deal coalition or the class cleavage sufficient to explain the pattern of citizen interests and political alliances. Political interests have diversified and proliferated. Still, this very fragmentation of interests reflects the growing sophistication of contemporary publics in developing new issue concerns. Political systems may find it difficult to respond to an abundance of new issue interests rather than the predictable politics of the past; but this is the challenge that democracies face in responding to the new style of citizen politics.

Notes

1. Data from recent Gallup surveys show a marked increase in the proportion of Britons who want government services to be extended even if it means some increases in taxes:

1979	1983	1985
37%	52%	63%

2. The most visible example of this New Politics trend is the West German Green party. The Greens were founded in 1980 and in 1983 won 27 seats in the West German parliament. From this forum, the Greens have become spokespersons for a wide range of New Left causes, and encouraged similar developments in other European nations. See the discussion of the Greens in chapter 7 and Buerklin (1985).

3. Data from the American General Social Surveys indicate a conservative trend on some of the antisystem issues of the 1970s, such as legalization of marijuana, and a renewed attentiveness to societal needs. In most instances, however, beliefs are fairly stable across the last decade or have become more liberal (*Public Opinion,* December/ January 1984, pp. 21-37).

4. A good example is the abortion issue in the United States. Since the 1973 Supreme Court decision, there has been much apparent fluctuation in the popularity of pro- and antiabortion groups. Yet, time-series data from the Gallup poll and the National Opinion Research Center display very little change in the opinions of the American public on this issue (*Public Opinion,* April/May 1985, pp. 26-27).

PART THREE

The Electoral Connection

7. Parties and Party Systems

Citizen influence is a complex process and can occur in many ways. Voting is the most obvious means of influence, since it enables the public to select political leaders who will represent their opinions. Citizens also contact government officials, write letters to the media, and engage in other forms of political participation. Public influence flows through a variety of formal and informal political groups. These groups vary both in the scope of their issue interests and their methods of action — from single-issue groups to broad political movements, from conventional participation to protest activities.

Although all these means of influence are important, the electoral connection through political parties is still the primary basis of citizen influence in representative democracies.[1] Elections are one of the few available methods to reach a collective decision based on individual choices. The voting choice between parties aggregates the individual preferences of the electorate for political leadership, thereby converting public opinion into specific political decisions. Other forms of citizen participation may exert substantial influence, but they lack this representative quality.

Elections are also important because of what they decide. Electoral outcomes determine who will manage the affairs of government and make public policy. The selection of leaders and the ability to "throw the rascals out" at the next election are the public's penultimate power. Political leaders may not always act as they promise, but the choice of elites provides some popular control of policy outcomes.

Voting research also attracts disproportionate attention from social scientists because it is the most common political activity. Because voting is a regular activity for most citizens, voting research provides an opportunity to study the link between political attitudes and actual behavior. Individuals have to translate their beliefs and opinions into a specific decision. Hence, attitudes toward voting are likely to be relatively well thought out, intelligible, and predictable. The electoral connection is useful for examining public opinion and political behavior.

Any study of electoral politics must begin with an examination of political parties. Parties are the primary institutions of representative democracy, especially in Europe (Sartori, 1976; Rose, 1984; Beyme, 1985). Parties define the structure of electoral competition. Candidates in most European nations are selected by the parties and elected as party representatives, not as individuals. Open primaries and independent legislators are virtually unknown outside the United States. Indeed, a large proportion of Europeans (including the West Germans) vote directly for party lists and not for individual candidates. Once in government, parties exercise control over the policymaking process. This control is often absolute, as in the parliamentary systems of Britain and West Germany; American parties are less united and less decisive. Political parties and party leaders identify and articulate many of the public's issue concerns. Parties also perform an education function by informing the public. Consequently, E.E. Schattschneider once concluded that democracy without parties is unthinkable.

Political parties provide the focus for our study of the electoral connection. This chapter presents an overview of the history and structure of contemporary party systems and the party options available to the voters. Chapter 8 examines the social bases of partisan support and the trends in these social alignments. The following chapter describes public images of the parties and the source of these images. Finally, chapter 10 measures the functioning of the electoral connection by comparing the opinions of party supporters and party elites.

The History of Party Systems

Discussions of political parties normally focus on the present, the policy positions and political leaders that define current party images. And yet it is also clear that historical factors have deeply etched their features on the framework of party systems. The Democratic preferences of American southerners, for example, can be traced back to the consequences of the Civil War. The Democratic tendencies of American Catholics can be explained by their class and ethnic origins and the history of how these groups were integrated into American society and politics.

The legacy of history is even more evident in Western Europe. To many observers of the French party system the Left/Right cleavage continues the divisions of the 1789 French Revolution. The liberal, republican, and secular forces of the Left compete against the conservative, statist, and religious forces of the Right. There are similar historical linkages for the British and West German party systems. Contemporary party politics stands in the shadow of past events.

Seymour Martin Lipset and Stein Rokkan (1967) described the development of party systems in a study combining theoretical richness and impressive historical detail. Modern party systems, they maintained, are largely derived from the historical conditions of national and socioeconomic development. Contemporary political cleavages reflect the consequences of two successive revolutions in the modernization of Western societies: the *National Revolution* and the *Industrial Revolution*. Although their discussion deals primarily with Western Europe, the approach has relevance to other Western democracies including the United States.

The National Revolution refers to the process of nation building that transformed the map of Europe in the eighteenth and nineteenth centuries. The development of nation-states stimulated conflicts over boundaries and the limits of government control. More important, it involved conflicts over values and cultural identities. Were Alsatians to become Germans or French; was Scotland a separate nation or a region within Britain? The westward expansion of the United States in the nineteenth century generated similar tensions between regional cultures.

The National Revolution stimulated two kinds of social cleavage. The first was the *center-periphery* cleavage. It pitted the dominant national culture against resisting ethnic, linguistic, or religious minorities in the provinces and the peripheral sectors of society. This cleavage is visible today in persisting regional differences in political orientations; between the English, Welsh, and Scots; between Bretons and the Parisian center; between the "Free State of Bavaria" and the Federal Republic of Germany; and between the distinct regional cultures in the United States.

A second cleavage involved *church-state* conflict. The centralizing, standardizing, and mobilizing national government often faced opposition from the Catholic church, which sought to protect its established corporate privileges. Furthermore, Protestants often allied themselves with nationalist forces in the struggle for national autonomy. Thus the divisions between religious denominations and between secular and religious groups were continuing sources of political conflict and even open warfare.

The Industrial Revolution in the nineteenth century also generated new social tensions. The rural, agrarian social structure was threatened by the mass migration into the cities and the creation of an industrial class system. This process first developed a *land-industry* cleavage, which matched the agricultural interests of large estate owners against the economic concerns of the rising class of industrial entrepreneurs. The Ruhr industrialists challenged the power of the Prussian Junkers; the landed gentry of Britain and the United States were challenged by the barons of industry.

As the industrial sector became dominant, a second cleavage developed between *owners and workers*. This cleavage furnished the basis of the Marxian class conflict between the working class and the middle class composed of business owners and the self-employed. The struggle for the legitimization and representation of working-class interests by labor unions often generated intense political and physical conflict in the late nineteenth and early twentieth centuries.

Differences in the timing and character of the Reformation, the National Revolution, and the Industrial Revolution produced diverse national patterns of political conflict. Specific national conditions led to a variety of alliance patterns among the leaders of the various social groups.

In Britain the early conflicts over nation building often overlapped with regional and religious differences. The Anglican church supported the nation-building process and became identified with the English political establishment. Opposition to the central government was concentrated among Welsh members of nonconformist religions, Scottish Presbyterians, and Irish Catholics. The Industrial Revolution created new conflicts between agrarian and industrial elites, but these groups eventually formed an alliance to oppose the growing influence of the industrial working class. Religious and regional cleavages faded, and the social-class cleavage played a predominate role in structuring British political alignments.

A similar conservative alliance of industrial leaders and Prussian agricultural interests gradually developed in Germany. The result was a deep division between economic elites and the working class. In this case, however, sharp religious differences also existed between the Lutheran majority and a large Catholic minority. The Lutheran church allied itself with the economic elites in support of the nation-building process. The Catholic minority supported regional movements in opposition to the national establishment. Thus, two cross-cutting dimensions of conflict existed: class and religion.

French political alignments followed a third pattern. The nation-building forces in Paris drew their support from urban, industrial, and secular interests. The opposition was composed of Catholics, agricultural, and regional groups. This meant that in contrast to Britain and Germany, the French nation-state had a liberal image. France experienced successive democratic and authoritarian regimes while searching for a national consensus between contending forces. Many specialists say that these divergent views are still unresolved. The Industrial Revolution then overlaid a new class cleavage onto these previous divisions, producing a highly polarized and fragmented system of political alignments.

Although social divisions also exist in the United States, the political consequences of these social cleavages have been muted (Lipset, 1963). Religious and moral conflicts have been a central element in American social history, but the formal separation of church and state limited the impact of religion on politics. Similarly, the openness and mobility of the economic system attenuated class differences, and the federal system produced inconsistent patterns of alignment across regions. Class, religion, and region influence political alignments, but social differences are smaller than in most European systems.

These historical events may seem far removed from contemporary party systems, but Lipset and Rokkan (1967) demonstrated that a linkage exists. These four dimensions of cleavage define the potential social bases of political conflict. As social groups related to these cleavages developed, they won access to the political process before the extension of the voting franchise. When mass voting rights were granted to most Europeans around the turn of the century, this political structure was already in place. In most instances citizens were mobilized into supporting the party groups that already were represented in the political process. New voters entered the electorate with preexisting partisan loyalties. The Conservative party in Britain, for example, became the representative of the middle-class establishment, and the Labour party catered to the interests of the working class. The working class in France and Germany were mobilized into Communist and Socialist parties. The development of the American party system was less abrupt because the voting franchise was granted earlier and social groups were less polarized; still, the modern party system clearly reflects the experiences of the Civil War and class alignments created in the 1920s. The formation of mass political parties thus tended to institutionalize the existing elite coalitions, creating the framework for modern party systems. Once voters formed party loyalties and interest groups established party ties, the potential for dramatic partisan change lessened and the parties became self-perpetuating institutions. In one of the most often cited conclusions of comparative politics, Lipset and Rokkan (1967) stated that "the party systems of the 1960s reflect, with but few significant exceptions, the cleavage structures of the 1920s" (p. 50).

Early electoral research tended to substantiate Lipset and Rokkan's claims. Regional voting patterns from early in this century were mirrored in more recent election returns (Converse, 1969a; Clubb et al., 1980; Miller, 1977, chap. 5). Survey research found that social cleavages exerted a potent effect on voting, especially class and religious differences. Richard Rose and Derek Urwin's (1970) comparative study of postwar party systems found striking stability in electoral results. Their conclusion echoed Lipset and Rokkan's:

> Whatever index of change is used . . . the picture is the same: the electoral strength of most parties in Western nations since the war has changed very little from election to election, from decade to decade, or within the life span of a single generation. In short, the first priority of social scientists concerned with the development of parties and party systems since 1945 is to explain the *absence* of change. (Italics in original; Rose and Urwin, 1970, p. 295)

Just as Rose and Urwin wrote their conclusions, dramatic changes began to affect these same party systems. The established parties were presented with new demands and new challenges, and the evidence of substantial partisan change became obvious (Dalton et al., 1984; Daalder and Mair, 1983). Party systems became more fractionalized; there was a breakup of many established parties and a growing number of new parties. Fluctuations in voting results also increased. Voting is now characterized by higher levels of partisan volatility at the aggregate and individual levels (Crewe and Denver, 1985). Popular attachments to political parties weakened and discussions of the crisis of party systems are commonplace (see chapter 9). In sum, within a single decade the major research question changed from explaining the persistence of party systems to explaining their instability.

A number of unique national circumstances contributed to these patterns: the Vietnam war in the United States, regional and economic tensions in Britain, the student movement in West Germany, and the May Revolts in France. At the same time, however, a similar set of new issues are visible across national boundaries. Party systems derived from the National and Industrial Revolutions are faced with the issues of environmental protection, social equality, nuclear energy, sexual equality, nuclear weapons, and alternative life styles. Citizens demand more opportunities to participation in the decisions affecting their lives and press for a further democratization of society and politics. Once these trends began, they evoked a conservative counterattack that opposed the liberalization of social norms, women's rights, environmentalism, and related issues. As the pace of social change quickens, calls for the preservation of old values also increase. These new political conflicts are an important aspect of contemporary politics.

A major factor in the destabilization of these party systems was the initial inability or unwillingness of the major parties to respond fully to the demands being placed on them. As a result, several established parties fragmented and new parties were formed specifically to represent these new political perspectives, such as the ecologist parties in West Germany and France (Mueller-Rommel, 1982). It is unclear whether these developments reflect temporary adjustments to new issues or a more long-lasting realignment of political conflict. American history is filled with third-party movements that were successfully incorporated into the established parties. Is the present partisan instability in Western democracies just another case of this recurring pattern?

Several scholars claim that we are witnessing a permanent restructuring of political alignments as a result of the socioeconomic trends of advanced industrialism. They maintain that Western democracies are experiencing a third revolution, the Postindustrial Revolution (Bell, 1973; Touraine, 1971). The general character of postindustrial politics has been widely debated, and there are several suggestions of the form new political alignments will take. Ronald Inglehart (1977, 1984b) suggests that postmaterial values can furnish a new basis of political cleavage. Indeed, new issue interests, new styles of participation, and new expectations about the citizen's role in society seem to flow from the value changes discussed in chapter 5. Samuel Huntington (1974) predicts an intensification of the conflict between the declining manual labor force and rising knowledge workers, the shrinking old middle class and the expanding new middle class, and the economically decaying central cities and affluent suburbs. Zbigniew Brzezinski (1970) and Alain Touraine (1971) see a technology-based cleavage between the technologically knowledgeable and the technologically superfluous, between the information-rich and the information-poor. Erik Allardt (1968) suggests that education may provide the new basis of social cleavage, subsuming many of the above points.

Party systems are in a state of flux, and it is difficult to determine how fundamental and long lasting these changes will be. It is clear, however, that the new political conflicts of advanced industrial societies have contributed to this situation. While we wait for history to determine the significance of these trends, we can look more closely at the political alignments that now exist in America, Britain, West Germany, and France. These analyses also provide a brief introduction to the political parties in each nation.

The Structure of Political Alignments

Most parties and party systems are still oriented primarily toward the traditional political alignments described by Lipset and Rokkan. We shall refer to these alignments collectively as the *Old Politics* cleavage. The Old Politics cleavage is based on the political conflict between Old Left and Old Right coalitions. Lipset and Rokkan maintained that the class cleavage played the primary role in structuring the Old Politics alignment because class issues were the most salient during the extension of the franchise. The Old Left is therefore identified with the working class and labor unions, as well as secular groups and urban interests. The Old Right is synonymous with business interests and the middle class; in some nations this conservative coalition also includes religious and rural voters. When political issues tap the concerns of the Old Politics cleavage—for example, wage settlements, employment programs, social security programs, or abortion legislation—party positions reflect their traditional social orientations.

The political conflicts of advanced industrial societies have created a new dimension of cleavage in recent years. This *New Politics* dimension involves conflict over a new set of issues—environmental quality, alternative life styles, minority rights, participation, and social equality. This dimension represents the cleavage between proponents of these issues, the New Left, and citizens who feel threatened by these issues, the New Right.

The Old Politics cleavage is likely to remain the primary basis of partisan conflict in most Western democracies for the immediate future. The New Politics dimension is significantly affecting these party systems, however, because it cuts across the established Old Politics cleavage. Despite their differences, labor unions and business interests occasionally join forces to fight the opponents of nuclear energy. Farmers and students sometimes become allies to oppose industrial development projects that may threaten the environment. Fundamentalist blue-collar and white-collar workers unite to oppose changes in moral codes. A New Left and New Right are emerging whose potential may restructure social-group alignments and party coalitions. In sum, the simple dichotomy between Old Left and Old Right is no longer adequate to describe present patterns of political competition. The contemporary political space is now better described by at least two dimensions.

In order to map present party images on both the Old Politics and New Politics dimensions, we relied on surveys in which respondents were asked to evaluate the major political parties and a set of sociopolitical groups. Although the selection of groups is not ideal for our purposes, these data can be used to identify the structuring of major social groups and the political parties in relation to Old Politics and New Politics dimensions. A statistical analysis method was used to represent the interrelationship of group ratings in graphic terms.[2] This technique produces a mapping of the political space as defined by the citizens of each nation. When there is a strong similarity in how two groups are evaluated, they are located near each other in the space. When groups are evaluated in dissimilar terms, they are located a distance apart in the space.

We start with a description of the West German political space, since it presents the clearest representation of both dimensions (also see Buerklin, 1981; Dalton, 1984b). The horizontal axis in figure 7.1 is based on the traditional political alignments of the Old Politics, primarily class and religion. At one pole the electorate perceives the Old Left coalition of Social Democrats (SPD) and labor unions. The SPD emerged from the socialist working-class movement and still consistently represents working-class interests. Although West German labor unions no longer have institutional ties to the SPD, the relationship nevertheless remains close. For instance, over half of the SPD Bundestag deputies belong to a labor union; labor union members constitute the SPD's core voters *(Stammwahler)*; and the campaign support of labor unions is crucial to the SPD's electoral chances. Thus, the SPD's control of the national govern-

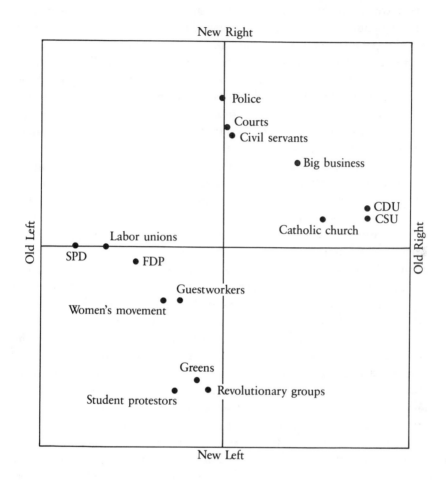

FIGURE 7.1
WEST GERMAN SOCIOPOLITICAL SPACE, 1980

SOURCE: 1980 Political Action Study.

ment from 1969 until 1982 resulted in a series of policies designed to improve the situation of the average worker: expanded social programs, retirement benefits, health-care insurance, and worker self-management *(Mitbestimmung)*.

At the other extreme of the Old Politics dimension is the traditional Old Right coalition. The Christian Democratic Union (CDU) was formed after the war as a conservative-oriented catchall party *(Volkspartei)*. In the state of Bavaria the CDU has allied itself with the Christian Social Union (CSU), which shares its political orientations. As their names imply, both conservative parties represent religious voters on the church-state cleavage. West Germans therefore see a close relationship between the Catholic church and the CDU/CSU. The Union parties are also advocates of conservative economic policies and a free market economy. For instance, when the CDU/CSU captured the national government in 1982, they moved to limit the social programs enacted by the previous Social-Liberal government in order to lessen the government's budget deficit and pursued a policy of economic reform based on incentives to investors, restructuring the tax system, and encouraging industrial growth. Business interests are therefore identified as part of the CDU/CSU's Old Right coalition.

As representatives of the major social forces in West Germany, the SPD and CDU/CSU are the dominant actors in the party system (table 7.1). The CDU/CSU has maintained a fairly stable electoral base of 45 to 50 percent of the popular vote since the 1950s. After a long growth in support, the SPD normally averages better than 40 percent of the vote. The smaller Free Democratic party (FDP) captures between 5 and 10 percent of the vote and acts as a junior coalition partner for the two larger parties. These three parties have accounted for more than 90 percent of the popular vote since 1961. From 1961 until 1983, only these three parties were represented in the West German parliament.

In recent elections this established party system has been altered by the emergence of a new dimension of political cleavage. The vertical axis in figure 7.1 represents a New Politics cleavage based on the issues of environmental protection, women's liberation, greater democratization of society, guestworker rights, and opposition to West Germany's participation in the arms race. Because the established parties were hesitant to represent these new issue concerns, a new political party, the Greens, was created in 1980 (Buerklin, 1985). The party initially united various environmental groups under a single banner and has since extended its program to include a large number of New Left issues. The party fared quite well in the 1983 and 1987 elections, and now holds 42 seats in the parliament. The Greens provide one of the clearest examples of the New Left ideology. The youthful, antiestablishment character of the New Left is seen in the electorate's placement of student protesters, the women's movement, and revolutionary groups near the Greens. Distinctly New Right groups were not included in the survey, but figure 7.1 indicates that opposition to the New Left is linked to positive feelings toward the political establishment: police, courts, civil servants, and business interests.

This mapping of groups highlights the political tensions and volatility of the West German party system. In 1980 the alignment of the two major parties, the SPD and CDU/CSU, remained almost exclusively oriented to the Old Politics dimension of class and religion. This necessitated the creation of the

TABLE 7.1
PARTY VOTE SHARES IN ELECTIONS TO THE GERMAN BUNDESTAG, 1949-87

Party	1949	1953	1957	1961	1965	1969	1972	1976	1980	1983	1987
CDU/CSU	31.0	45.2	50.2	45.4	47.6	46.1	44.8	48.6	44.5	48.8	44.3
FDP	11.9	9.5	7.7	12.8	9.5	5.8	8.4	7.9	10.6	7.0	9.1
SPD	29.2	28.8	31.8	36.2	39.3	42.7	45.9	42.6	42.9	38.2	37.0
Greens	–	–	–	–	–	–	–	–	1.5	5.6	8.3
Other parties	27.9	16.5	10.3	5.6	3.6	5.4	.9	.9	.5	.5	1.3

Greens to represent the New Politics concerns of young, postmaterial, and better-educated West Germans. In the few years since these data were collected, the West German party system has undergone further change. In 1982 the FDP reversed its policy priorities and moved from an SPD alliance to support a new CDU-led government. If this study were repeated today, the FDP would undoubtedly be part of the Old Right coalition. As the SPD moved into the opposition, it adopted many of the policies proposed by the Greens and has even formed SPD-Green coalitions at the state and local levels. The Old Politics and New Politics cleavages are showing some signs of convergence in the West German party system.

Political alignments in Britain exemplify the persistence of social cleavages that Lipset and Rokkan described (figure 7.2). Social class became the major basis of the Old Politics cleavage as the voting franchise was granted to the working class early in this century. The Labour party rapidly mobilized these new voters and became a viable political force. The party's working-class orientation became institutionalized through formal ties to the labor unions. Normally, membership in a union automatically includes a dues-paying membership in the Labour party; union leaders then control this large bloc of votes at Labour party conventions. Past Labour governments have nationalized several major industrial sectors, expanded social welfare programs, and vigorously defended the interests of their working-class supporters. Thus the Labour party and labor unions together are seen as anchoring the Left end of the Old Politics dimension.

As the Labour party mobilized the newly enfranchised working class in the early 1900s, the Conservative party emerged as the representative of the middle class and business interests. Up to the present day the party still depends on the financial support of the business community and the votes of the middle class. Recent Conservative party governments have challenged the political influence of labor unions while enacting a probusiness program: restructuring taxes, limiting social programs, and privatizing some government-owned industries. Britons consequently see the Conservative party and company directors as defining the Old Right coalition. In contrast to West Germany and France, religion has not been a significant source of British party competition since before World War I, and the clergy are not viewed as part of the Old Politics cleavage.

A New Politics cleavage also appears in the British political space; a New Left coalition of student protesters and the women's movement is paired against a variety of establishment groups: police, clergy, and civil servants. However, the New Politics cleavage has had a limited impact on British politics. While some New Left groups are active in Britain, such as the antinuclear movement and environmental groups, these issues have not had large-scale partisan con-

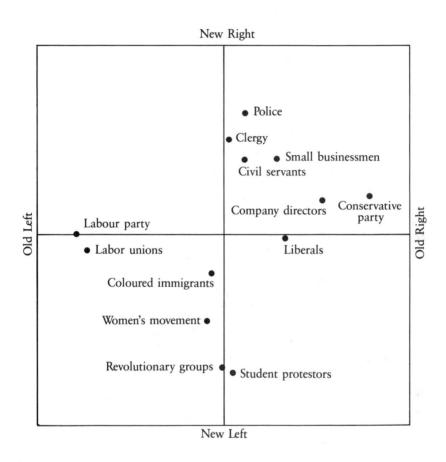

FIGURE 7.2

BRITISH SOCIOPOLITICAL SPACE, 1974

SOURCE: 1974 Political Action Study.

sequences. Britons have lagged behind other Europeans in the development of citizen action groups, the women's movement, consumer groups, and similar New Left organizations—and in linking the existing groups to the established political parties. Conversely, the major parties have not distinguished themselves on the New Politics axis.

The general stability of party fortunes is seen in the record of postwar election results (table 7.2). The Labour and Conservative parties each routinely

TABLE 7.2

PARTY VOTE SHARES IN ELECTIONS TO THE BRITISH HOUSE OF COMMONS, 1945-87

Party	1945	1950	1951	1955	1959	1964	1966	1970	February 1974	October 1974	1979	1983	1987
Conservative	39.8	43.5	48.0	49.7	49.4	43.4	41.9	46.4	37.9	35.7	43.9	42.4	42.3
Liberals[a]	9.0	9.1	2.5	2.7	5.9	11.2	8.5	7.5	19.3	18.3	13.8	25.4	22.8
Labour	47.8	46.1	48.8	46.4	43.8	44.1	47.9	43.0	37.1	39.3	36.9	27.6	30.8
SNP/Plaid Cymru	—	—	—	—	.4	.5	.4	1.7	2.6	3.5	2.0	1.5	1.7
Other parties	3.4	1.3	.7	1.2	.5	.8	1.3	1.5	3.2	3.2	3.4	3.1	2.4

a. In 1983 and 1987 the Liberal percentage represents the Liberal/SDP Alliance.

receive between 40 and 50 percent of the national vote, while the small Liberal party often garners 10-15 percent. Shifting vote margins led to a regular alternation of government between Labour and Conservatives, but the basic structure of the party system seemed fairly constant.

Changing socioeconomic conditions began to inject new volatility into the stable British party system during the 1970s (Finer, 1980). These effects were first apparent in the remobilization of Old Politics cleavages. Revived regional movements strengthened the nationalist parties in Scotland (Scottish Nationalist party) and Wales (Plaid Cymru) in the mid-1970s. This increased the fractionalization and volatility of the British party system. The polarization between the major established parties intensified as Margaret Thatcher moved the Conservative party rightward and Labour leaders became "born again" socialists. As a result, a new Social Democratic party (SDP) was created in 1981. The SDP is perceived as a Center-Left party on the Old Politics dimension, with a slight New Left tendency (Crewe, 1982). In the 1983 and 1987 elections the Social Democrats formed an electoral alliance with the centrist Liberal party and captured over 20 percent of the vote, but only 3 percent of the parliamentary seats because of Britain's plurality-based electoral system. The Labour party recorded its worst showings since the 1920s. With the opposition vote divided, Thatcher has maintained control of the government with barely 40 percent of the vote.

The American political space is depicted in figure 7.3. The same two dimensions of political cleavage again appear. The Old Politics cleavage reflects a continuation of the New Deal coalitions created by the Great Depression: the Democratic party and its labor union supporters against the Republicans and big business. Despite the inroads the Republican party has made in attracting labor voters and increased business support for the Democrats, the American electorate clearly perceives the Old Politics alignment fifty years after the New Deal.

A distinct New Politics dimension also structures this space; student protesters, the women's movement and blacks are aligned against symbols of the political establishment. Although the New Politics cleavage is dramatically affecting the nature of American politics, the major parties are only slightly differentiated on this dimension. In this 1974 survey the Democrats are seen as having slight New Left tendencies, while the Republicans are closer to the New Right. This is because the New Politics cleavage exists *within* both of the American parties, rather than *between* the parties. Recent American presidential primaries illustrate this point.

The 1984 Democratic primaries featured a confrontation between the Old Politics and the New Politics. Walter Mondale was identified with the traditional New Deal policies of the Democratic party and won early endorsements

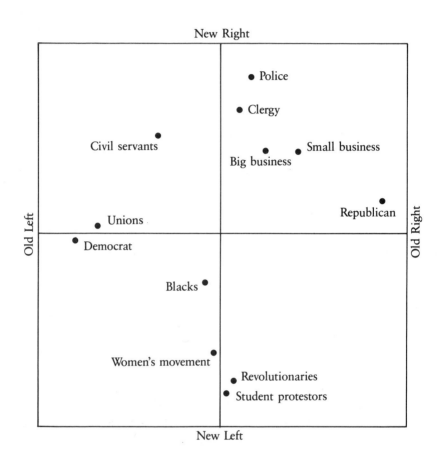

FIGURE 7.3
AMERICAN SOCIOPOLITICAL SPACE, 1974

SOURCE: 1974 Political Action Study.

from labor unions and the party establishment. Gary Hart, on the other hand, explicitly claimed that he was the New Politics candidate, the representative of new ideas and a new generation. Hart's core voters were the *Yuppies*—young, urban, upwardly mobile professionals—one of the groups linked to the New Politics cleavage. Many of the other Democratic candidates also can be classified in broad Old Left (Glenn, Askew) or New Left (Cranston, McGovern) terms. In the 1976 and 1980 primaries Jerry Brown championed New Left issues such as opposition to nuclear power and women's rights. In 1972 a New Left candidate, George McGovern, actually won the Democratic nomination.

The Republican party contains similar ideological divisions. Representative Philip Crane of Illinois, chairman of the American Conservative Union, was the New Right candidate in 1980; the liberal policies of John Anderson often reflected New Politics themes. The eventual winner of the nomination and the election, Ronald Reagan, successfully assembled a coalition of traditional Old Right business interests and New Right groups such as the Moral Majority and the antiecologist Rocky Mountain Defense Fund.

The public's perceptions of the American parties were primarily based on the Old Politics cleavage in 1974. The policies of the Reagan administration probably have moved the Republican party closer to its New Right supporters. At the same time, the New Left constituency is being integrated into the Democratic party. Preliminary analyses of data from the 1981 Political Action survey (not shown) suggest a growing overlap between Old Politics and New Politics cleavages in the American party system.

American electoral trends are difficult to categorize because congressional and presidential results vary so greatly (table 7.3). Elections to the House of Representatives reflect the broad and stable bases of party support. There appears to be a basic equilibrium in party strengths in these elections; the fluctuations in party outcomes has averaged less than a 3 percent vote change between elections. The Democrats have won every House election since World War II with two exceptions (1946 and 1952). In contrast, the results of presidential elections vary widely, from Lyndon Johnson's Democratic landslide in 1964 to Richard Nixon's Republican majority in 1972. Presidential elections are heavily influenced by the candidate's own attributes, instead of serving as strict partisan contests. Therefore, our cross-national analyses of electoral patterns in subsequent chapters analyze American congressional elections because they are more similar to West European parliamentary contests.

A comparable mapping of the French political space is not available. But data on party and candidate images from a 1978 survey enable us to map the French party space at that election.[3] Figure 7.4 displays the familiar Old Politics dimension on the horizontal axis. The French Communist party (PCF) and its leader, Georges Marchais, were the major political representatives of the Old Left. The PCF depends very heavily on working-class votes and has formal ties with the Communist labor union, the CGT. The Communists still claim that a Marxian class analysis can explain France's current socioeconomic problems and that these problems can be solved by a rigid application of Communist doctrine. In many ways it is surprising how little the PCF has changed since it was founded in 1920.

TABLE 7.3
PARTY VOTE SHARES IN AMERICAN NATIONAL ELECTIONS, 1948-84

Party	1948	1952	1956	1960	1964	1968	1972	1976	1980	1984
Presidential election										
Republican	45.1	55.1	57.4	49.5	38.5	43.4	60.7	48.0	50.7	58.8
Democrat	49.5	44.4	42.0	49.7	61.0	42.7	37.5	50.1	41.0	40.6
Other parties	5.4	.5	.6	.8	.5	13.9	1.8	1.9	8.3	.6
House elections										
Republican	45.5	49.3	48.7	44.8	42.3	48.2	46.4	42.1	48.0	46.8
Democrat	51.9	49.2	50.7	54.7	57.2	50.0	51.7	56.2	50.4	52.3
Other parties	2.6	1.5	.6	.5	.5	1.8	1.9	1.7	1.6	.9

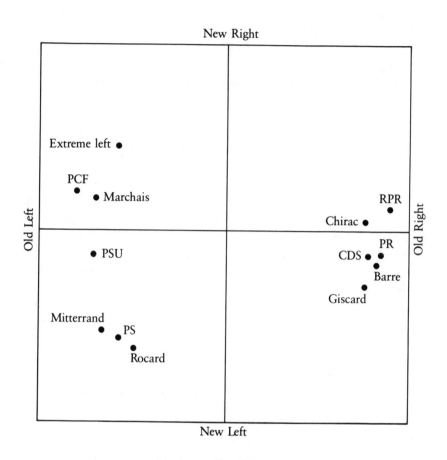

FIGURE 7.4
FRENCH PARTY SPACE, 1978

SOURCE: 1978 French Election Study.

At the beginning of the Fifth Republic in 1958, Charles de Gaulle assembled business, middle class, and religious interests to support his Gaullist party. These groups historically comprised the conservative coalition on the Old Politics cleavages of class and religion. The Rally for the Republic (RPR) has inherited this Old Right coalition and is a major force in French politics. The other major conservative party in 1978 was the Republican party (PR), headed by then-president Giscard d'Estaing. Together the RPR and the PR formed the conservative *Majorite,* which governed France from 1958 until 1981. If social groups could be added to figure 7.4, we would expect an alignment of labor unions, business groups, and the Catholic church along the horizontal Old Politics dimension.

A second dimension of cleavage also exists in the French party space. The Socialist party (PS), its leader, Francois Mitterrand, and Michel Rocard constitute a separate political grouping to the French public. Previous research normally found that the PCF and PS were placed together in voter images of the French party space (Campbell, 1976). Both parties have a long history of representing working-class interests and supporting Old Left policies. In the 1978 election, however, the Socialist party balanced its Old Left image with new attention to a non-Marxist, decentralizing, and antiauthoritarian brand of socialism. The public's association of Rocard with the Socialists implies that these issues were developing a New Politics image for the PS even in 1978. Rocard was a former leader of the left-wing PSU, the only party that supported the students during the May Revolts. He became a spokesperson for New Left issues such as worker self-management *(autogestion)* and opposition to nuclear power, and he opposed the Old Left political philosophy favored by the Communists. This pattern of party images therefore suggests that the New Politics dimension already had emerged in the French party system by 1978. Furthermore, a distinctly New Left ecologist party, the MEP, was also formed that year.

The instability of French partisan politics has continued since this 1978 survey. In recent elections the Republican party of Giscard d'Estaing has allied with the Center party (CDS) to form the Union for French Democracy (UDF). A variety of new Leftist parties also have been created. The most significant recent development, however, is the formation of a new Right party, the National Front. The party is headed by a former army general with a checkered past, involving an uncertain war record and support for radical causes. The National Front has attracted voters opposed to the social changes occurring in France, and may be the prototype of a reactionary New Right party.

The electoral record of the Fifth Republic depicts a growing bipolarization of party support (table 7.4). A large bloc of voters supported centrist parties during the 1950s and early 1960s. These voters gradually migrated to parties of the Left or the Right, leaving the center depopulated. The Gaullist party was the original benefactor of this trend and participated in conservative governments for the first two decades of the Fifth Republic. The tide shifted toward the Left in the late 1970s, especially toward the PS with its broad program of Old Politics and New Politics reforms. The Socialist party took control of the government in 1981 following its victories in the presidential and legislative elections. The Socialists' programs reflected a mix of Old Politics and New Politics

TABLE 7.4

PARTY VOTE SHARES IN ELECTIONS TO THE FRENCH NATIONAL ASSEMBLY, 1958-86

Party	1958	1962	1967	1968	1973	1978	1981	1986
Gaullists	20.4	32.0	37.7	46.0	26.9	22.5	20.8	41.0
UDF (RI, etc.)	—	4.4			11.2	21.4	19.2	—
MRP	11.1	9.1	—	—	—	—	—	—
Center parties	22.1	9.6	13.4	10.3	12.6	—	—	—
Radicals	7.3	7.5				—	—	—
Left-Radicals	—	—			1.5	2.1	—	1.4
Socialists	15.7	12.4	18.7	16.5	17.7	22.6	37.6	31.0
Communists	19.2	21.7	22.4	20.0	21.2	20.5	16.2	9.8
Other parties	4.2	3.3	7.8	7.2	8.8	10.9	6.2	16.8

issues. The government nationalized several sectors of the economy (an Old Politics goal) while also restraining France's massive nuclear power program (a New Politics goal); and expansion of social welfare benefits was paired with policies for political decentralization.

The pendulum of French politics swung again in 1986. The Socialist government found it difficult to implement policy reforms that satisfied all of their supporters, and government policies at least temporarily worsened economic conditions. The conservative parties played on this discontent; a coalition of the RPR and UDF won a narrow three-seat majority in the 1986 elections for the National Assembly. Government power is now divided between a conservative legislature and socialist president. Internal differences still exist within the governing coalition and the Socialist party, and the future prospects for the French party system remain uncertain.

Contemporary Party Systems

This chapter presents broad similarities in the ideological structure of contemporary party systems. Most political parties are still organized around the Old Politics cleavages of class and religion. Even if these cleavages have become less central to party programs, the group ties and institutional structure of the parties have perpetuated these images. Parties are, after all, still turning to the same interest groups and associations for the core of their support. Western publics see Rightist parties as linked to business interests (and sometimes the Catholic church), and Leftist parties are allied with the labor unions.

While major party differences exist on the Old Politics dimension, there are also indications of the increasing importance of the New Politics cleavage. Earlier chapters (5 and 6) found that Western publics are developing postmaterial values that lead to new policy interests. These new issue demands initially manifested themselves outside the established parties. The growth of citizen action groups, for example, often reflected a mix of the new style of citizen participation and New Politics issue concerns. These interests are now seeking representation through partisan politics, which places new demands on the established parties.

Some indications of partisan change along the New Politics dimension are already evident. New parties, such as the West German Greens and French ecologists, have been formed to represent New Politics concerns. These small parties have drawn their support from the young, the better educated, and postmaterialists — key groups in defining the New Politics cleavage (chapter 8). A more basic change would occur if the larger established parties adopt clearer positions on New Politics issues. There is some evidence of this change in the recent actions of the West German SPD and French Socialists. Both parties are attempting to combine Old Left and New Left issue appeals into a single program; the French PS found this an especially difficult task for a governing party. The Democratic and Republican parties in the United States also seem to be developing closer ties to New Left and New Right groups respectively.

Despite these indications of partisan change, we should not underestimate the difficulty of integrating the New Politics cleavage into party systems based on the Old Politics cleavage. The established parties have been understandably hesitant to formalize close ties to New Left or New Right groups. Parties are naturally cautious about taking clear stands on a new dimension of conflict until the costs and benefits are clear. When the Democratic party unabashedly supported New Left causes in 1972, they suffered a major electoral defeat because the party alienated its traditional Old Politics clientele. Similarly, the major European Leftist parties are deeply divided on many issues that involve Old Politics/New Politics conflicts. While most industrial labor unions favor economic development projects that will strengthen the economy and produce jobs, environmentalists within the Leftist parties often oppose these same projects because of their ecological consequences. These conflicts contributed to the SPD's losses in the recent elections and the growing alienation of environmentalists from the French PS. Many conservative parties also face divisions between conservative business elites and a more liberal middle-class constituency. Political alliances between Old Politics and New Politics groups have so far been of a temporary nature because of the conflicting values of these groups.

Given the uncertainties facing the parties and the difficulties in integrating a new political cleavage into the existing Western party systems, future partisan change is likely to follow a slow and uncertain course. Continuing changes in citizen values and issue interests mean that the potential for further partisan change is substantial.

Notes

1. The American Enterprise Institute has sponsored an excellent series of books describing party actions and public opinion in recent non-American elections (Penniman, 1975a, 1975b, 1980, 1981; Ranney, 1985; Cerny, 1978, forthcoming). In addition, there are several good analytic studies of recent American elections (Pomper, 1981, 1985; Abramson et al., 1986).

2. Factor analyses were computed on the group sympathy scores using the procedures described in Barnes, Kaase, et al. (1979, pp. 581-83); also see Inglehart (1984b) for similar analyses of a larger group of nations. Figures 7.1 to 7.3 represent the varimax rotations of the principal axes solutions.

3. The mapping is based on a factor analysis of seven-point sympathy scales. Figure 7.4 presents the unrotated principal components solution.

8. The Social Bases of Party Support

Partisan politics is built on a social base. The preceding chapter discussed how party systems were formed to represent class, religious, and other social groups in the political process. Contemporary parties maintain political ties to clientele groups and project images in group terms: The Communists are a working-class party, the Republicans are the party of business, the CDU represents religious voters, and so forth. Although the issues and personalities of the campaign change from election to election, parties generally maintain their institutional and ideological ties to specific social groups. Most parties depend on the votes of their clientele groups to provide a stable base of electoral support.

Because of the group orientation of most parties, the social characteristics of an individual are often an important guide to voting behavior. The significance of social characteristics is based on two factors. First, one's position in the social structure often indicates one's values and political beliefs. A French steelworker is more likely than a shopkeeper to favor an expansion of social services or government regulation of the economy. Opposition to liberal abortion laws is more likely among devout Catholics than nonreligious citizens. Thus, social characteristics are an indirect measure of attitudinal differences between groups of voters and voter perceptions of which party best represents these policy positions. Second, social groups can be an important reference point in orienting the individual to political issues and providing information about politics. In other words, social characteristics indicate some of the political cues to which an individual is exposed. A British mineworker, for example, hears about politics from his coworkers or other working-class neighbors and friends; he is also exposed to the political education program of the union representative at work and union publications at home. This social milieu provides repeated cues on which policies will benefit people like oneself, and which party best represents one's interests — a strong Labour party bias in these cues is inevitable. Similarly, a Bavarian Catholic hears about political issues at weekly church services, from Catholic social groups, and from his or her predominately conservative Catholic friends. This information generally encourages a favorable opinion of the CSU and its program. For many citizens, the cues provided by such social networks can be a potent influence on political attitudes and voting behavior.

Voter reliance on group-based political orientations is an example of the model of satisficing decision making presented in chapter 2. Social cues are used to narrow the voting choice to parties that are consistent with the individual's social characteristics. Attention focuses on the party (or parties) that historically have supported the class or religious groups to which the voter belongs, while excluding parties with unsupportive records from the decision-making process. Voters can then decide between competing parties based on the cues provided by social groups—the endorsements of labor unions, business associations, religious groups, and the like—as well as the group appeals of the parties themselves. The stable group bases of the parties means that many voters develop standing partisan predispositions that endure across elections, simplifying the decision process still more.

Reliance on social characteristics is a shortcut to making voting decisions. A citizen who is fully informed on all the issues and all the candidates is better prepared to make a rational voting choice and justify this decision in issue-oriented and ideological terms. Social characteristics provide a simpler, but less certain, method of choosing which party best represents the voter's interests. Still, when strong social-group identities are matched by clear party positions on these social cleavages, as they are in most European nations, then social characteristics can provide a very meaningful guide for citizen voting behavior.

From the beginning, electoral research has stressed social-group attachments as an important influence on voting behavior. One of the first empirical studies of American voting focuses on the social bases of American partisanship (Lazarsfeld et al., 1948). This study found that an *Index of Political Predispositions* based on social class, religion, and rural/urban residence was a strong determinant of voting choice. Moreover, most voters apparently have already-formed partisan loyalties before the campaign begins, based on past electoral experiences. Social stratification is greater in Europe, producing even sharper group differences in voting patterns. Descriptions of British electoral politics emphasize the distinct class images of the Labour and Conservative parties, and the sizable class differences in voting behavior. Both class and religion are strong correlates of voting in West Germany and France.

This chapter's examination of group voting patterns highlights both the stability and change in Western party systems. On the one hand, the partisan loyalties generated by social characteristics produce a basic stability in the composition of party coalitions, since the same kinds of individuals are continually attracted to a party. This constancy in the bases of party support reinforces the partisan images presented in chapter 7.

On the other hand, this chapter also examines whether the social bases of partisanship are changing. The socioeconomic and political trends discussed in earlier chapters have often been linked to a realignment in the group bases of party support (Inglehart, 1977; Dalton et al., 1984). In addition, the increasing sophistication of contemporary electorates may be lessening voter reliance on social cues, as individuals are now better able to make their own political decisions. Thus, a general erosion in group-based voting patterns may constitute another element in the new style of citizen politics. These theories are examined by tracking group voting patterns over time and across nations.

The Class Cleavage

Class politics taps the essence of what we described as the Old Politics — a conflict between the haves and have-nots. The class cleavage represents the economic and material problems of industrial societies: providing for the economic security of all citizens and ensuring a just distribution of economic rewards. Issues such as unemployment, inflation, social services, tax policies, and government management of the economy reinforce class divisions.

Social scientists have probably devoted more attention to the class cleavage than to any other social characteristic as a predictor of mass voting behavior. This emphasis reflects the historical importance of class-based politics. Lipset and Rokkan (1967), for example, described how the class cleavage influenced the structure of party systems because these issues were most salient during the development of modern party systems. The last chapter documents the public's persisting association of Leftist parties with labor unions and Rightist parties with business interests. Seymour Martin Lipset's cross-national study of mass politics describes the class cleavage as one of the most pervasive bases of party support:

> Even though many parties renounce the principle of class conflict or loyalty, an analysis of their appeals and their support suggests that they do represent the interests of different classes. On a world scale, the principal generalization which can be made is that parties are primarily based on either the lower classes or the middle and upper classes. (1981a, p. 230)

Similarly, Arend Lijphart's (1981) overview of modern party systems identifies the class cleavage as a major dimension of ideological cleavage in virtually all democracies. Subsequent empirical studies generally support these conclusions (Rose, 1974b; Powell, 1982).

Research on the class cleavage often defines social class in terms of occupation. Following Karl Marx's still influential writings on class politics, occupations are classified on the basis of their relationship to the means of production. The bourgeoisie are the owners of capital and the self-employed; the proletariat are the workers who produce capital through their labor. This schema is then generalized to define two large social classes: the middle class and working class. This pattern of class differences provided the basis for the creation of Socialist and Communist parties that represent the interests of the working class; conservative parties, in turn, defend the interests of the middle class.

The changing structure of advanced industrial societies has revised the traditional bourgeoisie/proletariat cleavage through the creation of a "new" middle class. This stratum consists primarily of civil servants and salaried white-collar employees (Bell, 1973; Lipset, 1964). The new middle class rapidly expanded in size along with the general postwar growth in the service industry and government employment. This group now constitutes the largest sector of the labor force in most Western democracies, even exceeding the size of the traditional working class.

The new middle class is an important addition to the class structure because it lacks a clear position in the traditional class conflicts between the working class and the old middle class. The separation of management from capital ownership, the expansion of the service sector, and the growth of government (or nonprofit) employment created a social stratum that does not conform to Marxian class analysis (Dahrendorf, 1959). The new middle class does not own capital like the old middle class, but also differs in life style from the blue-collar workers of the traditional proletariat. Members of the new middle class seem less interested in the economic conflicts of the Old Politics and are more attuned to New Politics issues (Baker et al., 1981). Consequently, the identity of the new middle class differs from both the bourgeoisie and proletariat.

Table 8.1 presents the varying partisan preferences of these social classes.[1] The persistence of historical class alignments is clearly evident. The working class in each nation gives disproportionate support to Leftist parties, ranging from 54 percent in Britain to 72 percent in France (the combined PCF, PS, and other Left vote). At the other extreme, the old middle class is the bastion of support for conservative parties. Overall class differences appear largest in Britain and France, although signficant differences also exist in the United States and West Germany.

The ambiguous social position of the new middle class is also apparent in their partisan preferences. The new middle class is always located between the working class and old middle class in terms of its Left/Right voting preferences. In addition, the new middle class gives disproportionate support to parties that represent a New Politics ideology: the West German Greens, French Ecologists, and the SDP/Liberal Alliance in Britain. The new middle

TABLE 8.1

SOCIAL CLASS AND PARTY SUPPORT (IN PERCENT)

Country	Working Class	New Middle Class	Old Middle Class
United States, 1984			
Democrat	60	55	53
Republican	40	45	47
	100	100	100
Great Britain, 1983			
Labour	54	25	15
Liberal/SDP	18	23	19
Conservative	28	52	66
	100	100	100
West Germany, 1987			
Green	6	8	12
SPD	53	41	27
FDP	2	6	7
CDU/CSU	39	45	54
	100	100	100
France, 1981			
PCF	18	7	4
PS	44	40	31
Other left	10	9	5
Ecologists	11	16	16
UDF	10	16	21
Gaullists	7	12	23
	100	100	100

SOURCES: *United States,* CPS 1984 Election Study; *Great Britain,* 1983 British Election Study; *West Germany,* 1987 West German Election Study; *France,* Eurobarometers 15 and 16. American data are based upon congressional vote in this and subsequent tables. Note that social class is based on the occupation of the head of the household.

class is a key element in the changing political alignments of advanced industrial societies.

Table 8.1 presents only a snapshot image of the dynamics of class voting. The recent history of this cleavage can be tracked over time with separate national series of voting surveys. In order to ensure the comparability of these data, we focus on the Left/Right voting patterns of the working class versus the combined middle class (old and new).[2] Table 8.2 displays the Leftist voting preferences for these two strata over several decades in each nation. Class lines

TABLE 8.2
TRENDS IN CLASS VOTING[a]

United States	1948	1952	1956	1960	1964	1968	1972	1976	1980	1984
Working class	76	61	58	65	76	60	62	66	60	60
Middle class	35	42	45	50	56	43	50	49	52	54

Great Britain			1959	1964	1966	1970	February 1974	October 1974	1979	1983
Working class			62	64	69	58	57	57	50	38
Middle class			22	22	26	25	22	25	23	17

West Germany	1953	1957	1961	1965	1969	1972	1976	1980	1983	1987
Working class	59	61	57	58	59	70	58	67	61	60
Middle class	29	24	29	32	47	53	42	51	51	51

France			1955	1958	1962	1967	1968	1973	1978	1981
Working class			60	44	58	55	52	65	65	72
Middle class			35	29	39	37	37	51	46	53

SOURCES: *United States*, SRC/CPS Election Studies; *Great Britain*, British Election Studies; *West Germany*, West German Election Studies; *France*, 1955, MacRae (1967, p. 257); 1958, Converse and Dupeux study; 1962, IFOP survey; 1967, Converse and Pierce study; 1968, Inglehart study; 1973-81, European Communities studies.

a. Table entries are the percentages preferring a Leftist party (in West Germany only the SPD and CDU/CSU voters are included until 1980 and later when the Greens are included among Leftist voters). American data are based on congressional elections, except for 1948 which is presidential vote.

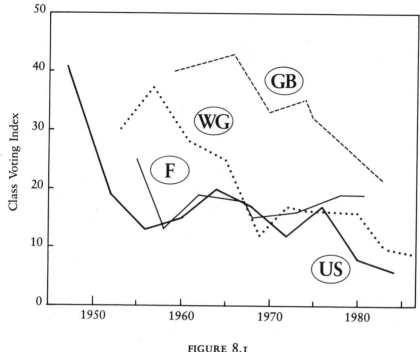

FIGURE 8.1

TRENDS IN CLASS VOTING

SOURCE: See table 8.2. Note that entries are the Alford Class Voting Index; that is, the percentage of the working class voting for Leftist parties minus the percentage of the middle class voting for the Left.

are clearly drawn. Leftist parties draw greater support from working-class voters than from the middle class. This pattern holds for all elections in the table. Regardless of the specific issues of each election campaign, the personalities of party leaders, or even the variety of competing parties, the direction of class voting is the same.

Although social class is clearly influencing voting behavior, the data in table 8.2 also indicate a general narrowing of class voting differences over time. This pattern can be seen more clearly in figure 8.1, which presents the Alford index of class voting for each election series. The Alford index measures the magnitude of class voting as the simple difference between the percentage of the working class voting for the Left and the percentage of the middle class voting Left.

The general trend in figure 8.1 is obvious; class differences are declining. The size of the class voting index in Britain and West Germany has decreased by almost half over the past three decades (Rose, 1986; Saarlvik and Crewe, 1983; Franklin, 1985; Baker et al., 1981). Class voting patterns follow a less regular decline in American congressional elections, but the downward trend is clear. Social class had a modest impact on voting behavior during the French Fourth Republic (MacRae, 1967). The turbulent events surrounding the formation of the Fifth Republic—including the creation of a broad-based Gaullist party—abruptly lowered class voting in 1958. Since then, class voting has stabilized at a level significantly below pre-1958 levels (Lewis-Beck, 1984; Michelat and Simon, 1977a).

The decline in class voting reflects a general trend of weakening socioeconomic cleavages. Voting differences based on union membership, income, education, and other class characteristics display a similar downward trend in their influence on voting choice. A similar erosion in socioeconomic cleavages has developed in the Netherlands, Norway, Sweden, Denmark, and other Western democracies (Andeweg, 1982; Borre, 1984). The decline in the class alignment is a common feature of politics in advanced industrial societies.

There are several reasons for the weakening of the class cleavage. One factor is the changing composition of social classes. The new middle class, for example, has progressively increased its share of the combined middle class. This is important because the old middle class and new middle class have differing values and voting patterns. The more moderate voting record of the new middle class means that the growth of this class has lessened overall working-class/ middle-class polarization. Kendall Baker and his colleagues (1981, chap. 8) credit the growth of the new middle class as a major source of narrowing class differences in West Germany. Similarly, a more refined analysis of the French data presented in table 8.1 finds that the French new middle class has shifted to giving a majority of its votes to Leftist parties.[3]

The changing composition of the middle class is a specific example of a more general decrease in the social differences between classes. Improving incomes and the spread of middle-class life styles are leading to the *embourgeoisement* of some sectors of the working class. At the same time, the expanding ranks of low-paid and low-status white-collar employees and the growth of white-collar unions are producing a *proletarianization* of the middle class. Few individuals possess exclusively middle-class or working-class social characteristics, and longitudinal studies indicate that the degree of class overlap is increasing (Rose, 1974c).[4] In sum, a convergence of life conditions contributes to the convergence of class voting patterns.

A related theory explains the decline of class voting as a function of social and occupational mobility. All the nations in this study experienced a decline in the agricultural sector and an increase in middle-class employment during the postwar period. Dramatic changes in the size of economic sectors often occurred within a few decades. High levels of social mobility mean that an individual's ultimate social position is often different from that of his or her parents. Many farmers' children from conservative political upbringing moved into unionized, Leftist, working-class environments in the cities; many working-class children from urban, Leftist backgrounds have careers in traditionally conservative, white-collar occupations. Some socially mobile individuals will change their adult class identity and voting behavior to conform to their new social contexts; others will not. This mix of social forces tends to blur traditional class and partisan alignments.

Another reason for the erosion of class voting is the convergence of party positions on class-based issues. Many democratic party systems experienced a trend away from ideological politics in the decades following World War II. Parties became interested in broadening their electoral appeals, which led to more moderate party programs to attract centrist voters. Socialist parties in Europe shed their Marxist programs and adopted more moderate domestic and foreign policy goals. Conservative parties also tempered their views and accepted the basic social programs proposed by the Left. Socialist parties vied for the votes of the new middle class, and conservative parties sought votes from the working class. These developments created a collectivist consensus (Beer, 1978) in Britain; the two major West German parties similarly competed to become broad-based *Volksparteien* (people's parties). Thomas's (1980) historical analysis of party programs documents a general convergence of party positions on socioeconomic issues during the last half century (also see Robertson, 1976). With smaller actual policy differences between the parties, it is only natural that class cues would become less important as a guide to voting behavior.

In sum, the decline in class voting patterns represents both a weakening of the voters' class identities and a narrowing of party positions on class-based issues. The nature of these forces implies that the downward trend in class voting may be a continuing process. For instance, the public's increased attention to economic issues in recent years has not led to a revival in class voting; the trends in figure 8.1 continue downward. The long-term impact of these societal trends is suggested by a comparison of class voting differences across generations (figure 8.2). Strong and persisting relationships between class and vote are generally found among older generations socialized during earlier periods of substantial economic problems, sharp class differences, and clear party positions on class issues. But among younger generations, these relationships are weak and decreasing. Among the youngest West German cohort, the traditional class alignment is actually reversed in 1983; support for the SPD and Greens is greater among middle-class youth than their blue-collar peers. A shifting socioeconomic

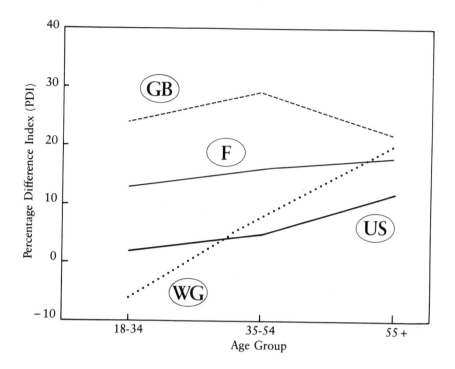

FIGURE 8.2

CLASS VOTING BY AGE GROUP

SOURCES: *United States,* 1984 CPS American Election Study; *Great Britain,* 1979 British Election Study; *West Germany,* 1983 West German Election Study; *France,* 1978 French Election Study. Note that entries are the Percent Difference Index (PDI), the percentage voting for a Leftist party among the working class minus the percentage of the middle class voting for the Left.

environment has stimulated a change in voting patterns among the young because their values are less conditioned by the Old Politics cleavage and they place less reliance on class cues when deciding how to vote. Moreover, longitudinal analyses indicate that these generational patterns in class voting are fairly stable over time (Abramson, 1975; Dalton, 1984b; Butler and Stokes, 1974, chap. 4). The erosion of bourgeoisie/proletariat class divisions is therefore likely to be an ongoing trend in advanced industrial democracies as older generations are replaced by younger cohorts who are less oriented to class-based politics.

The Religious Cleavage

The relationship between religion and politics arises from a centuries-old interplay of these two forces. The Reformation created divisions between Catholics and Protestants that carried over into politics. Control of the nation-building process often became intermixed with the religious cleavage. In Anglican England, for example, the Protestant church supported national independence and became identified with the dominant national culture. In Germany the tensions between Lutherans and Catholics were a continuing source of conflict and even open warfare; this delayed national unification until late in the nineteenth century. Gradually the political systems of Europe accommodated themselves to the changes wrought by the Reformation, and a new status quo was institutionalized. But then the French Revolution renewed religious conflicts in the nineteenth century (Martin, 1978). Religious forces—both Catholic and Protestant—mobilized to defend church interests against the liberal, secular movement spawned by the events in France. Conflicts over church/state control, the legislation of mandatory state education, and disestablishment of state religions occurred across the face of Europe.

As was true with the class cleavage, conflicts over religion defined the structure of elite conflict and political alliances that existed in the late nineteenth century. The political parties formed with the extension of mass suffrage often allied themselves with specific religious interests—Catholic or Protestant, religious or secular. As previously argued, the Old Politics party alignments developed at the start of the twentieth century institutionalized the religious cleavage, and many features of these party systems have endured to the present.

Empirical research on mass voting behavior underscores the continuing importance of the religious cleavage. Richard Rose and Derek Urwin (1969) examined the social bases of party support in sixteen Western democracies. Their oft-cited conclusion maintains that "religious divisions, not class, are the main social bases of parties in the Western world today" (p. 12). Additional evidence comes from Arend Lijphart's (1979) comparison of the religious, class, and linguistic cleavages in four democracies where all three cleavages exist. He finds that religion was the strongest influence on voting choice. The persisting importance of the religious cleavage has been documented by numerous other cross-national and longitudinal studies (Rose, 1974b; Baker et al., 1981, chap. 7; Miller, 1977; Michelat and Simon, 1977a).

Despite this evidence of a strong relationship between religious values and partisan preferences, there are indications that the religious cleavage may be following the same pattern of decline that we just described for the class cleavage. The modernization process may have disrupted religious alignments in the same manner that social-class lines have blurred. A change in leisure patterns is important; church life is no longer the focus of social activities. More generally, the increased social and geographic mobility of industrial societies has undermined community integration, and social bonds of all sorts—class,

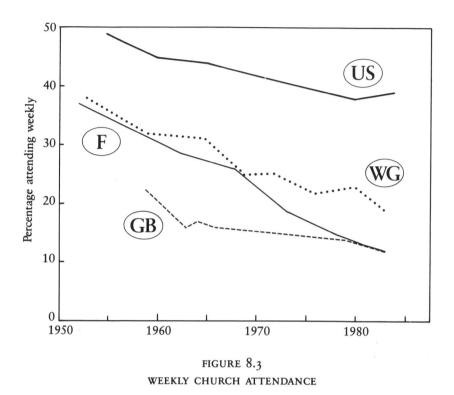

FIGURE 8.3
WEEKLY CHURCH ATTENDANCE

SOURCES: *United States,* Gallup (1980); *Britain,* Civic Culture Study, British Election Studies; *West Germany,* Civic Culture Study, West German Election Studies; *France,* IFOP Polls, Inglehart 1968 Election Study, European Community Studies.

religious, and linguistic—have generally moderated. As a result of these factors, contemporary mass publics are not well integrated into religious networks, and their behavior is less likely to follow a bloc pattern.

One example of this secularization process is the public's involvement in church activities. Participation in church activities exposes the individual to the clergy's views on political issues and to the social cues of the religious milieu (Sani, 1974), much as union involvement indoctrinates the working class. Figure 8.3 displays the trends in church attendance for our set of nations. The downward trend is unmistakable. In West Germany, for example, weekly church attendance drops from almost 40 percent in 1953 to less than 20 percent of the present public (1983). Even when church attendance is initially quite low, as in Britain, a further decline occurs during the 1960s and 1970s. This trend exists across nations and for both Catholics and Protestants; it is a general feature of advanced industrial societies.

The decline in church attendance is replicated with numerous other measures of religious involvement. There has been a postwar decline in the proportion of West Germans who have church weddings, and the percentage of interdenominational weddings is increasing. Participation in religiously based associations and social clubs is dropping in most Western democracies. And, nearly everywhere, the number of young men entering a religious vocation is decreasing.

The public's declining involvement in the established churches is paralleled by the churches' declining involvement in politics. Conflict between secular and religious forces has moderated since World War II. On the one hand, socialists in many European nations reached a rapprochement with religious groups, especially with the Catholic church in countries with a large Catholic population. On the other hand, the churches sought to normalize political relations if church interests could be guaranteed as part of the process. West Germany provides an example of this reconciliation. The SPD consciously modified its antireligious image in the 1960s, and the Catholic church responded. A series of political agreements were negotiated between church representatives and the Social Democrats. Beginning with the 1969 election, most Catholic bishops refrained from their traditional election-day sermons in support of the CDU/CSU.

Measuring the present impact of religious cues on voting behavior requires more complexity than the analyses of the class cleavage. Although the class composition of most industrial democracies is fairly similar, their religious composition is more varied. Britain is a predominately Protestant nation, and nearly two-thirds of the population are nominally Anglicans. In contrast, nearly all French citizens are baptized Catholics, and the Protestant minority is very small. West Germany is a mixed denominational system, with nearly an equal number of Catholics and Lutheran Protestants. The United States represents yet another pattern of religious pluralism. The United States lacks a dominant national religion; there are a significant number of Catholics, Reformation-era Protestants (Anglicans, Calvinists, Lutherans, etc.), Pietist Protestants (Methodist, etc.), other Protestant and Christian groups (Southern Baptists, Pentecostals, Mormons, etc.), and Jews.

In addition to the diverse religious composition of nations, the partisan tendencies of religious denominations also vary cross-nationally. Catholics normally support parties of the Right, and Protestants normally support parties of the Left. While this pattern generally holds for Western democracies, historical events often led to a different pattern of religious and partisan alignments (Lipset and Rokkan, 1967; Dalton, forthcoming). This means that the voting cues provided by religious affiliation may differ across national boundaries, in contrast to the consistent working-class/middle-class pattern on the class cleavage.

TABLE 8.3

RELIGIOUS DENOMINATION AND PARTY SUPPORT (IN PERCENT)

United States, 1984	No Religion	Jewish	Catholic	Pietist Protestant	Other Christian	Reformation Protestant
Democrat	68	80	61	52	55	43
Republican	32	20	39	48	45	57
	100	100	100	100	100	100

Great Britain, 1983	No Religion	Catholic	Other Protestant	Church of Scotland	Anglican
Labour	32	45	28	41	23
Liberal/SDP	26	21	30	26	25
Conservative	42	34	42	33	52
	100	100	100	100	100

West Germany, 1987	No Religion	Lutheran	Catholic
Greens	17	8	6
SPD	49	52	36
FDP	1	5	4
CDU/CSU	33	35	54
	100	100	100

France, 1981	Non-Catholic	Catholic
PCF	20	5
PS	44	45
Other left	12	6
Ecologists	13	9
UDF	5	17
Gaullists	6	17
	100	100

SOURCES: *United States,* CPS 1984 Election Study; *Great Britain,* 1983 British Election Study; *West Germany,* 1987 West German Election Study; *France,* Eurobarometer 16.

Table 8.3 presents the relationship between religious denomination and party support in each nation. Religious differences in voting behavior are often substantial; however, each nation displays its unique pattern for the religious cleavage.

West Germany exhibits the strongest relationship between denomination and partisanship. The historical conflict between the Catholic church and Liberal/Socialist parties still appears in voting alignments. Catholics give disproportionate support to the CDU/CSU, which has defended traditional values and the church's perogatives. The SPD and Greens receive greater support from Protestants and nonreligious voters.

Even though France is a predominately Catholic nation—over 80 percent of the population has been baptized in the Catholic faith—sizable differences in voting behavior still separate French Catholics and non-Catholics. Only 11 percent of non-Catholics vote for conservative parties, as compared to 34 percent among Catholics. Because the public is overwhelmingly Catholic, the political consequences of this imbalance on election outcomes is limited.

In Britain the religious cleavage follows a different pattern (Miller, 1977; Wald, 1983). The Anglican church historically has been identified with the political establishment; thus most Anglicans vote for the Conservative party. Catholics are aligned with the Labour party because of their minority status and the question of Irish independence. Non-conformist Protestants have long given disproportionate support to the Liberal party.

Religious and moral conflicts have been a central element in American history (Lipset, 1981a); yet the formal separation of church and state has limited the impact of religion on partisan politics. The table indicates that the Protestant denominations from the Reformation era predominately support the Republicans; the other major religious blocs support the Democrats. These differences are modest, however, and may reflect other factors more than religion per se. Neofundamentalist Protestants are a heavily Democratic group, but this largely reflects regional cleavages in American politics and the concentration of this denomination in the conservative, though Democratic, South. Similarly, the Democratic ties of American Catholics are primarily the result of ethnic and class influences rather than explicitly religious values.

A second aspect of the religious cleavage is the division between secular and religious voters. In predominately Catholic nations, such as France, this dimension represents a voter's integration into the Catholic culture. In mixed denominational systems the secularization process has often stimulated an alliance between Protestants and Catholics in a joint defense of religious interests, so that denominational differences are being replaced by a secular/religious cleavage. In West Germany, for example, the Christian Democratic Union bridged the historic religious cleavage by uniting both Catholics and Protestants in a single religious party. Even in the United States, similar phenomena have been observed. In 1980 and 1984 Ronald Reagan campaigned for the votes of religious conservatives from all denominations. The Republicans hoped to tap a common concern with the preservation of traditional values and opposition to abortion and the supposed moral decline of American society.

The relationship between religious involvement, measured by the frequency of church attendance, and party preference is presented in table 8.4. The voting

TABLE 8.4

CHURCH ATTENDANCE AND PARTY SUPPORT (IN PERCENT)

Country	Never	Occasionally	Weekly
United States, 1984			
Democrat	56	56	53
Republican	44	44	47
	100	100	100
Great Britain, 1983			
Labour	34	24	28
Liberal/SDP	24	26	26
Conservative	42	50	46
	100	100	100
West Germany, 1987			
Green	10	7	3
SPD	55	43	25
FDP	4	5	5
CDU/CSU	31	46	67
	100	101[a]	100
France, 1981			
PCF	14	6	0
PS	47	47	28
Other left	11	4	3
Ecologists	12	9	9
UDF	8	16	34
Gaullists	9	18	26
	100	100	100

SOURCES: *United States,* CPS 1984 Election Study; *Great Britain,* 1983 British Election Study; *West Germany,* 1987 West German Election Study; *France,* Eurobarometer 16.

a. Does not add to 100% because of rounding.

gap between religious and nonreligious citizens is considerable in both France and West Germany. For instance, only 31 percent of French citizens who attend church on a weekly basis prefer a Leftist party, compared to 72 percent among individuals who never go to church. Not a single regular church attender in the survey expresses support for the Communist party!

Religious involvement has little impact on voting patterns in Britain. Because of the Erastian nature of the Anglican church, religious conflicts have not been a major factor in partisan politics since early in this century. As we saw in chapter 7, evaluations of the clergy are virtually unrelated to party im-

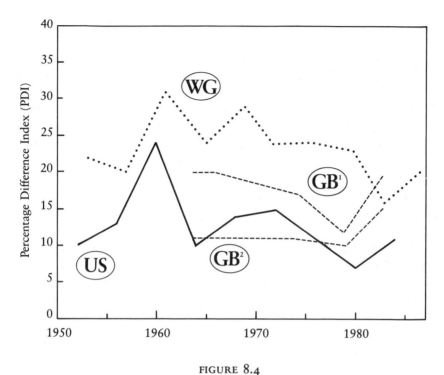

FIGURE 8.4

INDICES OF DENOMINATIONAL VOTING

SOURCES: *United States,* SRC/CPS Election Studies; *Great Britain,* British Election Studies; *West Germany,* West German Election Studies. Note that comparisons for the United States and West Germany are between Protestants and Catholics. GB[1] is a comparison of the Labour party vote of Anglicans and Catholics; GB[2] is a comparison of the Conservative party vote of Anglicans and nonconformists.

ages. Similarly, the formal separation of church and state in America limits the partisan implications of religious feelings. Despite the recent attempts of the Republican party to court religious voters, church attendance and vote are virtually unrelated in the 1980s.

These tables underscore the diversity of the religious cleavage across these four nations. Both religious denomination and church attendance are strongly related to partisan preferences in West Germany. The religious cleavage in France is based on the voting differences between devout Catholics and the nonreligious. In the United States and Britain there are modest partisan differences between religious denominations but only marginal differences by church attendance.

The relationships between religious characteristics and partisan preference are apparent evidence of the persistence of religious cleavages despite the secularization process. These expectations can be tested by observing the pattern of religious voting differences over time.

Analogous to the class voting index, figure 8.4 plots a religious voting index based on the difference in party preferences between religious groups. For instance, the gap in SPD voting support between West German Catholics and Protestants remains within the 20-25 point range for most of the past three decades. Similarly, the differences in Conservative party support between Anglicans, non-conformist Protestants, and Catholics have changed only slightly since 1959. The partisan tendencies of American Catholics and Reformation-era Protestants vary across elections; the religious cleavage intensifies with John Kennedy's candidacy in 1960, while other elections display fairly weak religious voting. Overall, however, there is only a slight convergence in religious voting patterns in American congressional elections.

Further evidence of the persistence of the religious cleavage is presented in figure 8.5, which displays the difference in Leftist voting between citizens who attend church weekly and those who seldom or never attend church. Religious involvement in West Germany and France has a strong and persisting impact on voting preferences, averaging over a 40 percent difference in Leftist party support. American and British party differences on the religious voting index are initially quite small and display little change over time.

Against the backdrop of contemporary politics in these nations, the persistence of the religious cleavage is a cause for some surprise. Despite the paucity of explicitly religious issues and the lack of religious themes in most campaigns, religious beliefs are often a strong predictor of party choice. Where religious voting patterns are weak, as in the United States and Britain, this reflects an ongoing characteristic of the party system rather than the recent erosion in religious voting. The stability of religious voting indices is all the more surprising because advanced industrial societies have become more secularized during the past few decades. In addition, many of the societal changes that have weakened the class cleavage presumably should have the same effect on religious voting.

In fact, the importance of religion as a basis of voting behavior is declining, but the pattern of decline is less obvious than was the case for the class cleavage. The persisting strength of religious voting indices does not mean that the secularization process has not affected voting behavior. Comparisons of voting patterns between religious denominations ignore the growing nonreligious segment of society. Furthermore, even though voting differences between religious and secular voters have remained fairly constant for the past generation, secularization is steadily increasing the absolute number of nonreligious citizens. Individuals who attend church regularly are still well integrated into

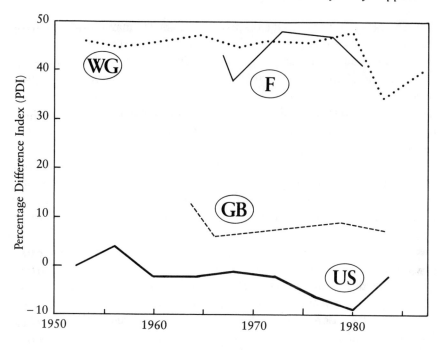

FIGURE 8.5

INDICES OF RELIGIOUS VOTING (CHURCH ATTENDANCE)

SOURCES: *United States*, SRC/CPS Election Studies; *Great Britain*, British Election Studies; *West Germany*, West German Election Studies; *France*, 1967 Converse and Pierce Study, 1968 Inglehart Study, European Community Studies. Note that entries are the Percentage Difference Index (PDI), comparing the Leftist voting preferences of those who attend church weekly to those who never attend.

a religious network and maintain distinct voting patterns; but there are fewer of these individuals today. By definition, the growing number of secular voters are not basing their party preferences on religious cues. Thus the changing composition of the electorate is lessening the partisan significance of religious cues by decreasing the number of individuals to whom these cues are relevant.

The New Politics Cleavage

The weakening of party bonds based on Old Politics cleavages of class and religion creates the potential for new political cleavages to develop. Many citizens are open to different political appeals and might be mobilized by new issues and innovative programs. The rigid social divisions that long structured Western party systems are beginning to fade.

The New Politics cleavage discussed in chapter 7 may provide the basis for a new partisan alignment. The erosion of Old Politics cleavages is at least partially the result of the increasing salience of New Politics issues. Environmental protection, women's rights, social issues, and disarmament are not easily related to traditional class or religious alignments. Furthermore, New Politics issues attract the attention of the same social groups that are weakly integrated into the Old Politics cleavages: the young, the new middle class, the better educated, and the nonreligious.

The development of a new basis of partisan cleavage is a long and difficult process (Dalton et al., 1984, chap. 15). Social groups must organize to represent New Politics voters and mobilize their support; the group bases of these issues are still ill defined. The parties must also develop clear policy images on these issues. So far, many established parties have been hesitant to identify themselves with these issues because the stakes are still unclear and many parties are internally divided on the issues.

Despite these limiting factors, the partisan impact of the New Politics has increased in recent years. Small, but influential, New Left parties are appearing in many West European democracies. In response, the established parties are becoming more receptive to the political demands of New Politics groups, although clear party alignments on New Politics issues are not fully developed. The public also seems more willing to base their voting choices on New Politics concerns. A cross-national survey in 1982 found that a considerable number of Americans, Britons, and West Germans said that a party's environmental policy would affect their voting decisions (Milbrath, 1984). Several researchers are already suggesting that the New Politics cleavage will eventually become an institutionalized aspect of party politics and may supplant (or join) class and religion as a major basis of party competition (Inglehart, 1977; Miller and Levitin, 1976; Touraine, 1971).

Chapter 7 suggested that the initial structure of this new cleavage will likely be based on the conflict between New Politics and Old Politics adherents. To measure the present development of this cleavage, we relied on the material/ postmaterial values index presented in chapter 5. Materialists emphasize security, stability, economic well-being, and other Old Politics objectives. Postmaterialists place greater stress on New Politics goals, such as participation, social equality, and environmental protection.

Table 8.5 displays the relationship between value priorities and party preferences in each nation. A consistent pattern of political alliance is apparently developing between postmaterialists and Leftist parties. In every nation, postmaterialists favor the Left by a significant margin. The influence of changing values is especially evident for the New Left environmental parties in West Ger-

TABLE 8.5

VALUE PRIORITIES AND PARTY SUPPORT (IN PERCENT)

	Postmaterial	Mixed	Material
United States, 1984			
Democrat	66	53	50
Republican	34	47	50
	100	100	100
Great Britain, 1983			
Labour	52	30	26
Liberal/SDP	25	19	17
Conservative	23	52	56
	100	100	100
West Germany, 1983			
Green	23	5	2
SPD	54	48	37
FDP	6	6	5
CDU/CSU	16	41	56
	100	100	100
France, 1981			
PCF	14	13	8
PS	40	38	41
Other left	15	8	7
Ecologists	21	13	8
UDF	5	16	21
Gaullists	5	13	15
	100	100	100

SOURCES: *United States,* CPS 1984 Election Study; *Great Britain,* Eurobarometer 19; *West Germany,* 1983 West German Election Study; *France,* Eurobarometers 15 and 16.

many and France. For example, 23 percent of the West German postmaterialists supported the Greens, as compared to only 2 percent of the materialists.

The overall magnitude of these voting differences is substantial, often exceeding the Alford index scores for class or religious voting. There is a 38 percentage point gap in Leftist voting (Greens and SPD) between West German materialists and postmaterialists. Sizable PDI scores also appear in Britain (27) and France (26), while value differences are less pronounced in the United States (16).

Long-term trend data are not available for the New Politics cleavage, but some idea of these trends emerges from a comparison of voting patterns across

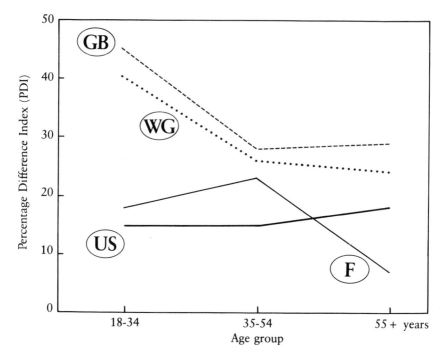

FIGURE 8.6

VALUES VOTING BY AGE GROUP

SOURCES: *United States,* 1984 CPS American Election Study; *Great Britain,* Eurobarometer 19; *West Germany,* 1983 German Election Study; *France,* Eurobarometer 16. Note that entries are the Percentage Difference Index (PDI), the percentage of postmaterialists voting for a Leftist party minus the percentage of materialists voting for the Left.

generations (figure 8.6). In contrast to class voting, which is decreasing among younger cohorts, the impact of the values cleavage is generally stronger among the young. A similar pattern of generational change comes from an analysis of political alignments in twelve Western democracies (Dalton and Flanagan, 1982). Class position has the strongest impact on the political behavior of older generations who experienced the intense class conflicts of the pre-World War II era; value priorities are generally more important in determining the political orientation of the post-World War II generations. Consequently, the relative weight of the values cleavage should increase through the continuing process of generational change. The bases of partisan cleavage are changing in advanced industrial democracies—the long-standing class cleavage is being challenged by a new values cleavage.

It would be a mistake simply to equate the New Politics cleavage with increased support for Leftist parties. We have repeatedly stressed that the Old Politics cleavages will remain the major forces structuring party competition for some time. Furthermore, the partisan consequences of the New Politics depends on how parties respond to these issues. For instance, while American environmentalists normally feel closer to the Democratic party, an early Republican President (Teddy Roosevelt) nurtured the modern environmental movement and another Republican President (Richard Nixon) created the Environmental Protection Agency. Similarly, the Christian Democratic government has taken more forceful action than its SPD predecessors in dealing with acid rain, pollution of the North Sea, and other environmental problems in West Germany. Environmentalism is not a Left or Right issue in the traditional Old Politics meaning of these terms; the partisan consequences of these issues depend on how parties respond. The real lesson of these data is that public interests and party alignments are changing, and the party systems in Western democracies are affected by these trends.

The Transformation of Social Cleavages

This chapter describes a general decline in the social cleavages that have traditionally structured Western party systems. Throughout much of this century, the dominant social cleavage in most democracies distinguished between working-class and middle-class parties. But the socioeconomic transformation of advanced industrial societies is weakening class alignments. Similarly, the number of churchgoers available for mobilization by confessional parties is decreasing, leading to a declining influence of religion on voting behavior. These class and religious trends are often accompanied by declines in the influence of regional, residential, and other social cleavages (Abramson et al., 1986, chap. 5; Baker et al., 1981, chap. 8; Butler and Stokes, 1974).

The general erosion of these social cleavages has fueled speculation about a potential *realignment* in Western party systems. A realignment is defined as a significant shift in the group bases of party coalitions, usually resulting in a shift in the relative size of party-vote shares. For example, the New Deal realignment in the United States is traced to the entry of large numbers of blue-collar workers, Catholics, and blacks into the Democratic party coalition. Realignments have been a regular feature of American electorate politics for well over a century, and probably since the emergence of the first mass party coalitions around 1800 (Clubb et al., 1980). Similar historical realignments have occurred in European party systems (Butler and Stokes, 1974, pp. 155-210; Robertson, 1976).

As old social cleavages weaken, the realignment approach leads us to search for potential new social bases of partisan alignment. The emergence of non-economic value conflicts — issues of environmental protection, nuclear energy, sexual equality, consumer advocacy, disarmament, and human rights — may provide the necessary catalyst. These issues may eventually coalesce into broad social movements that will realign electorates as well as the respective party systems.

The realignment perspective is apparently supported by the growing partisan polarization along the New Politics value cleavage. Value priorities have become a more important influence on voting choice, and new parties have even formed to represent these new political perspectives. Nevertheless, the realigning potential of the New Politics cleavage so far has been limited because these values are linked only weakly to specific demographic groups. The process of partisan realignment is normally based on clearly defined and highly cohesive social groups that can develop institutional ties to the parties and provide clear voting cues to their members (Zuckerman, 1982). There are few indications of growing polarization between social groups that might signal a New Politics realignment. Generational differences in voting patterns have increased in several nations in a manner consistent with the New Politics cleavage, but age groups provide a very transitory basis for party alignment. Other potential group bases of partisan cleavage so far remain speculative, without firm evidence of realigning effects.

The lack of a group basis for the New Politics cleavage highlights another aspect of the new style of citizen politics. The kinds of cleavages that divide modern electorates and the kinds of groups they define are changing. Electoral politics is moving from cleavages defined by social groups to value and issue cleavages that identify only communities of like-minded individuals. The growing heterogeneity, secularization, and *embourgeoisement* of society is weakening social-group identifications generally. Increasing levels of urbanization, social mobility, and geographic mobility mitigate against the continued existence of exclusive social-group networks. The revolutions in education and cognitive mobilization work against the survival of disciplined, hierarchic, clientelist associations.

The New Politics value cleavage is unlikely to provide a basis of mobilization into exclusive, cohesive associational frameworks. Indeed, postmaterial values are antithetical to such massive disciplined organizations as unions and churches. Instead, a vast array of single-issue groups and causes are developing to represent New Politics concerns: from the women's movement to peace organizations to environmental groups. These groups generally are loosely organized with ill-defined memberships that wax and wane.

In sum, two kinds of changes are affecting the durability of a potential realignment and its extensiveness (the proportion of the population affected). First, the shift from the Old Politics to the New Politics marks a transformation from social-group cleavages to issue-group cleavages. Because issue-group cleavages are more difficult to institutionalize or "freeze" via social-group identifications linked to mass organizations, they may not be as stable. Because many of the new issue concerns involve only a narrow sector of the public, the linkage between these cleavages and party support may remain less clear. Some parties may adopt vague issue stands to avoid offending various narrow interests; other parties may cater to special interest groups and lose their broader programmatic image.

A second change affects all cleavages. Several possible social cleavages may still emerge to represent the changing political interests of contemporary electorates. Nevertheless, all forms of political mobilization are subject to the atomizing influences of advanced industrial societies. Interest mobilization along any cleavage dimension necessarily will be characterized by more complex, overlapping, and cross-cutting associational networks; more fluid institutional loyalties; and looser, more egalitarian organizational structures. In other words, the question is not whether labor union leaders support Leftist parties (they do) but whether the union rank and file will follow their leaders any more. This change affects the breadth, effectiveness, and stability of any future partisan alignment. Not only is the style of the Old Politics cleavages fading but the prognosis for an eventual recovery is not optimistic.

The new style of citizen politics therefore includes a more fluid and volatile pattern of party alignments. Political coalitions and voting patterns will lack the permanence of past class and religious cleavages. Without clear social cues, voting decisions will become a more demanding task for voters, and voting decisions will become more dependent on the individual beliefs and values of each citizen.

Notes

1. Most American voting studies are based on analyses of presidential elections. Because of the importance of candidate image, presidential elections reflect a different set of electoral forces than normally found in European parliamentary elections. To ensure comparability of American and European results, the American data in this chapter are based on voting patterns in congressional elections.

2. In the United States, this is the percentage voting Democratic in congressional elections; in Britain, the percentage voting Labour; in West Germany, the percentage voting SPD (after 1976 the SPD and Greens) among SPD and CDU/CSU voters; in France, the percentage voting for Leftist parties.

3. The following table gives the percentage of the Leftist party vote among members of the new middle class at each election:

1962	1967	1968	1973	1978	1981
42	40	42	54	51	57

4. Three-quarters of the public in each nation possess a mix of middle-class and working-class characteristics across four measures of social status: occupation, income, education, and union membership.

9. Attitudes and the Vote

A sociological analysis of politics formed the basis for many early studies of voting behavior. Election outcomes were explained in terms of the political alignment of economic classes, religious blocs, and other sociological groups. This sociological model of voting has been examined in the two previous chapters. Despite the value of such sociological analyses, there are also several weaknesses to this approach. Elections represent a dynamic process; researchers and policymakers are often concerned with explaining changes between elections. Since social characteristics are relatively stable traits, a sociological model has limited value in explaining short-term electoral change. Furthermore, recent survey research documents a substantial decline in the impact of social characteristics on voting choice (see chapter 8). Social characteristics are becoming less important in explaining even the stable aspects of voting patterns.

The limitations of a purely sociological approach to voting shifted researchers' attention to voting models based on psychological factors. While social cleavages may define the broad structure of party alignments, citizen voting behavior is more dependent on the attitudes and perceptions of each individual. Most elections are not presented as conflicts over historical cleavage alignments, but deal with more contemporary problems (which may reflect long-term conflicts). Citizens make judgments about which party best represents their interests, and these perceptions guide individual behavior. Attitudes toward the issues and candidates of an election are a necessary element in any realistic voting model. Attitudes are also changeable, and their incorporation into a voting model helps explain stability and change in voting patterns. Thus the study of voting behavior evolved from the sociological to the psychological, from social characteristics to attitudes.

A team of researchers at the University of Michigan were the first to formalize a model of voting behavior integrating both sociological and psychological influences on voting (Campbell et al., 1960, 1966). This sociopsychological model describes the voting process in terms of a *funnel of causality* (figure 9.1). At the wide mouth of the funnel are the socioeconomic conditions that generate the broad political divisions of society: the economic structure, social

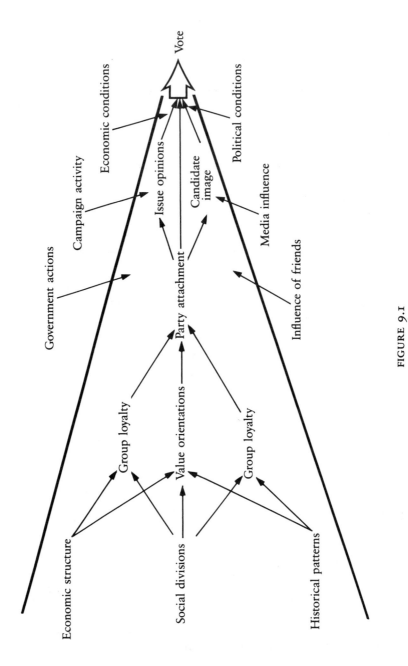

FIGURE 9.1

THE FUNNEL OF CAUSALITY PREDICTING VOTE CHOICE

divisions such as race or religion, and historical alignments such as the North-South division in the United States. These factors influence the structure of the party system (see chapter 7) but are far removed from the voting decisions of individual citizens.

As we move down the causal funnel, socioeconomic conditions influence the public's group loyalties and basic value orientations. For instance, economic conditions may bond an individual to a social class, or regional identities may form in reaction to social and political inequalities. Thus social conditions are translated into attitudes that can directly influence the individual's political behavior.

The causal funnel narrows further as group loyalties and value priorities are linked to more explicitly political attitudes. Angus Campbell and his colleagues explained individual voting decisions primarily in terms of three attitudes: partisanship, issue opinions, and candidate images. These beliefs are most proximate to the voting decision and therefore have a direct and very strong impact on the vote.

Although the funnel of causality appears quite simple by contemporary standards of social science, it represented a major conceptual breakthrough for voting research. This model provides a useful heuristic device for organizing the factors that influence voting behavior. In order to understand voting decisions, one has to recognize the causal relationship between the many factors involved. The wide end of the funnel represents broad social conditions that structure political conflict but are temporally and psychologically far removed from the actual voting decision. As we move down the funnel, attention shifts to factors that are explicitly political, involve individual beliefs, and are more proximate to voting choice. Social characteristics are therefore seen as an important aspect of the voting process, but their primary influence is in forming political attitudes; most of the direct impact of social characteristics on voting is mediated by attitudinal dispositions. Attitudes, in turn, are dependent on the group loyalties and value orientations of the individual, as well as external stimuli such as friends, media, government actions, and the activities of the campaign. In the funnel of causality there is a place for each element of the voting process, and each element is understood in terms of its relation to others.

In addition to the heuristic value of the model, the sociopsychological approach is also very successful in predicting the public's voting choices. Attitudes toward the parties, issues, and candidates of an election are psychologically very close to the actual voting decision and therefore are strongly related to voting choices. In fact, the model can predict voting decisions more accurately than individuals can predict their own behavior (Campbell et al., 1960, p. 74)!

The sociopsychological model has defined a paradigm of voting behavior that has structured how we think about elections and how researchers analyze the voting process. The basic elements of the model have been tested and applied in a variety of nations. This chapter examines the attitudinal bases of voting within the framework of this model.

Partisan Attitudes

The sociopsychological model focuses on the specific issue opinions and candidate evaluations that determine voting behavior. Yet it soon became clear that for many citizens these political beliefs were conditioned by feelings of party loyalty. As one elderly voter once commented to me while waiting to vote, "I vote for the candidate and not the party. It just seems like the Democrats always choose the best candidate." Many voters begin each electoral season with already-formed partisan predispositions. These partisan loyalties become a central element in an individual's belief system, serving as a source of political cues for other attitudes and behaviors.

The Michigan researchers describe these party attachments as a sense of *party identification*, analogous to identifications with a social class, religious denomination, or other social group. Party identification is defined as a long-term, affective, psychological identification with one's preferred political party (Campbell et al., 1960, chap. 6).[1] These party attachments are distinct from voting preferences, which explains why some citizens vote for the presidential candidate of one party while expressing loyalty to another party. Indeed, it is the conceptual independence of voting and party identification that initially gives the latter its theoretical significance. Partisanship constitutes the psychological basis of stable party alignments and influences other citizen attitudes and behaviors (Miller, 1976). The discovery of party identification is heralded as one of the most significant findings of public opinion research. The concept has become a key to understanding citizen political behavior.

The export of party identification to study public opinion in other democracies has yielded mixed results (Butler and Stokes, 1974; Baker et al., 1981; Budge et al., 1976). The problem is finding an equivalent measure of partisanship in multiparty systems or in nations where the term *partisanship* holds different connotations for the voters. The limited voting opportunities in unitary parliamentary states also makes it difficult to separate long-term partisan loyalties from present voting preferences. Still, most studies agree voters hold some sort of party allegiances that endure over time and strongly influence other opinions.

The importance of party identification for citizen political behavior is partially the result of the early origins of party attachments. Socialization studies find that children develop basic partisan orientations at a very early age, often during the primary school years (Hess and Torney, 1967, p. 90; Greenstein and Tarrow, 1969). Children learn party loyalties before they can understand what the party labels stand for, a process similar to the development of many other group ties. These early party attachments then provide a reference structure for future political learning (which often reinforces early partisan biases).

The early-life formation of party identities means that parents play a central role in the socialization of these values. The transmission of partisanship within the family can be seen by comparing the party identifications of parents and their children. A recent cross-national socialization study documents relatively high levels of partisan agreement within American, British, and West German families.[2] Parents and their children were both interviewed so that their opinions could be compared directly (table 9.1). In the United States, for example, 70 percent of the 16-to-20-year-old children of Democratic parents are themselves Democrats, and 54 percent of Republican parents have Republican children. Less than 10 percent of the children actually express loyalty to the party in opposition to their parents. These levels of partisan agreements are quite similar to those found in a larger and more representative study of the socialization pattern of American adolescents (Jennings and Niemi, 1973). The British and West German surveys also indicate that the party attachments of these parents are frequently re-created in the values of their offspring. Conservatives beget Conservatives, and Social Democrats rear new Social Democrats. Measures of partisan transfer are not available for French family pairs, but Left/Right ideological orientations display substantial generational agreement (Percheron and Jennings, 1981). Parents apparently have a strong formative influence on the partisan values of their children, even before most children become active in the political process.

There are many reasons why parents are so successful in transmitting their partisan loyalties to their children. Partisan loyalties are formed at a time when parents are the dominant influence in a child's life, and the exposure to partisan cues from the parent is quite common. Parties are very visible and important institutions in the political process, and virtually all political discussion includes some partisan content: Candidates are identified and judged by their party affiliation, and policies are evaluated in terms of their party sponsor. It does not take long for a child to realize the parents' partisan leanings from their reactions to television news and statements in family discussions. Furthermore, most parents have strong party attachments that endure across elections. Children are consequently exposed to consistent and continuous cues on which party is preferred by their parents. Either through explicit reinforcement or subconscious internalization of parental values, many children learn of their parents' partisan preferences and take them as their own.

TABLE 9.1

THE TRANSMISSION OF PARENTAL PARTISANSHIP (IN PERCENT)

Child	Parent		
United States	Democrat	Republican	Independent
Democrat	70	25	40
Republican	10	54	20
Independent	20	21	40
	100	100	100
(N)	(128)	(77)	(30)

Great Britain	Labour	Liberal	Conservative	None
Labour	51	17	6	29
Liberal	8	39	11	6
Conservative	1	11	50	6
None	40	33	33	59
	100	100	100	100
(N)	(83)	(18)	(54)	(17)

West Germany	SPD	FDP	CDU/CSU	None
SPD	53	8	14	19
FDP	4	59	1	3
CDU/CSU	9	–	32	12
None	34	33	53	66
	100	100	100	100
(N)	(68)	(12)	(78)	(67)

SOURCE: Political Action Study.

Once party ties are established, electoral experience normally reinforces these partisan tendencies because most citizens cast ballots for their preferred party. Partisan loyalties consequently strengthen with age or, more precisely, with continued electoral support of the same party (Converse, 1976).[3]

This increasing strength of party identification with age is portrayed in figure 9.2. Regardless of which party one supports, party bonds are generally stronger among older age groups. The majority of the public in the United States and Britain develop a strong sense of party identity by middle age, which continues to strengthen through the rest of the life cycle. The strength of French partisanship also increases with age, but the level of partisanship is limited by the general instability of the French party system. French parties frequently change their names or political orientations, and this impedes the development of strong party attachments as occurs in stable party systems such as the United States and Britain.

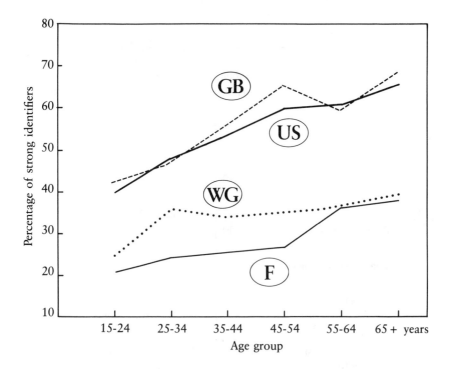

FIGURE 9.2

STRENGTH OF PARTY ATTACHMENT BY AGE

SOURCES: *France,* Eurobarometers 9 and 10; *other nations,* Political Action Study.

The one exception to the age pattern, West Germany, lends credence to the partisan learning model (Baker et al., 1981, chap. 9; Norpoth, 1983). Older Germans spent a significant portion of their lives under the nondemocratic regimes of the Wilhelmine Empire or Third Reich. The turbulent democratic interlude of the Weimar Republic also was not conducive to developing strong party ties. Consequently, older voters were unable to accumulate partisan loyalties at a "normal" rate. So, the partisan attachments of older Germans are only marginally stronger than the attachments of younger citizens raised during the democratic years of the Federal Republic. As the generational composition of the West German electorate gradually shifts to voters raised exclusively under the postwar system, the age distribution of German partisanship should more closely resemble the normal life-cycle pattern of the longer-established democracies.

Partisan attachments are thus learned early in life, become deeply embedded in a child's belief system, and are reinforced by subsequent partisan experiences. Partisanship may change in reaction to later life experiences, but

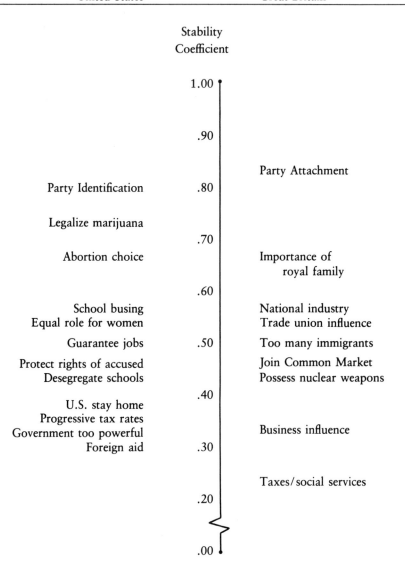

United States		Great Britain
	Stability Coefficient	
	1.00	
	.90	
		Party Attachment
Party Identification	.80	
Legalize marijuana		
	.70	
Abortion choice		Importance of royal family
	.60	
School busing Equal role for women		National industry Trade union influence
Guarantee jobs	.50	Too many immigrants
Protect rights of accused Desegregate schools		Join Common Market Possess nuclear weapons
	.40	
U.S. stay home Progressive tax rates Government too powerful		Business influence
Foreign aid	.30	
		Taxes/social services
	.20	
	.00	

FIGURE 9.3

THE STABILITY OF POLITICAL BELIEFS

SOURCES: CPS 1972-76 American Election Panel Study; 1964-66 British Election Panel Study. Note that entries are two-year stability coefficients or estimates based on four-year stability measures.

these attachments are not easily altered once they have been formed. For example, figure 9.3 displays the stability coefficients for several attitudes from the 1972-76 American election panel study. Party identification is the most stable political attitude, far exceeding the stability of opinions on several policy issues of long-standing national concern: race relations, economic programs, and foreign policy. Only issues that touch strongly held moral values, such as opinions on abortion, rival the stability of partisanship. Over 90 percent of the American electorate retains the same partisan loyalties between most pairs of elections. Additional evidence of long-term partisan constancy comes from Jennings and Niemi's (1981) eight-year American panel study. They find that 78 percent of the adult sample and 58 percent of the adolescent sample do not change their partisan ties across one of the most turbulent political periods in recent American history (1965-73).

Evidence from other nations mirrors this pattern. Party attachments are significantly more stable than other political beliefs across a two-year British panel survey (figure 9.3). On the average, between 80 and 90 percent of the British public retain constant party ties from one election to the next. Hilde Himmelweit and her colleagues (1981) present additional evidence of the continuity of British partisanship. Reinterviewing a sample of British middle-class males over a twelve-year period, they find that a clear majority of voters supported the same party in 1959 and 1974; conversions between Labour and Conservative partisans were exceedingly rare. A several-year panel study in the West German Saarland indicates that partisanship is the most stable political attitude measured in the survey (Kaase, 1973), and shorter national panels present the same pattern. The limited evidence for France indicates that below the surface of substantial turbulence in the actions of party leaders, there is considerable continuity in the partisan orientations of the French public (Converse, 1969a). The process of partisan change moves slowly in most established party systems.

Important evidence on the relative permanence of partisan attitudes comes from comparing the stability of partisanship and voting preferences (table 9.2). For instance, reinterviews with the same American voters in 1972 and 1976 indicates that 93 percent had stable party identifications, while only 75 percent had stable congressional voting preferences. Moreover, when there was some variability, more voters maintain a stable party identification while changing their vote (22 percent) than the other way around (4 percent). Party preferences are also more stable than voting preferences in Britain and West Germany, but this difference is more modest than in the United States (LeDuc, 1981; Norpoth, 1978). In Europe there is a greater tendency for partisanship and vote to travel together; when one changes, so does the other. Because of their limited amount of electing, Europeans are less likely to distinguish between partisanship and

TABLE 9.2

THE RELATIVE STABILITY OF PARTY ATTACHMENTS AND VOTE (IN PERCENT)

United States, 1972-76

	Vote	
Party Identification	Stable	Variable
Stable	71	22
Variable	4	3

100

N = 539

Great Britain, 1970-74

	Vote	
Party Identification	Stable	Variable
Stable	75	10
Variable	5	10

100

N = 795

West Germany, 1976

	Vote	
Party Identification	Stable	Variable
Stable	83	8
Variable	1	8

100

N = 707

SOURCES: LeDuc (1981, p. 261); Berger (1977, p. 504).

NOTE: Tables are based on those who were voters and identified with a political party at each time point. American and British results are based on changes between two elections; West German data are based on changes during a three-wave 1976 election panel.

current voting preferences. Still, partisanship generally appears to provide a political orientation that continues over time, even in the face of vote defections.

In sum, party attachments are the most stable political attitude in the belief system of most individuals. This enduring sense of party attachment serves as a valuable guidepost in managing the complexities of politics for many voters.

Partisanship provides a fairly constant reference structure in an ever-changing political world, and researchers have stressed the functional value of these party cues for the electorate (Miller, 1976; Borre and Katz, 1973; Baker et al., 1981). Partisanship serves a reference-group function as a source of cues for evaluating issues and other aspects of politics. Moreover, in comparison to social-group cues such as class and religion, party attachments are relevant to a much broader range of political phenomena, since parties are so central to the political process. Issues and events frequently are presented to the public in partisan terms, as the parties take positions on the political questions of the day or react to the statements of other political actors. Party ties also perform a mobilizing function; attachment to a political party draws an individual into the political process. Interest in politics, voting turnout, and participation in campaign activities is normally higher among strong party identifiers (see chapter 2).

The cue-giving function of partisanship is strongest in the case of voting behavior. Elections in most democracies almost always are partisan contests. Partisanship provides a clear and low-cost voting cue for the unsophisticated voter. When additional information is unavailable, one votes for the candidate of one's preferred party. Even for the sophisticated citizen, a candidate's party affiliation normally signifies a policy program that the candidate represents.

Surveys generally find an exceedingly close relationship between partisanship and voting in legislative elections. For example, only 11 percent of British partisans defected from their preferred party in the 1979 election, and only 5 percent of West German partisans defected in 1983. This is to be expected because the limited voting opportunities in most European nations lessen the separation between partisanship and vote.[4] The American elector, on the other hand, "has to cope simultaneously with a vast collection of partisan candidates seeking a variety of offices at federal, state, and local levels; it is small wonder that he becomes conscious of a generalized belief about his ties to a party" (Butler and Stokes, 1969, p. 43). Consequently, the separation between attitudes and behavior is most noticeable in American elections, especially at the presidential level. Presidential elections attract great public interest, and candidate image exerts an important influence on voting choice. Party defections are most common in this kind of election. The recent Republican presidential candidates have been successful because they have been able to attract defectors from the Democratic majority. In 1984 over 14 percent of American partisans cast presidential votes contrary to their party identification. A similar situation exists in France. The two-candidate runoff in French presidential elections is decided by the size of the vote the candidates can attract from parties other than their own. Still, even in the case of these two presidential elections, partisanship has a strong influence on American (1984 eta = .75) and French (1974 eta = .71) voting patterns. Party ties routinely are the strongest predictor of voting behavior in virtually all Western democracies.

Partisan Dealignment

Partisanship has emerged as a central variable in the study of many different aspects of citizen political behavior. For the individual citizen, partisanship is an enduring and very useful source of political guidance. For the political system, widespread party attachments promote continuity in party alignments and reinforce the stability of the political process. If any change in this situation was foreseen, most researchers predicted a strengthening of this partisanship model (e.g., Converse, 1969b; Rose and Urwin, 1970).

It thus came as some surprise when party ties abruptly began to weaken in many democracies during the 1970s. At first, the signs of partisan decline were difficult to detect against the normal background of partisan change between elections. Gradually, the evidence of substantial change became more obvious. In many nations, new political parties emerged to challenge the established partisan order. The fluctuations in party fortunes between elections increased in magnitude (Crewe and Denver, 1985). Discussions of a crisis of confidence facing parties and party systems became commonplace.

Partisan change is a normal element of the electoral process, and periods of heightened partisan volatility and fragmentation dot the electoral histories of most democracies. In this instance, however, partisan decline apparently reflects a more fundamental change in citizen political behavior. Many Western democracies are experiencing a process of *partisan dealignment* (Dalton et al., 1984). Voters are not simply defecting from their preferred party in one or two elections. Partisan dealignment means that there is more than just a temporary erosion in partisan loyalties.

The weakening of party ties first became apparent in the United States (figure 9.4). American partisanship was extremely stable during the early 1960s; the percentage of strong party identifiers remained within the 35-37 percent range. Partisan loyalties began to weaken after the 1964 election; by 1980, only a quarter of the American electorate expressed a strong sense of partisanship (Beck, 1984; Abramson, 1983). Even a partial increase in partisanship in 1984 leaves the percentage of strong partisan far below the pre-1964 level. An almost identical pattern of declining party ties occurs in Britain. Over 40 percent of the British public were strong partisans during the late 1960s. This percentage was cut in half within less than a decade. The series of comparable French survey data is much shorter, but it too follows a downward trend in the proportion of strong partisans (see Lewis-Beck, 1984, for a discussion of trends in France).

188

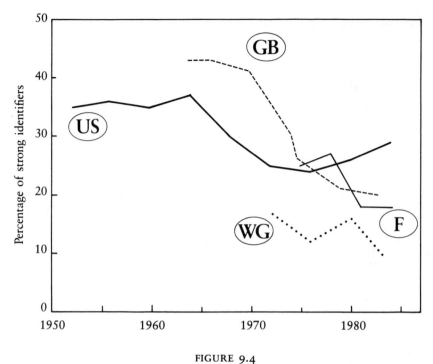

FIGURE 9.4

THE PERCENTAGE OF STRONG PARTISANS

SOURCES: *United States,* SRC/CPS American Election Studies; *Great Britain,* British Election Studies; *West Germany,* West German Election Studies; *France,* Eurobarometer studies.

West Germany again deviates from the pattern of partisanship found in other nations. Surveys over the past decade fail to detect significant evidence of dealignment among West German voters. Furthermore, extensive longitudinal analyses of another partisanship measure actually indicate a substantial increase in partisanship between 1961 and 1976, as West Germans developed initial commitments to the postwar party system (Baker et al., 1981, chap. 8). Still, other data will show that the signs of the dealignment process are also evident in West Germany.

The symptoms of partisan dealignment are visible in most nations, even when popular attachments to parties have not weakened. For instance, studies of American voting behavior plot a consistent and dramatic decline in the impact of partisanship on voting in presidential, congressional, senatorial, and state elections (Nie et al., 1979). This downward trend partially reflects the increasing number of nonpartisans who, by definition, lack clear party cues. In addition, defection rates have steadily increased even among strong and weak

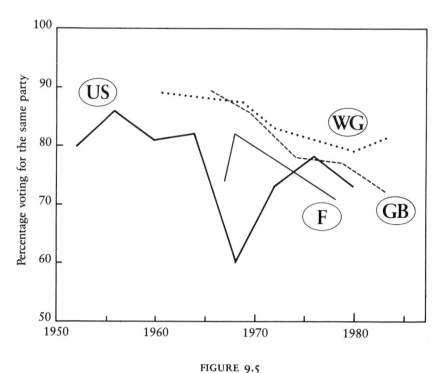

FIGURE 9.5

THE STABILITY OF VOTING PREFERENCES BETWEEN ADJACENT ELECTIONS

SOURCES: *United States,* recall data for presidential vote SRC/CPS American Election Studies; *Great Britain,* British Election Studies; *West Germany,* recall data from the West German Election Studies; *France,* recall data from the Converse and Pierce 1967 survey, Inglehart 1968 survey, and 1978 Election survey.

party identifiers. Split-ticket voting has similarly risen in recent American elections, as weakened party attachments lead fewer voters to cast straight party ballots (Wattenberg, 1984).

The erosion of partisanship is also visible in the declining stability of voting patterns. Figure 9.5 displays the percentage of voters participating in two adjacent elections who support the same party each time. Although most voters continue to support the same party over time, the number of stable voters is generally declining in each nation.

Indications of partisan dealignment appear in other aspects of partisan behavior. There is a significant decrease in voting turnout in Britain and the United States; at least partially the result of weakened partisanship. Instead of basing voting choices on standing partisan preferences, more electors are delaying their voting decision until later in the campaign. Partisanship was once a stable guidepost for citizen political behavior, and now fewer individuals are following its guidance.

There are several explanations for the spreading pattern of partisan dealignment. One factor involves the declining role of parties as political institutions. Many of the parties' traditional input functions have been taken over by other institutions. A myriad of special-interest groups and single-issue lobbies have developed in recent years, and political parties have little hope of representing all these groups. Instead, these groups are organizing to press their interests without relying on partisan channels. Similarly, the mass media are assuming many of the information and input functions that political parties once controlled. Party leaders are even losing some control over the selection of elected party representatives. The most advanced example is the United States, where the introduction of open primaries and nonpartisan elections undermined the parties' hold on recruitment. The British Labour party has experienced a similar shift in nomination power away from the party in Parliament to party conventions and local constituency groups. These and other developments lessen the importance of parties in the political process and therefore weaken the significance of parties as political reference points.

Partisan dealignment is also encouraged by the failure of parties to deal successfully with contemporary political issues. On the one hand, many parties remain rigidly committed to outdated policies on the economic and welfare issues associated with the traditional class cleavage. On the other hand, the agenda of advanced industrial societies often appears unsuited for mass political parties. Many of these issues, such as nuclear energy, minority rights, university reform, or local environmental problems, are too narrow to affect mass partisan alignments. The rise of single-issue groups does not translate well into mass political organizations. We have discussed how parties are reluctant to take clear positions on these issues because of the uncertain electoral benefits. Thus the parties are not entirely fulfilling their critical programmatic function of aggregating and articulating political interests.

Not only do parties perform fewer system-level functions, but party attachments and partisan cues are also becoming less important to individuals as a source of political cues. W. Phillips Shively (1979) suggests that the development of party ties partially depends on the functional value of partisanship. He maintains that voters develop party identifications as a shortcut to help them handle difficult and often confusing political decisions. By relying on cues emanating from a party identification, the costs of political involvement are lessened.

Several socioeconomic trends occurring in contemporary societies are making party identifications less necessary, and perhaps less relevant, for many voters. Rising levels of education have increased the voters' sophistication and ability to deal with the complexities of politics. At the same time, the growing availability of political information through the media reduces the costs of making informed decisions. Moreover, the present instability of parties and party systems, the rise of new parties, and shifting party positions make long-standing party attachments less reliable as political guides. Thus the functional need for partisan cues to guide voting behavior, evaluate political issues, and mobilize political involvement is decreasing for a growing sector of society.

This interpretation of partisan dealignment is supported by the pattern of weakening party ties. Educational level is significantly related to dealignment in Britain. Between 1964 and 1974, the decrease in partisanship among British citizens with advanced education was three times as great as among those with minimal education (Alt, 1984). Dealignment in the United States is largely concentrated among the young (Beck, 1984; Abramson, 1983). Paul Beck traces this decline to a breakdown in family socialization and a general increase in anti-party sentiment.

An extension of these analyses presents cross-national evidence of a new kind of nonpartisan in advanced industrial societies (Dalton, 1984a). These *apartisans* are sophisticated and active citizens who remain unattached to any political party. In contrast to the traditional partisan independents, who were uninformed and uninvolved in politics, apartisans are active participants (though often outside party-related activities such as campaigns and elections). These new independents are also less consistent in their voting patterns because voting behavior is not dependent on long-standing party predispositions. Because apartisans are concentrated among the young, the better educated, and citizens with postmaterial values, the continuing socioeconomic development of advanced industrial societies may reinforce the dealignment trend that has emerged over the past decade.

Issue Voting

As the electoral impact of long-term partisan attachments has eroded, many political scientists have emphasized a corresponding increase in the influence of candidate preferences and issue opinions on voting choice. These two factors are located at the end of the causal funnel and are more dynamic components of the voting model. In addition, these factors may be easily integrated into the new style of politics because decisions are based on individual beliefs and evaluations.

While candidate images are often an important factor in American elections, their impact in Europe is substantially limited by party control of parliamentary elections. For example, it is not uncommon for parties to assign candidates to run in a district they have never visited previously; the French describe this situation as "parachuting" a candidate into the district. This does not mean that candidate image is an unimportant influence on voting decisions; the expanding role of the media in European elections and the personalization of party programs have made images of party leaders a more visible aspect of electoral politics. Because of the uncertain influence of candidate image on parliamentary contests and the difficulty of comparing this influence cross-nationally, our analyses of short-term voting influences are limited to the impact of issue voting.[5]

The study of issue voting has been closely intertwined with the scholarly debate on the political sophistication of contemporary publics; research studies often differ widely in their evaluation of issue voting. Three requirements are generally needed before meaningful issue voting can exist: citizens should be interested in the issue, they should hold an opinion on the issue, and they should know the party/candidate positions on the issue. The authors of *The American Voter* maintained that on almost all policy issues, the majority of voters failed to meet these criteria. These researchers classified a third of the public, or less, as possible issue voters on each of a long list of policy topics (Campbell et al., 1960, chap. 8). Moreover, the Michigan researchers believed that the small numbers of issue voters reflected the conceptual and motivational limits of the electorate; the lack of issue voting was presumably an intrinsic aspect of mass politics. These political scientists therefore rejected the notion that election results represent the policy choices of the public.

Even from the beginning of empirical voting research, there were critics of this negative image of issue voting. A leading scholar, V.O. Key, was one of the first to present survey evidence indicating that citizens were "moved by concern about the central and relevant questions of public policy, of government performance, and of executive personality" (Key, 1966, pp. 7-8). In short, Key's unorthodox argument was that "voters are not fools." Key's position gradually has become less unorthodox as our understanding of citizen voting behavior has grown.

Because only a minority of the public may fulfill the criteria of rational issue voting for each specific issue, this does not mean that only a third of the total public are capable of any issue voting at all. Contemporary electorates are comprised of overlapping issue groups, or *issue publics* (see chapter 2). These issue publics vary in size and composition. A large and heterogeneous group of citizens may be interested in fundamental political issues such as taxes, inflation rates, budget deficits, and the threat of war. On more specific issues — agricultural policy, nuclear energy, immigration policy, foreign aid — the issue

publics normally are smaller and politically distinct. Most voters are politically attentive on at least one issue, and many voters may belong to several issue
publics. When citizens are able to define their own issue interests, most electors can fulfill the issue-voting criteria for their issues of interest. For example,
David RePass (1971) shows that only 5 percent of the public is interested in
medical programs for the elderly, but over 80 percent of this group can be classified as potential issue voters. By adopting a more diversified view of the electorate — not all citizens must be concerned with all issues — the evidence of issue
voting is substantially strengthened.

Several political trends have further increased the extent of issue voting
by contemporary electorates. There have been real changes in the nature of
electorates (and politics itself) that facilitate issue voting. The process of cognitive mobilization is increasing the number of voters who possess the conceptual ability and political skills necessary to fulfill the issue-voting criteria. The
growth of citizen action groups, new issue-oriented parties, and the general
renaissance of ideological debate at election time are obvious signs of the public's greater issue awareness. Political elites have become more conscious of the
public's preferences and more sensitive to the results of public opinion polls.

The public's changing issue interests also stimulate increased issue voting.
The development of new issue interests that conflict with established party allegiances means that citizens are tempted to vote on the issues, which may lead
them to cross party lines. Often these issues arise from long-standing political
controversies that reenter the political process, such as the racial issue in the
United States and regional differences in Great Britain (Carmines and Stimson, 1988; Rose, 1982). New issue interests also were born from the political
turmoil and policy changes of the 1960s and 1970s — the Vietnam war,
decolonialization in France, and *Ostpolitik* in West Germany.

Over the last decade the OPEC price increases and resulting recession of
Western economies have revived interest in the traditional economic issues of
unemployment, inflation, and the size of government. This trend has stimulated
academic interest in the impact of economic issues on voting behavior (Kiewiet,
1983; Eulau and Lewis-Beck, 1985; Alford and Leege, 1984). Economic conflicts
historically provided the basis for many party systems, and yet these new issue
interests often seem to develop independent of partisan ties and even social-
class position. Therefore, rather than reinforce existing party lines, these new
economic concerns contribute to the further weakening of party alignments.

A more gradual and enduring growth of issue interests has centered on
a set of New Politics issues — nuclear energy, women's liberation, environmental
protection, democratization — that are injecting new issue interests into the electoral process of most Western democracies. These issues have played a special

role in providing a political base for many new parties and reorienting the voting patterns of the young.

As a result of these forces, numerous longitudinal studies have documented the growing electoral impact of issues. Several American studies describe a general increase in issue voting in the 1970s (Nie et al., 1979; Pomper, 1975; Declercq et al., 1976). The Republican party's victories in 1980 and 1984 are the result, at least in part, of the appeal of issues counteracting the Democrats' partisan majority (Pomper, 1981, 1985). The use of policy criteria to evaluate the major West German parties steadily expanded between 1969 and 1980 (Klingemann, 1983). Mark Franklin's (1985) sophisticated longitudinal analysis of British electoral behavior uncovers a similiar increase in the independent influence of issue beliefs on voting decisions (see also Rose, 1986; Heath et al., 1985).

This general trend toward greater issue voting in most Western nations is a self-reinforcing process. Issue voting contributes to, and benefits from, the concomitant decline in party voting patterns. As party ties weaken, this increases the potential for issue opinions to influence voting choice. As policy preferences become more important to the voter, this inevitably encourages some party defection and erodes party attachments.[6] Thus the rise of issue voting and the decline of partisanship are normally viewed as interrelated trends.

Although the issues of each specific election campaign are different, the general impact of policy preferences on voting behavior can be estimated by examining the relationship between Left/Right attitudes and vote. Chapter 6 described Left/Right attitudes as a sort of "super issue"; that is, a statement of positions on the issues that are currently most important to each voter. The salient issues might vary across individuals or across nations, but Left/Right attitudes provide a single measure of each citizen's overall policy views.

Most citizens can position themselves along a Left/Right scale, and these attitudes are linked to specific policy views, fulfilling the first two criteria of issue voting. Figure 9.6 indicates that the publics in each nation are also able to locate the major political parties on this Left/Right scale. The figure presents the electorate's average self-placement and the average score assigned to political parties within each nation. American voters perceive fairly modest political differences between the Democrats and Republicans, a reflection of the large policy overlap between both parties. The perceived party differences are more substantial in the three European party systems. The French Communist party is at the far left of the political spectrum, counterbalancing the RPR on the far right. The West German partisan landscape ranges from the Greens on the far Left to the conservative CSU.[7] In Britain the Labour and Conservative parties have recently assumed more distinct positions on the Left/Right scale, opening a void in the center that the SDP/Liberal Alliance occupies. Most political

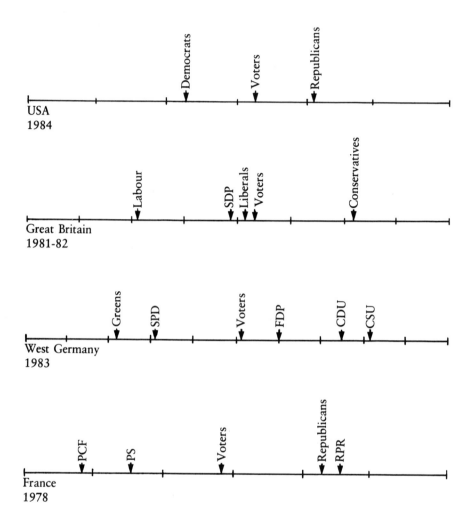

FIGURE 9.6

LEFT/RIGHT PLACEMENT OF THE PARTIES AND VOTER SELF-PLACEMENT

SOURCES: *United States,* CPS 1984 American Election Study; *Great Britain,* Crewe (1983); *West Germany,* 1983 West German Election Study; *France,* Jaffre (1980, p. 52). Note that in the United States the endpoints of the continuum were labeled Liberal/Conservative; in the other nations, Left/Right was used.

TABLE 9.3

LEFT/RIGHT ATTITUDES AND PARTY PREFERENCES (IN PERCENT)

Country	Left	L/C	Center	C/R	Right
United States, 1984					
Democrats	86	66	62	46	30
Republicans	14	34	38	54	71
	100	100	100	100	100
Great Britain, 1983					
Labour	84	65	30	8	9
Liberal/SDP	9	21	32	9	2
Conservative	7	14	38	83	89
	100	100	100	100	100
West Germany, 1983					
Greens	21	19	6	0	0
SPD	55	72	32	11	6
FDP	9	0	8	4	1
CDU/CSU	14	9	54	85	93
	100	100	100	100	100
France, 1981					
PCF	52	14	5	3	0
PS	26	67	30	9	7
Other Left	14	7	10	1	7
Ecologists	7	10	19	4	3
UDF	1	2	26	52	47
RPR	0	1	10	31	37
	100	100	100	100	100

SOURCES: *United States,* 1984 CPS Election Study; *Great Britain,* Eurobarometer 19; *West Germany,* Eurobarometer 19; *France,* Eurobarometer 15.

observers would agree that these party placements are fairly accurate portrayals of actual party positions. Therefore, in overall terms citizens also fulfill the third issue voting criterion: knowing party positions.

Table 9.3 presents the relationship between Left/Right attitudes and voting choice. Left/Right attitudes are strongly related to voting choice in every nation, but the impact of these attitudes is greatest in France and West Germany, where the parties offer the clearest policy options. In the United States, for instance, 86 percent of the self-identified Liberals voted for a Democratic congressional candidate in 1984, compared to only 30 percent for the Democrats among self-identified Conservatives. This voting gap is much larger than the effects of social characteristics noted in chapter 8. In part, the substantial influence of Left/Right attitudes is because policy evaluations are located closer to the end of the funnel of causality. In addition, longitudinal trends suggest that the relative impact of Left/Right attitudes has been increasing (Miller and Levitin, 1976; Lewis-Beck, 1984).

More detail can be added to this general picture of policy voting by studying the relationship between policy attitudes and party preferences. A recent Eurobarometer survey included a list of policy attitude items that tap most of the central issues of current political debate (though not all). Table 9.4 describes the impact of issues on party preferences in Britain, West Germany and France.[8] For several reasons, we should be cautious about overinterpreting these data. The strength of each relationship reflects both the varying size of the relevant issue public and the clarity of party positions. The dynamic, short-term

TABLE 9.4

THE CORRELATION BETWEEN ISSUE OPINIONS AND PARTY PREFERENCE

	Great Britain	West Germany	France
Left/Right placement	.39	.36	.33
Old Politics			
Public ownership of industry	.23	.08	.33
Government manages economy	.18	.13	.17
Co-determination	.17	.15	.25
Control multinationals	.17	.06	.18
Reduce income inequality	.16	.11	.29
Liberalize abortion	.08	.15	.17
Foreign Aid			
Aid EC regions	.09	.09	.14
Aid Third World	.10	.10	.17
Security			
Strengthen defense	.15	.15	.24
Action against terrorists	.10	.12	.20
New Politics			
Nuclear energy	.07	.14	.24
Protect environment	.06	.10	.10
Free expression	.09	.09	.23

SOURCE: Eurobarometer 11. Table entries are Kramer's V coefficients.

nature of issue beliefs means that either of these factors, and thus the impact of an issue, may change substantially between elections. These data therefore provide only a momentary description of the relationship between issue opinions and party preferences, and not an explanation.

The traditional economic issues of the Old Politics generally display the strongest relationships with party preferences. The largest correlation in every nation is based on an economic issue. This pattern probably holds for most elections because economic topics have relatively large issue publics and most political parties have defined the party program around issues of the government's role in the economic and related economic policies. The impact of these issues is greatest in France, where a Communist party represents a distinctly different economic program. In contrast, the weak correlations for the West German electorate may reflect the general consensus on structural aspects of the economy that exists within the German public.

Foreign policy issues are only weakly related to party preferences in all three nations. This is a normal pattern in most electoral analyses. Foreign policy issues attract the primary attention of only a small share of the public, except at times of international crisis. Party differences on issues such as foreign aid and regional aid are also modest in comparison to party polarization on many other topics. At the same time, the European consensus on foreign policy is breaking down at least partially (Flynn and Rattinger, 1983) and this may explain the surprisingly strong relationship between defense attitudes and party preference.

New Politics issues have only a modest impact on party choice. Although topics such as nuclear energy and environmental protection have attracted substantial public attention, the translation of these policy attitudes into party preferences has been limited by the hesitancy of most parties to adopt clear policies on these issues (Dalton et al., 1984, chap. 15). This is another reflection of the tendency of New Politics issues to cut across traditional party lines (see chapter 7). New Politics issues are significant more for their potential impact than for their present influence on electoral outcomes.

A much richer compendium of information on issue voting exists for American electoral politics and we need only review these results (Abramson et al., 1986; Nie et al., 1979). The general pattern of the American findings follows the broad contours of the European results. Economic issues such as support for government spending or government guaranteed living standards are strongly related to voting results. The racial issue is also a prominent aspect of American electoral politics. Foreign policy topics such as relations with the Soviet Union have a much weaker impact on party choice. The notable feature of American politics is that the influence of issues is much stronger in presidential elections, where candidate positions are more visible, than in congressional campaigns.

The brief overview of issue voting indicates that many issues influence the partisan preferences of contemporary electorates. Although the impact of any one issue for the entire public is often modest, this is because not all issues are salient to all voters. A more refined analysis based on the concept of *issue publics* would find that individual voting decisions are heavily influenced by each voter's own specific issue interests. When these findings are combined with evidence of increasing issue voting overall, V.O. Key's positive assessments of the public's voting decisions no longer appear so unorthodox.

Citizen Politics and Voting Behavior

The chapters in this section present a consistent picture of the changing patterns of voting behavior in these nations. One major change involves a general decline in the long-term determinants of voting choice. The influence of social class on voting preferences has decreased in virtually all Western democracies, as has the impact of religion, residence, and other social characteristics. Similarly, dealignment trends signal a decrease in the impact of enduring party attachments on voting decisions. Fewer voters now approach elections with standing party predispositions based either on social characteristics or early-learned partisan ties.

As the long-term determinants of party choice have decreased in influence, there has been a counterbalancing growth in the importance of short-term attitudes such as issue opinions (and possibly candidate image). A legion of researchers has described the growth of issue voting in the United States. Studies of European voting patterns also stress the increasing role of issues in contemporary elections.

The shifting balance of long-term and short-term voting influences may represent another aspect of the new style of citizen politics as it applies to voting behavior. As modern electorates have become more sophisticated and politically interested, and as the availability of political information has expanded, many citizens are now better able to reach their own voting decisions without relying on broad external cues such as social class or family partisanship. In short, more citizens now possess the political resources to follow the complexities of politics; they have the potential to act as the independent issue voters described in classic democratic theory but seldom observed in practice.

Changing styles of citizen voting behavior are illustrated by the changing impact of economics on the vote. Traditionally, economic conflicts have been structured by social divisions: the working class versus the middle class, industrial versus agrarian interests. In this situation, one's social position was often a meaningful guide to voting decisions. As social divisions have narrowed and the group bases of political interests have blurred, social class has decreased as a source of voting cues. This does not mean that economic issues have also eroded in importance. Quite the opposite. As recessions weakened the economies of the industrial nations in the late 1970s and early 1980s, economic issues again rose to the top of the political agenda for many citizens. Contemporary evidence of economic voting is widespread (Kiewiet, 1983; Lewis-Beck, 1984; Eulau and Lewis-Beck, 1985), but now issue positions are individually based rather than group derived. The political cues of a union leader or business association must compete more equally with the voter's own opinions on economic policy and party programs. That a partial return to the old issues of economic growth and security has not revived traditional class divisions provides compelling evidence that a new style of citizen politics now affects voting patterns.

This new style of individually based voting decisions may signify a boon or a curse for contemporary democracies. On the positive side, sophisticated voters should inject more issue voting into elections, increasing the policy implications of electoral results. In the long term, greater issue voting may make candidates and parties more responsive to public opinion. Thus the democratic process may move closer to the democratic ideal.

On the negative side, many political scientists have expressed concerns that the growth of issue voting and single-issue groups may place excessive demands on contemporary democracies (see chapter 11). Without the issue-aggregating functions performed by party leaders and electoral coalitions, democratic governments may be faced with conflicting issue demands from their voters. Governments may find it increasingly difficult to satisfy unrestrained popular demands.

Another concern involves the citizens who lack the political skills to meet the requirements of sophisticated issue voting. This sector of the electorate may become an atomized collection of voters if traditional political cues (party and social groups) decline in usefulness. Lacking firm political predispositions and a clear understanding of politics, these individuals may be easily mobilized by charismatic elites or fraudulent party programs. Indeed, the development of television facilitates unmediated one-on-one contacts between political elites and voters. Despite its potential for encouraging more sophisticated citizen involvement, television also offers the possibility of trivialized electoral politics in which video style outweighs substance in campaigning.

In sum, the trends we have discussed here do not lend themselves to a single prediction of the future of democratic party systems. But the future is within our control, depending on how political systems respond to these new challenges. It does appear, however, that the new style of citizen politics will be characterized by a greater diversity of voting patterns. A system of frozen social cleavages and stable party alignments is less likely in advanced industrial societies where voters are sophisticated, power is decentralized, and individual choice is given greater latitude. The diversity and individualism of the new style of citizen politics constitutes a major departure from the structured partisan politics of the past.

Notes

1. The standard party identification question is one of the most frequently asked questions in American public opinion surveys. It measures both the direction of partisanship and the strength of party attachments:

> Generally speaking, do you think of yourself as a Republican, a Democrat, an Independent, or what? (For those expressing a party preference:) Would you call yourself a strong Republican/Democrat or a not very strong Republican/Democrat? (For Independents:) Do you think of yourself as closer to the Republican or Democratic party?

The question yields a seven-point measure of partisanship ranging from strong Democratic identifiers to strong Republican identifiers.

2. These data are drawn from the Political Action Study. The study supplemented its national sample of adults with additional parent-child interviews in families where a 16-to-20-year-old was still living in the parent's home. For additional analyses, see Jennings et al. (1979).

3. The question of whether age differences in American partisanship represent generational or life-cycle effects has been intensely debated by researchers (Converse, 1976; Abramson, 1979). We emphasize the life-cycle (partisan learning) model because the cross-national pattern of age differences seems more consistent with this explanation.

4. This has led some researchers to question the usefulness of the partisanship concept in parliamentary systems (Budge et al., 1976). Should we question the value of partisanship because it works too well in explaining voting behavior? Partisanship is also valuable in explaining other, less obvious aspects of political behavior.

5. The vast majority of American electoral research has studied voting in presidential elections, where candidate image plays an obvious role. The French presidential elections may pose an analogous situation. Davidson (1982) has compiled important evidence of how candidate image in American presidential elections has also changed in content toward more evaluative aspects (issues and candidate abilities).

6. The conventional wisdom holds that partisanship is often a strong influence on issue opinions, while the reverse causal flow is minimal (figure 9.1). As issue voting has increased, we have also become aware of the ability of issues to remold basic party attachments. Recent studies show that the causal influence of issues in changing partisanship is substantial.

7. The position of the Greens on the far left is additional evidence that the meaning of Left and Right in West Germany is changing to include New Politics issues as well as the Old Politics cleavages of class and religion.

8. The relationship is described in terms of a Kramer's V correlation statistic. A value of .00 means that issue opinions are unrelated to party preference. A Kramer's V or .20 is normally interpreted as a moderately strong relationship, and .30 is considered a strong relationship.

10. Political Representation

Contemporary mass democracies owe their existence to a relatively modern invention: representative government. From the ancient Greeks up through the time of Rousseau, democracy was equated with the direct participation of the citizenry in the affairs of government. Political theorists believed that democracies must limit the definition of citizenship or the size of the polity so that the entire public could assemble in a single body and decide political issues. The Greek city-state, the self-governing Swiss canton, and the New England town meeting exemplified the democratic system.

The invention of representative government freed democracies from these constraints. Instead of directly participating in political decision making, groups of citizens selected legislators to represent them in government deliberations. The functioning of the democratic process depended on the relationship between the representative and the represented.

The case for representative government is largely one of necessity. Democracy requires citizen control over the political process, but in a large nation-state the town meeting model is no longer feasible.[1] Proponents of representative government also stress the limited political skills of the average citizen and the need for professional politicians. Citizen control over political elites is routinized through periodic, competitive elections to select these leaders. Elections are intended to ensure that elites remain responsive and accountable to the public. By accepting this electoral process, the public gives its consent to be governed by the elites selected.

Many early democratic theorists were critical of the concept of representative government and felt that it undermined the very tenets of democracy. Representative government transferred political power from the people to a small group of designated elites. Voters had political power only on the day that their ballots were cast and then waited in political servitude until the next election—four or five years hence. Under representative government the citizens may control, but elites rule. Jean Jacques Rousseau warned in the *Social Contract* that "the instant a people allows itself to be represented it loses its freedom."

Recent proponents of direct democracy are equally critical of representative government. The West German Green party, for example, criticizes the structure of representative government while calling for increased citizen influence through referendums, citizen action groups, and other forms of "basic" democracy. Populist groups in the United States display a similar skepticism of electoral politics in favor of direct action. Benjamin Barber has articulated these concerns:

> The representative government principle steals from individuals the ultimate responsibility for their values, beliefs, and actions. . . . Representation is incompatible with freedom because it delegates and thus alienates political will at the cost of genuine self-government and autonomy. (1984, p. 145)

The democratic principle of popular control of the government is replaced by a commitment to routinized electoral procedures; democracy is defined by its means, not its ends. It is claimed that other opportunities for increasing popular control are not developed because elections provide the accepted standard of citizen influence. These critics are not intrinsically opposed to representative government, but they oppose a political system that stops at representation and limits or excludes other (and perhaps more influential) methods of citizen influence.

The linkage between the public and political decision makers is one of the essential questions for the study of democratic political systems. The commitment to popular rule is what sets democracies apart from other political systems. While one cannot resolve the debate on the merits of representative government, this chapter determines how well the representation process functions in Western democracies today.

Collective Correspondence

In the broadest sense of the term, the representativeness of elite attitudes is measured by their similarity to the overall attitudes of the public. Robert Weissberg (1978) refers to this comparison as *collective correspondence*. When the distribution of public preferences is matched by the distribution of elite views, the citizenry as a collective is well represented by elites as a collective.

The complexity of the representation process obviously goes beyond a definition based simply on citizen-elite agreement. Some political leaders may stress their role in educating the public instead of merely reflecting current public preferences. In other instances, the opinions of voters may be contradictory, and the policymaking role of elites may lead them to adopt more consistent, but less representative, opinions. Policy preferences also are not necessarily equivalent to policy outcomes. Other qualifiers could be added to this list. Still, it is clear that citizen-elite agreement is the normal standard for judging the representativeness of a political system. This is a meaningful test of representation because it determines whether political decision makers enter the policy process with the same policy preferences as the public. This is a basic goal of representative democracy.

Several data sources are available that enable us to compare the beliefs of top-level political leaders and the public for our set of nations (also see Reif and Cayrol, 1988; Verba and Orren, 1985; Miller and Jennings, 1987). In 1979 the European Communities conducted a survey of European voters and candidates for seats in the first directly elected European Parliament (Dalton, 1985). Because of the historic nature of this election, it attracted many well-known and influential party leaders as candidates. The Eurocandidate study thus provides a sample of elites for the various national parties.

The distribution of citizen and elite opinions in Britain, West Germany, and France are presented in table 10.1. The broadest measure of political orientations is the Left/Right self-placement scale discussed in chapter 6. The first row in the table indicates that elites in each nation are significantly more likely than the public to identify themselves as Leftists. This liberal tendency among political elites is a common finding in elite studies. Research in West Germany, France, and the Netherlands indicates that political elites consistently locate themselves to the Left of their own supporters (Hoffmann-Lange, 1984; Converse and Pierce, 1986; Van de Geer and de Mann, 1974). Political elites apparently consider themselves to be more progressive than their constituencies.

Collective correspondence on specific issues is more varied across these three nations. This sample of British elites is more liberal than the public on most issues. This elite bias is strongest for foreign aid and security issues. Abortion policy is the only area where the British public is substantially more liberal than elites. In comparison, data presented by Richard Rose (1980b, p. 273) also find that members of the British Parliament are more liberal than voters on issues such as the death penalty, coloured immigrants, and the Common Market.

The West German public tends to be slightly more liberal than political elites on the Old Politics issue conflicts of economics and abortion. Conversely, elites are significantly more liberal on foreign aid, dealing with terrorists, and the free-speech issue. This general pattern is verified by the results of another recent comparison of citizen-elite opinions in West Germany. Ursula Hoffmann-Lange (1984) finds that West Germans are more liberal than elites on economic issues such as price controls, government regulation of banks, and codetermination; elites are more liberal on foreign aid and legislation aimed at controlling political radicals.

TABLE 10.1

THE DISTRIBUTION OF OPINIONS FOR THE EUROPEAN PUBLIC AND ELITES
(IN PERCENT)

	Great Britain		West Germany		France	
	Public	Elites	Public	Elites	Public	Elites
Leftist self-placement	42	46	42	57	47	68
Old Politics						
Public ownership of industry	30	35	34	27	41	48
Goverment manages economy	44	38	45	32	56	44
Codetermination	52	54	69	60	73	52
Control multinationals	50	66	66	75	72	86
Reduce income inequality	65	64	76	88	93	93
Liberalize abortion	77	58	75	65	77	74
Foreign Aid						
Aid EC regions	45	90	47	98	71	90
Aid Third World	35	85	40	93	52	82
Security						
Strengthen defense	18	25	30	22	34	32
Action against terrorists	5	29	12	30	8	15
New Politics						
Nuclear energy	21	23	34	19	34	15
Protect environment	94	92	88	97	94	92
Free expression	72	78	76	79	74	86
Average liberal issue response	46	57	53	60	60	62

SOURCES: 1979 Eurocandidate Survey, Eurobarometer 11; both studies have been weighted to produce representative national samples.

NOTE: Table entries are the percentages expressing a liberal opinion on each item.

The closest overall match between citizen and elite opinions occurs in France. French citizens and elites generally favor liberal policies on Old Politics issues, and there are no consistent differences between political strata on these issues. The pattern on New Politics and security issues is equally mixed. Only on the foreign aid issues are elites clearly more liberal than the French public.

Comparable data describing the views of American voters and political elites (candidates for Congress) are displayed in table 10.2. While the public

TABLE 10.2

THE DISTRIBUTION OF OPINIONS FOR

THE AMERICAN PUBLIC AND ELITES

(IN PERCENT)

	Voters	Elites
A law requiring a balanced budget	84	65
Large federal income tax cut	43	58
Tax break for tuition costs	67	54
National health insurance	51	38
Government-paid abortions for poor	42	31
Arms limit agreement with the USSR	70	66
Increase defense spending	36	34
A stronger commitment to Israel	33	19

SOURCES: CBS News/New York Times Congressional Poll and Voters Survey (Fall 1978).

NOTE: Table entries are the percentages agreeing with each policy statement.

and elites often differ in their policy views, there is not a systematic bias in the direction of these differences. The public is fiscally more prudent than elites; most voters favor legislation requiring a balanced federal budget while opposing large tax cuts. When Congress followed the opposite course—tax cuts without budget limits—record federal deficits resulted. The electorate is also significantly more liberal than elites on the social issues of government-funded abortions and national health insurance. Citizen and elite views are most similar on foreign policy issues.

If collective correspondence is judged by substantive criteria—for example, a 10 percent difference or less in issue opinions—then citizen-elite agreement is fairly common.[2] Most economic, security, and New Politics issues fall within the 10 percent range for the British, West German, and French comparisons.

Only the foreign policy issues display sizable opinion differences between citizens and Europarliament candidates. The samples of West German and French elites appear most representative of their respective publics. Overall, an average of 53 percent of the West German public give liberal responses on the thirteen issue questions, compared to 60 percent of elites. The match of citizen and elite opinions is even closer in France (60 percent versus 62 percent). The voter-elite gap in the United States appears somewhat larger, but this may be caused by the slight differences in question wording between the two sets of interviews (Bishop and Frankovic, 1981). Still, the general contours of opinion are similar between groups.

Dyadic Correspondence

Collective correspondence between the issue opinions of the public and the political elites does not occur as a collective process. Some degree of popular control is necessary to ensure the responsiveness of elites. Citizen-elite agreement without popular control is representation by chance, not democracy. The normal method of popular control makes political elites electorally dependent on a specific constituency. Weissberg (1978) defines the pairing of constituency opinion and elites as *dyadic correspondence.* In simple terms, liberal constituencies presumably select liberal representatives and conservative constituencies select conservative representatives.

In studying the connection between citizens and elites, past research generally treated the individual legislator as the primary means of dyadic linkage. One explanation for this approach lies in the historical development of political theory on representation. Edmund Burke's classic "Speech to the Electors of Bristol" in 1774 defined a paradigm of representation that still influences modern political science. Traditionally, a *delegate* model stated the legislator's role in a deterministic fashion. Representative government required that delegates be sent to Parliament and that voters instruct the delegate on constituency preferences. The legislator was obliged to follow the constituency's mandate. Burke proposed a more independent *trustee* role for legislators. He argued that, once elected, the legislators should be allowed to follow their own beliefs about what they thought was best for their constituency and for the nation.

This theoretical emphasis on the individual legislator was reinforced by the development of modern empirical research on political representation. Representation research, especially from the American perspective, largely treated the legislator as the basic source of political linkage (Miller and Stokes, 1963). In part, this reflects the weakness of American parties and the open structure of the American political process. Many American legislators can, and do, act as individual entrepreneurs. These studies generally focus on whether individual legislators follow the delegate or trustee model in representing their constituencies (Kuklinski, 1978; Wahlke et al., 1962).

Warren Miller and Donald Stokes (1963) conducted the seminal study of political representation in America. The design of the study was fairly complex because they were interested in the relationship between public opinion and elite actions. A small public opinion sample was interviewed in each of 116 congressional districts across the nation following the 1958 congressional elections. Members of the House of Representatives from these same districts also were interviewed. Finally, the voting records of the members of Congress were assembled for the next legislative session.

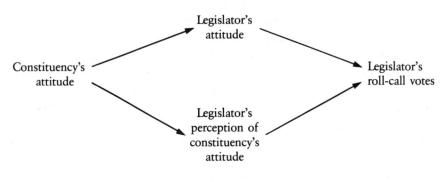

FIGURE 10.1

CONSTITUENCY INFLUENCE IN CONGRESS

This information was used to build a model of the representation process (figure 10.1). Broadly speaking, these researchers envisioned two pathways by which a constituency could influence the voting behavior of its representative (Miller and Stokes, 1963). One pathway defined the trustee model of representation; the constituency could select a legislator who shares its views, so that in following his or her own convictions the legislator represents the constituency's will. In this case the constituency's opinion and the legislator's actions are connected through the legislator's own policy attitudes. A second pathway is based on the delegate model. A legislator follows his or her perceptions of district policy preferences (which presumably were a fairly accurate reflection of the constituency's actual preferences). In this case the legislator's perception of constituency attitudes provides the linkage between actual constituency opinion and the legislator's voting behavior.

This model was applied to three policy areas: civil rights, social welfare, and foreign policy. Miller and Stokes found that the relationship between constituency opinion and the legislator's voting record was weakest in the foreign policy area, but that constituency influence was substantial for civil rights and social welfare issues. In addition, the path of constituency influence varied between policy domains. Civil rights issues primarily functioned in terms of a delegate model; the delegate path was at least twice as important as the trustee path. When the same procedure was applied to social welfare issues, the trustee path through the legislator's own attitude was the most important means of constituency influence.

This study provided hard empirical evidence of the representation process at work. Moreover, the process seemed to work fairly well. Most liberal constituencies were represented by liberal legislators, and vice versa. Although there have been many critics of the methodology of this study, its essential conclusions are still supported by most political scientists (for critiques, see Erikson et al., 1980; Achen, 1977).

The Miller-Stokes model was extended to representation studies in nearly a dozen other Western democracies (Barnes, 1977; Farah, 1980; Thomassen, 1976; Converse and Pierce, 1986). These other studies often found little evidence of policy agreement between constituencies and their legislators. Samuel Barnes compared the issue opinions of Italian deputies to district views from a parallel public opinion study. He found virtually no correspondence between citizen and elite views (average correlation across eight issues was .04). Barbara Farah documented a similar lack of correspondence between district opinions and the policy views of district-elected deputies in the West German Bundestag. The average correlation between district and deputy opinions was actually negative (average correlation across six issues was –.03). Preliminary results from the French representation study also suggested a weak linkage between district and legislator opinions.

The representation process is apparently not based on individual legislators in most non-American political systems. This is because the linkage process in these nations is based on the actions of political parties as collectives rather than individual legislators. This model of representation through parties — responsible party government — is built on several principles (Rose, 1974c). Elections should provide competition between two or more parties contending for political power. Parties must offer distinct policy options or programs so that voters are given meaningful electoral choices. Moreover, voters should recognize these policy differences among the parties. At the least, voters should be sufficiently informed to reward or punish the incumbent parties based on their performance (Stokes and Miller, 1962). National elections therefore serve as evaluations of the political parties and their activities.

Most descriptions of responsible party government also presume that members of a party's parliamentary delegation act in unison. Parties should vote as a single bloc in parliament, even though there may be internal debate before the party position is decided. Furthermore, parties should exercise control over the government and the policymaking process through party control of the national legislature. In sum, the choice of parties provides the electorate with indirect control over the actions of individual legislators and the affairs of government.

While the representation process may be based on individual legislators in the United States, political representation in Western Europe is largely structured along the lines of the party government model. In comparison to the United States, the party systems of most European democracies offer the voters greater diversity in party programs, which gives more meaning to party labels

(Harmel and Janda, 1982, p. 29). The vast majority of democracies are also parliamentary systems, where unified legislative parties play a crucial role in determining control of the executive branch. The available evidence indicates that party cohesion in European legislatures is considerably higher than in the American Congress (Harmel and Janda, 1982, p. 84). When a party votes as a united bloc, it makes little sense to discuss the voting patterns of individual legislators. Furthermore, public recognition of which party controls the government is more widespread in Western Europe than in the United States, probably as a result of the European parliamentary form of government. Giovanni Sartori maintains that "citizens in Western democracies are represented *through* and *by* parties. This is inevitable" (1968, p. 471; italics in original).

The party government model thus directs the voters' attention to parties as political representatives, rather than individual deputies. Indeed, many Europeans (including the West Germans) now vote directly for party lists. Dyadic correspondence is based more on a voter-party model than a district-legislator model. The voter half of the dyad is composed of all party supporters in a nation (even if there are geographic electoral districts); the elite half is composed of party leaders as a collective.

The importance of party linkage is a basic characteristic of democratic political systems, and we normally would expect a fairly close match between voters and party elites. Nevertheless, the last chapter discussed the general weakening of party organizations and popular attachments to parties. The erosion of party strength is most obvious for activities outside the electoral arena, such as providing political information, social services, and government employees. Although parties still remain the prime vehicle for electoral politics, even this area might display a pattern of partisan decline. Candidate images are playing a more prominent role in elections on both sides of the Atlantic; with the expanding influence of the media and reliance on candidate debates and similar activities, the personality of the candidates are a prominent part of elections. Especially in the United States, party campaign organizations are being replaced by the personal staff of the candidates. Similarly, citizen action groups and political action committees (PACs) are becoming important actors in the electoral process. In short, the functioning of the party linkage process deserves close study to see if the general weakening of parties has extended to electoral politics as well.

One other point should be stressed in comparing dyadic correspondence. While we occasionally speak in causal terms—voter opinions presumably influence party positions—it is clear that causal flow works in both directions. Voters influence parties as parties are trying to persuade voters. This is why researchers have adopted the causally neutral term *correspondence.* The essence

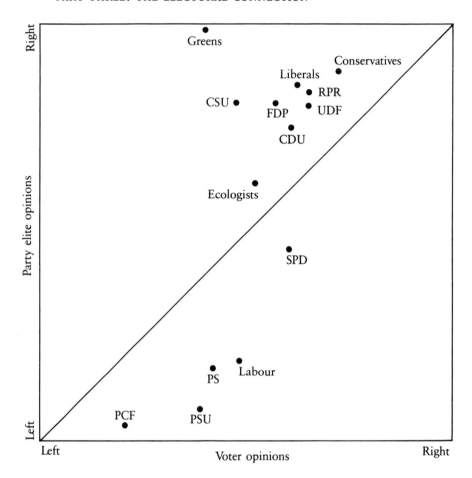

FIGURE 10.2
VOTER AND PARTY ELITE OPINIONS ON
FURTHER NATIONALIZATION OF INDUSTRY

SOURCE: 1979 Europarliament Study.

of the democratic marketplace is that like-minded voters and parties will search out each other and ally forces. Even if one cannot determine the direction of causal flow, the assessment of opinion similarity within parties is a meaningful measure of the representativeness of parties.

The party linkage model in Western Europe can be examined by comparing the opinions of voters and elites aggregated by party. This procedure yields comparisons for fourteen parties in Britain, West Germany, and France. The

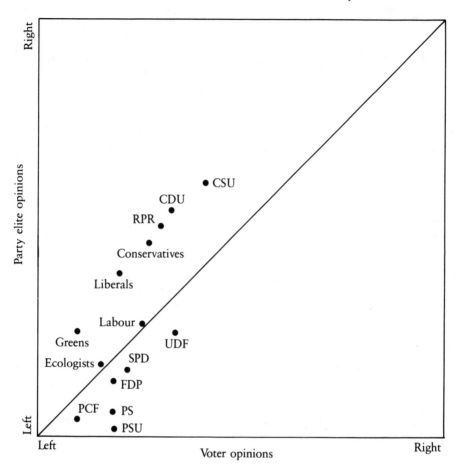

FIGURE 10.3

VOTER AND PARTY ELITE OPINIONS ON ABORTION

SOURCE: 1979 Europarliament Study.

following figures depict voter-party agreement on several issues. The horizontal axis in each figure plots the average issue position of the voters for a party; the vertical axis plots the average opinion of the party's elites. These two coordinates define a party's location in the figure. The 45-degree line represents perfect intraparty agreement: when the opinions of party elites exactly match those of their supporters.

Figures 10.2 and 10.3 display party patterns on two Old Politics issues: the economic issue of expanding government ownership of industry and the

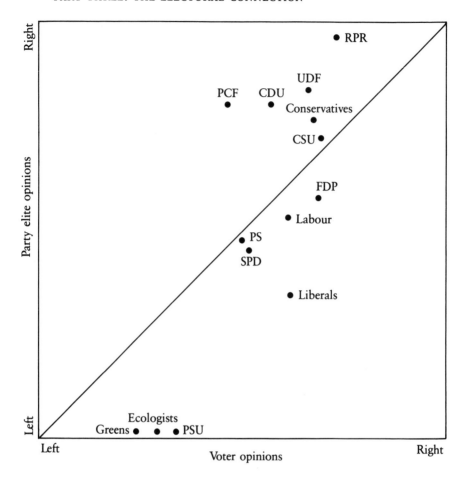

FIGURE 10.4

VOTER AND PARTY ELITE OPINIONS ON NUCLEAR ENERGY

SOURCE: 1979 Europarliament Study.

religious/moral issue of abortion. Party positions on these issues generally follow traditional Left/Right alignments. The Socialist and Communist parties
tend toward the lower-left quadrant; their voters and party leaders both hold
liberal opinions on these Old Politics issues. For example, supporters of the
French Communist party (PCF) are very liberal on the nationalization issues
(average score = 1.78) as are PCF elites (score = 1.08). Conversely, the voters
and leaders of the traditional Rightist parties generally share conservative opinions on these issues. Averaged across all parties, the opinions of party elites

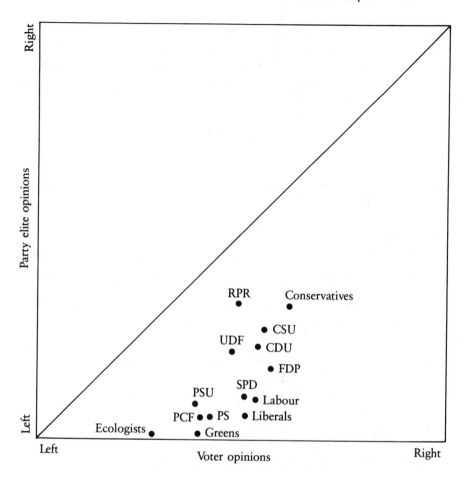

FIGURE 10.5
VOTER AND PARTY ELITE OPINIONS ON
AID TO THIRD WORLD NATIONS

SOURCE: 1979 Europarliament Study.

are less than one scale point (.85 on a five-point scale) from the voter opinions on the nationalization issue, and less than half a point (.45) on the abortion issue. The opinions of party elites on these two issues are fairly representative of their voters.

The issue of nuclear power provides an example of a salient New Politics issue. Figure 10.4 indicates a basic correspondence between party voters and party elites on this issue. A voter bloc that favors (or opposes) nuclear energy is represented by party leaders who generally share these opinions. The average difference (.74) between voter and elite opinions is fairly modest.

The significant aspect of the nuclear issue is the pattern of party alignment. The major established Left and Right parties had not taken clear positions on this issue as of 1979. The major Left parties—the West German SPD, British Labour, and the French PS—all hold centrist positions on this issue that are not much different from their conservative party rivals. In fact, the voters and party elites of the French Communist party favor nuclear power more than many conservative party groups. Opposition to nuclear power is represented by a set of new parties: the West German Greens, the French Ecologists, and French PSU. Thus, party alignments on nuclear power (and New Politics issues generally) tend to cut across the traditional Left/Right party lines defined by Old Politics issues.

The issue of aid for Third World nations presents an example of the lack of voter-party agreement (figure 10.5). Party elites are consistently more liberal than their voters. Only a single party is within one scale point of its supporters, and the average voter-party difference is substantial (1.33). In this area West European party elites display considerable independence from the policy opinions of their voters. This result is reminiscent of Miller and Stokes' (1963) finding that foreign policy exhibits the least evidence of dyadic correspondence for their sample of American legislators.

With the exception of foreign policy, party elites appear fairly responsive to the views of their voters. Yet there is also a systematic tendency for party elites to exaggerate the issue differences that exist among their supporters. The intensity and ideological commitment of political elites almost always generates greater issue differences among elites than among party supporters (McClosky, 1954; Dalton, 1985). On the nationalization issue, for example, party elites of the West German SPD are significantly to the Left of their voters, while CDU elites are to the Right of their constituency. The 45-degree line in the figures represents perfect intraparty agreement, and party elites are more polarized than their supporters on the issues of nationalization, abortion, and nuclear energy.

A pattern of accentuated elite polarization also can be seen in American voter-elite comparisons (table 10.3). Democratic and Republican voters display only minor differences in their issue opinions (average difference is 8 percent); but party elites accentuate these differences (average is 36 percent). In other words, party elites tend to overrepresent the opinions of their constituency by maintaining more extreme issue positions. This explains the greater clarity of party positions at the elite level and the greater intensity of party conflict among elites.

TABLE IO.3

THE DISTRIBUTION OF VOTER AND ELITE OPINIONS BY PARTY
(IN PERCENT)

	Democrats		Republicans	
	Elites	Voters	Voters	Elites
Balanced budget	48	82	87	85
Income tax cut	23	42	43	97
Tuition costs	36	69	64	26
National health insurance	63	63	37	9
Abortions for poor	45	46	37	16
Arms agreement with USSR	90	73	66	40
Increase defense spending	19	32	41	50
Commitment to Israel	18	35	31	21

SOURCES: CBS News/New York Times Congressional Poll and Voters Survey (Fall 1978).

NOTE: Table entries are the percentages agreeing with each policy statement; see table 10.2 for more complete question text.

Patterns of Political Representation

This chapter describes two distinct patterns of representative government among Western democracies. Political representation in the United States often depends on the relationship between individual legislators and their constituencies. Citizens in most other democracies are primarily represented through their choice of political parties at election time. Both models can provide an effective means of citizen-elite linkage, but they emphasize different aspects of representation.

The American system of representative government based on individual legislators allows for greater responsiveness to the interests of each legislative district. The political process is more open to new political interests and the representation of minority groups because electoral control at the constituency level is more easily accomplished than control of an entire party. The flexibility of the American style of representation also involves some costs. An entrepreneurial style of representation makes it more difficult for the public to monitor and control the actions of their representative between elections. This representation pattern also might encourage campaigns that focus on personalities and district service, rather than policy and ideological orientations. Indeed, studies of congressional elections suggest that personality and constituency service are important influences on voting patterns.

A party-government model yields a different pattern of political representation. The choice of parties provides the electorate with indirect institutional control over the actions of individual legislators through party discipline. When a party votes as a united bloc, political responsibility is more clearly established. If the public is satisfied (or dissatisfied) with the party's performance, the next election offers the opportunity to implement these evaluations. While the party model strengthens the policy linkage between citizens and elites, this may also produce rigidity and resistence to change. The highly cohesive European parliamentary parties place a necessary premium on party unity and disciplined voting. This hardly provides a fertile ground for experimentation and political change. Parties may be very responsive to their established clientele, but new social groups and internal party minorities may have difficulty gaining representation in the party-government framework.

This chapter has focused on how well parties perform their representation role. In some cases there is relatively close correspondence between the opinions of voters and party elites (e.g., economic, security, and New Politics issues), but in other instances the evidence of correspondence is substantially weaker (e.g., foreign policy). A large part of the correspondence that does exist must be attributed to the interactive linkage between voters and parties. Voters migrate to the party that best represents their views; parties change to reflect the opinions of their voters; or parties convince their supporters to accept party policy. The pairing of like-minded voters and parties provides the public with institutional representation in the policy process.

Just as important as the overall level of dyadic correspondence are the factors affecting voter-party agreement. Some parties consistently achieve a close match between the opinions of voters and party elites, while other parties display less correspondence. These variations in party representation determine the efficiency of the party linkage process.

A study of voter-party agreement for forty party groups across nine nations found that the clarity of party positions is an important influence on the representation process (Dalton, 1985). Characteristics that clarify party positions make it easier for voters to select a party compatible with their issue beliefs. Most policy areas display a strong and consistent tendency for centrally organized parties to be more representative of their supporters. Centralized parties may be less open to innovation and allow less internal democracy, as critics suggest, but centralized parties display greater dyadic correspondence. In addition, voter-party agreement is higher among ideological parties (of either the Left or Right). Apparently these characteristics clarify party positions and make it easier for voters to select a party consistent with their issue beliefs. A centralized party is more likely to project clear party cues, and an ideological image helps voters identify a party's general political orientation. At the system level, voter-party correspondence is greater in fractionalized party systems and nations with proportional representation. Diversity in party choices clarifies options and makes it more likely that voters can find a party that supports their mix of preferences.

Many roadblocks and pitfalls stand in the way of representation through parties. In these times of change and political turmoil the evidence of party failures is often obvious. Yet parties remain the dominant institution in the area of political representation. Citizen preferences on Old Politics issues are represented fairly well among the top stratum of political elites. When the established parties have avoided taking clear policy stances on New Politics issues, new parties have formed to represent these views (Mueller-Rommel, 1982). In general terms, therefore, parties continue to perform their role as representatives of voter interests.

Notes

1. The development of two-way cable television, teleconferencing, and other communication advances may lead us to reconsider the physical limits on direct citizen participation in large collectives. Indeed, the technology already exists for instantaneous national referendums and national town meetings (Poole, 1983).

2. In purely statistical terms, almost half of the citizen-elite issue comparisons in these tables yield statistically significant differences (.01 level). This, in part, is because of the large size of the public opinion samples.

PART FOUR

The Future of Democracy

11. Democracy in Crisis?

The changing nature of citizen politics described in this book presents new challenges for democratic political systems. The public's expanding issue interests involve governments in new aspects of the economy, society, and even family life. There is nearly unanimous agreement that governments are responsible for ensuring the economic and physical well-being of their citizens. Now governments must also protect the quality of the environment, guarantee the rights of consumers, arbitrate moral issues such as homosexuality and abortion, ensure equality for minorities and women, and deal with numerous other political concerns that were not on the political agenda a generation ago.

Not only do citizens expect more from their government, they also are more assertive in demanding a greater say in government decision making. Contemporary publics are less deferential to political elites and more likely to challenge the political establishment through citizen action groups and other direct-action techniques. Party leaders no longer can depend on inherited party attachments as a base of support, many voters now make party support conditional on a party's governmental performance. The new style of citizen politics means that individuals are more concerned with the outputs of the governing process, and more likely to act on these concerns.

Most Western democracies have had difficulties in responding to these new popular demands. First, a series of intense emotional issues strained the political consensus in these nations—issues such as desegregation and the Vietnam war in the United States, the Northern Ireland conflict in Great Britain, and *Ostpolitik* in West Germany. Cooperation and compromise were replaced by polarization and conflict; the public's image of government necessarily suffered. Second, even on less intense issues, governments lacked the financial or administrative resources to address new issues such as environmental protection, educational reform, consumer protection, and women's rights. The resources of modern states are committed to maintaining an extensive network of social welfare programs, supporting the corporate sector, and financing the defense establishment. Furthermore, the economic recessions of the last decade increased the needs for social programs and business incentives while decreasing government revenues — just as new, noneconomic issue interests proliferated. Political leaders were asked to cut taxes and increase social spending; to protect the jobs in polluting industries and improve environmental quality. In short, governments are seemingly overloaded by the new demands being placed on them.

At the same time that governments are struggling with these issue demands, political institutions are having a difficult time adjusting to calls for a more participatory democracy. Because the political process in most democracies presumes a passive and deferential public, there are insufficient opportunities for citizens to increase their participation in political decision making. Especially in Western Europe, democratic institutions were designed to limit and channel citizen participation, not to maximize popular control of elites.[1]

This situation has been described as the governability crisis of Western democracies (Crozier et al., 1975; Rose, 1980a; Lipset and Schneider, 1983). Public expectations exceed the present abilities of many democratic governments. This condition stimulates public criticism of political elites and the governing process. In the United States, trust in government began to erode during the 1960s. In 1979 President Jimmy Carter described the crisis in confidence as "a fundamental threat to American democracy." Carter believed that this situation reflected a malaise of the American spirit that struck at the very heart of society and politics.

Signs of a similar crisis of confidence have appeared across the map of Europe. Britons are less deferential and more open in their criticisms of the political process (Marsh, 1977; Kavanagh, 1980). Popular discontent in many nations has seemingly transformed the electoral advantage enjoyed by incumbent governments into a disadvantage. The Swiss worry aloud about the legitimacy of their extremely stable government. The West Germans seem one of the few exceptions to this trend, but even this is changing in recent years (Raschke, 1982; Kielmansegg, 1976). Furthermore, the unsettling impact of protest movements has been felt by governments across all of Europe.

In sum, a malaise seems to be spreading across Western Europe and North America. Many citizens are apparently losing faith in political institutions and the political process. These perceptions have fueled concerns about the future of democracy. Can democracies continue to exist while losing the confidence of their citizens? It is claimed that a former West German chancellor, Willy Brandt, stated that "Western Europe has only 20 or 30 more years of democracy left in it; after that it will slide, engineless and rudderless, under the surrounding sea of dictatorship" (quoted in Crozier et al., 1975, p. 2). Is this what the new style of citizen politics has wrought — political systems overloaded with citizen demands and becoming ungovernable, placing the future of democracy in jeopardy?

The Meanings of Political Support

Political support is a term with many possible meanings. Several political scientists have attempted to identify the essential aspects of this concept, and link these political attitudes to their consequences.

Gabriel Almond and Sidney Verba (1963) referred to attitudes toward politics and the political system as the *political culture* of a nation. Political culture encompasses everything from beliefs about the legitimacy of the system itself to beliefs about the adequacy and appropriateness of political input structures, government policies, and the role provided for the individual in the political process. The most important of these attitudes is a generalized feeling toward the political system, or *system affect*. Feelings of system affect were presumably socialized early in life (Easton and Dennis, 1969), representing a positive attitude toward the political system that was relatively independent of the actions of the current government. Almond and Verba felt that affective feelings toward the political system ensure the legitimacy of democratic governments and limit expressions of discontent with the political system.

David Easton (1965, 1975) extended several of these ideas into a theoretical framework describing the various elements of political support. Easton distinguished between support for three levels of political objects: political authorities, the regime, and the political community. Political authorities are the present incumbents of political office, or in a broader sense the pool of political elites from which government leaders are drawn. Support for political authorities focuses on specific individuals or groups of individuals. Regime support refers to public attitudes toward the offices of government rather than the present officeholders; attitudes toward the office of President of the United States rather than the present Chief Executive. This level of support also involves public attitudes toward the procedures of government and political institutions, such as the principles of pluralist democracy and support for parliamentary government. Finally, support for the political community implies a basic attachment to the nation and political system beyond the present institutions of government. A sense of being "English" (or "Scottish") exemplifies these attachments.

The distinction between levels of support is essential. Discontent with political authorities normally has limited political implications. Citizens often become dissatisfied with political officeholders and act on these feelings to select new leaders at the next election. Dissatisfaction with authorities, within a democratic system, is not usually a signal for basic political change. Negative attitudes toward political officials often exist with little loss in support for the office itself or the institutional structure encompassing this office. As the object of dissatisfaction becomes more general—the regime or political community—

the political implications increase. A decline in regime support might provoke a basic challenge to constitutional structures or the procedures of government. Weakening ties to the political community in a democratic system might foretell eventual revolution, civil war, or the loss of democracy. Therefore, "not all expressions of unfavorable orientations have the same degree of gravity for a political system. Some may be consistent with its maintenance; others may lead to fundamental change" (Easton, 1975, p. 437).

In addition to the objects of political support, Easton also discriminated between two kinds of support: diffuse and specific (also see Muller and Jukam, 1977). According to Easton, diffuse support is a state of mind—a deep-seated set of attitudes toward politics and the operation of the political system that is relatively impervious to change. For example, the sentiment "America, right or wrong" reflects diffuse support, a commitment to the political system that transcends the actual behavior of the government. In contrast, specific support is closely related to the actions and performance of the government or political elites. This kind of support is object specific in two senses. First, specific support normally applies to evaluations of political authorities; it is less relevant to support for the regime and political community. Second, specific support is based on the actual policies and general style of political authorities.

The distinction between diffuse and specific support is important in understanding the significance of public attitudes toward the political process. Democratic political systems must retain the support of their citizens if they are to remain viable. Yet, since all governments occasionally fail to meet public expectations, it is essential that short-term failures to satisfy public demands not be directly linked to evaluations of the regime or political community. In other words, a democratic political system requires a reservoir of diffuse support independent of immediate policy outputs (specific support) if it is to weather periods of public disaffection and dissatisfaction.

The significance of diffuse support is illustrated by the history of German democracy. The Weimar Republic was built on an unstable foundation. Many Germans felt that the creation of the republic at the end of World War I contributed to Germany's wartime defeat; from the outset, the regime was stigmatized as a traitor to the nation. Important sectors of the political establishment—the military, the civil service, and the judiciary—and large numbers of citizens questioned the legitimacy of the new regime and retained attachments to the political system of the former German Empire. The fledgling democratic state then faced a series of major crises: postwar economic hardships, attempted right-wing and left-wing coups, explosive inflation in the early 1920s, and French occupation of the Ruhr. The political system was never able to build up a pool of diffuse support for the republic. Consequently, the dissatisfaction created by the Great Depression in the 1930s easily eroded popular support for political authorities and the democratic regime. Communists and Nazis argued that the democratic political system was at fault, and the Weimar Republic succumbed to these attacks.[2]

Modern democracies are not the Weimar Republic and modern political problems are not as severe as the Great Depression. Yet this example makes it clear that popular support is essential for democracies to survive. Therefore, we need to assess the breadth and depth of the crisis of confidence facing these nations and discuss the implications of these findings for the future of these democracies.

Declining Confidence

A stable and well-functioning democratic polity normally presumes a supportive public. Specific political support is important for maintenance of the present government, diffuse support is essential for maintenance of the political system.

A linkage between public attitudes and the political system was seemingly confirmed by early cross-national opinion studies. Almond and Verba (1963) found that system affect in the late 1950s was most widespread in the long-established democracies of the United States and Great Britain. For example, 85 percent of Americans and 46 percent of Britons spontaneously mentioned their political system as a source of national pride. This system affect presumably was indicative of the diffuse support that had developed in these nations over their long democratic histories. Satisfaction with the policy outputs of government was also common in both nations. In contrast, system support was much more limited in the newly formed democracies of West Germany and Italy; only 7 percent of West Germans and 3 percent of Italians mentioned their political system as a source of national pride. These findings suggested that diffuse political support was underdeveloped in these political systems, raising fears that democracy was still fragile in these two formerly fascist states. The early years of the Federal Republic were closely watched by those who worried *Ist Bonn doch Weimar?* ("Is the Bonn government like Weimar?").

Another extensive cross-national study, by Hadley Cantril (1965), found a similar pattern in public opinions. Cantril showed that positive national self-images tended to be more common among the stable, well-run democracies. Although one can never be certain whether stable government produces popular support, or whether popular support produces stable government, these two phenomenona appear interrelated. Indeed, the advocates of an elitist theory of democracy (chapter 2) maintain that a benignly supportive public is a virtual prerequisite for the democratic process to function effectively.

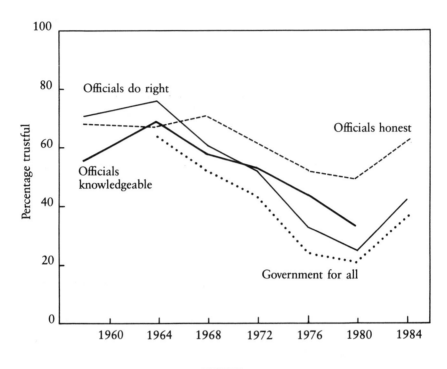

FIGURE II.I

AMERICAN TRUST IN GOVERNMENT

SOURCE: SRC/CPS American Election Studies.

The American Election Study series first began to measure political support in 1958 (figure 11.1). The early readings described a largely supportive public. Most Americans believed that one can trust the government to do what is right (71 percent), that there are not many dishonest people in government (68 percent), and that most officials know what they are doing (56 percent). These positive feelings remained relatively unchanged until the mid-1960s and then declined precipitously. Conflict over civil rights and Vietnam divided Americans and sapped support for the political system; Watergate, Koreagate, and a seemingly endless stream of political scandals pushed support even lower over the next decade. This decrease in political trust also corresponded to a period of worsening economic conditions and government inability to deal with this situation. Distrust of government reached a low point in 1980: Only 25 percent of the American public felt one could trust the government, only 21 percent believed the government is run for the benefit of all, and only 36 percent thought government officials know what they are doing (Abramson, 1983; Lipset and

Schneider, 1983). Opinions became more positive in 1984, but are still significantly below pre-1964 levels. One observer of these trends suggested that the political creed for contemporary American politics should read "In God we trust; everyone else pays cash."

This erosion of public confidence in politics is not unique to the United States. British citizens are well known for their deference to political elites and support of democratic institutions. Yet, during the 1970s, these aspects of the British political culture began to erode. The democratic political consensus weakened among signs of growing popular dissatisfaction with political parties and the other institutions of government (Kavanagh, 1980; Beer, 1982). During the 1950s and early 1960s most Britons approved of the "government's record to date"; disapproval became the majority opinion in the 1970s (Gallup, 1976a). Belief in the responsiveness of local and national government declined between the *Civic Culture* study in 1959 and the *Political Action* study in 1974 (Barnes, Kaase, et al., 1979, p. 141). By the 1979 election, a plurality (37 percent) felt the country was in poor shape and a sizable number (29 percent) believed something was seriously wrong in the country. A systematic study of British attitudes toward government described a public that was skeptical and distrustful of members of parliament, civil servants, and the political parties (Moss, 1980). In short, many political leaders and millions of citizens are asking, "What is wrong with Britain?"

Distrust between the citizen and the state is a basic aspect of the French political culture. The May Revolts dramatically symbolized the alienation that many French feel toward the overly centralized and bureaucratized political system. Throughout the past decade, most French citizens have been dissatisfied with the functioning of the political system (Eurobarometer series). Promised political reforms never materialized under conservative or socialist governments. A 1981 survey found open distrust of political parties in general (73 percent), politicians in general (65 percent), and government ministers (57 percent); only local representatives, mayors, and senators received the trust of most French citizens. More recent surveys indicate that, if anything, popular dissatisfaction with politics increased after Mitterrand came to power; *Le mal francais* continues.

West Germany is an exception to this general trend of declining public confidence in the democratic process. From an undemocratic beginning, popular support for the institutions of democratic government steadily grew during the postwar years (Baker et al., 1981; Conradt, 1980). This remaking of the political culture eventually produced nearly universal agreement that democracy is the best form of government, as well as growing commitment to democratic institutions and procedures. Despite this long-term growth in system support and democratic norms, signs of a new skepticism began to appear in the 1970s. The population became slightly less supportive of the political system and more hesitant to express their political views (Conradt, 1981). A surge of terrorist activities and spreading protest movements raised fears that the crisis in political support had reached the Federal Republic. The economic failures of the government drew on the popular support that previous administrations had accumulated. In 1981 and 1982, criticism of the government and political process became commonplace, contributing to the fall of the SPD-led government. The new CDU-led government has also been buffeted by policy problems and political scandals that have perpetuated the public's political skepticism (Dalton and Baker, 1985).

TABLE 11.1

CROSS-NATIONAL TRUST IN GOVERNMENT (IN PERCENT)

	United States	Great Britain	West Germany	France
Satisfied with working of democracy	32	13	35	12
Government benefits all	31	45	69	—
Trust government to do right	34	40	52	—
Officials care what people think	43	31	34	36
Parties interested in public opinion	37	29	39	—
Officials don't lose contact	30	26	22	—
Average	35	31	42	—

SOURCES: Satisfaction with democracy data from Gallup International Research Institute, 1977; other items from the Political Action Study and 1978 French Election Study.

Once-supportive publics are becoming generally critical of government and political authorities. Table 11.1 indicates how widespread these sentiments are now. Less than a third of the public in any of the four nations is very satisfied with the way democracy works. The other questions in the table document a popular skepticism and lack of trust in politics. Support levels are exceptionally low in Great Britain, while the remaking of the West German political culture produces higher, though still limited, levels of political trust.

The declining political trust of Western publics is a generally accepted fact, but political scientists disagree on whether these trends reflect a lack of support for political authorities or lack of support for the regime. The debate was first taken up by Arthur Miller (1974a, 1974b) and Jack Citrin (1974). Miller argued that popular dissatisfaction with the repeated policy failures and political scandals of government officials was being generalized into broader criticism of the political process as a whole. Miller spelled out the potentially grave consequences the loss of regime support could have for the American political process.

Citrin felt that Miller overstated the problem. The above trends were interpreted as a sign of popular disenchantment with the incumbents of government or political authorities in general, not distrust in the system of American government. Citrin claimed (1974, p. 987) that "political systems, like baseball teams, have slumps and winning seasons. Having recently endured a succession of losing seasons, Americans boo the home team when it takes the field." These boos do not indicate opposition to the process of democratic government, only for the players in the lineup and their recent performance on the field. Hence, a few new stars or a few winning streaks, and the decline in pub-

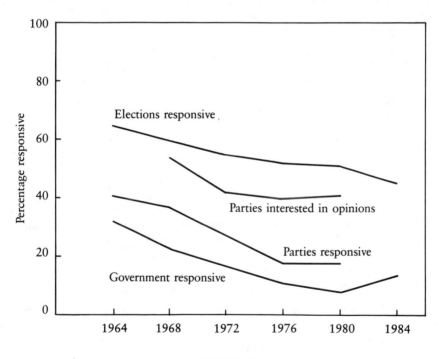

FIGURE 11.2

RESPONSIVENESS OF AMERICAN POLITICAL INSTITUTIONS

SOURCE: SRC/CPS American Election Studies.

TABLE II.2
CONFIDENCE IN AMERICAN INSTITUTIONS
(IN PERCENT)

	1966	1971	1973	1974	1976	1978	1980	1982	1984	1986	1987
Medicine	72	61	54	60	54	46	52	45	52	47	52
Higher education	61	37	37	49	38	28	30	33	29	28	35
Military	62	27	32	40	39	30	28	31	37	32	35
Organized religion	41	27	35	44	31	31	35	32	32	26	30
Supreme Court	50	23	32	33	35	28	25	30	35	31	37
Major corporations	55	27	29	31	22	22	27	23	32	25	31
Press	29	18	23	26	28	20	22	18	17	19	19
Executive branch	41	23	29	14	14	13	12	19	19	21	19
Congress	42	19	24	17	14	13	9	13	13	17	16
Organized labor	22	14	16	18	12	11	15	12	9	8	11
Average	48	28	31	33	29	24	26	26	28	25	28

SOURCES: 1966, 1971 from Harris Poll; 1973-87 NORC General Social Surveys.

NOTE: Table entries are the percentages expressing a great deal of confidence in the people running each institution.

lic confidence might be reversed; the trends of distrust thus have limited significance for Citrin.

Initially it was difficult to judge between these two contrasting explanations of declining political support, but a gradual accumulation of evidence suggests that the decline in public confidence is broader than just dissatisfaction with present political elites. The crisis of political confidence appears to be a general trait of Western democracies, not limited to the United States. In addition, questions that focus on political institutions and the political process also display decreasing political support. For example, several questions from the American election studies examine the perceived responsiveness of government and political institutions (figure 11.2 on page 233). These questions, too, track a trend of decreasing confidence in parties, elections, and the government in general.

Other survey evidence indicates that dissatisfaction has spread beyond the political system. A series of questions tap public confidence in major social, economic, and political organizations (table 11.2 on page 234). Confidence in the people running virtually all institutions has tumbled downward over the last two decades. For instance, in 1966 many Americans expressed a great deal of confidence in the executive branch (41 percent) and congress (42 percent); these positive evaluations dropped substantially over the next two decades. Confidence in business, labor, higher education, organized religion, the military, and the medical profession underwent a similar decline.

A 1981 cross-national survey provides the opportunity to compare confidence in institutions across our four nations (table 11.3).[3] A different question

TABLE 11.3

CONFIDENCE IN INSTITUTIONS (IN PERCENT)

Institution	United States	Great Britain	West Germany	France
Police	76	86	71	64
Armed forces	81	81	54	53
Legal system	51	66	67	55
Church	75	48	48	54
Education system	65	60	43	55
Legislature	53	40	53	48
Civil service	55	48	35	50
Major companies	50	48	34	42
Press	49	29	33	31
Labor unions	33	26	36	36
Average	59	53	47	49

SOURCES: 1981 European Values Survey; 1981 CARA Values Survey.

wording was used and a different set of institutions was examined, and so the results are not directly comparable to the findings in table 11.2. Still, the results present a familiar pattern. Barely a majority in each nation express confidence in the legal system, civil service, or national legislature. Europeans are noticeably more critical than Americans in their judgments of the church, major corporations, labor unions, and the press. Despite the American trends in table 11.2, European confidence in these institutions averages even lower than that in the United States. A sense of malaise touches many sectors of Western society.

Some hope for the future might be drawn from the improvement in American trust in government in the mid-1980s. Some recovery was perhaps inevitable with the passage of time. The 1970s were exceptionally turbulent years for most Western democracies, especially for the United States. A decade of social protest, a divisive and costly war, economic recession, and unprecedented corruption by government officials strained the fiber of American politics far beyond its regular bounds. As politics returns to more "normal" times and the memory of these earlier events fades, trust in government should improve (or at least stabilize). But as the Reagan administration worked to restore national pride, the Iran-Contra scandal rekindled public doubts about their government. The diversion of government funds to Swiss bank accounts, shredding parties in the White House basement, and efforts to deceive Congress and the American public revived the specter of Watergate. The majority of Americans doubted Reagan's accounts of his involvement. It is too soon to tell whether this latest scandal will reverse the gains in political confidence of the early 1980s, but even these gains were somewhat tenuous. The increase in support was greatest for the measures most closely tied to incumbent evaluations (figure 11.1). Measures of political responsiveness and confidence in political institutions displayed a smaller rebound and remained within the range of disaffection that existed during the Carter malaise period. In short, many Americans remained skeptical of politics even after a concerted government effort to revive the American spirit, but this certainly is not an inevitable occurrence.

System Support

Many of the survey questions analyzed so far have measured support for the incumbents of government, or could be interpreted in these terms. Trust in "politicians" or the "government in Washington" (or Westminster) focuses attitudes on the government or elites in general. Even questions assessing confidence in social and political institutions might be interpreted as evaluations of the present leadership of these institutions. Therefore, we sought out questions that

TABLE II.4

FEELINGS OF NATIONAL PRIDE

(IN PERCENT)

	United States	Great Britain	West Germany	France
Very proud	87	58	20	42
Quite proud	10	30	42	39
Not very proud	2	9	21	13
Not at all proud	—ᵃ	2	11	2
No opinion	1	1	6	4
Total	100	100	100	100
(N)	(1581)	(1001)	(987)	(965)

SOURCE: New York Times/CBS News Poll (October-November, 1985).

a. Less than 1 percent.

more clearly tap basic feelings of system support in order to determine whether the malaise reaches to the political system and society.

One aspect of system support involves the "system affect" described by Almond and Verba (1963). A strong emotional attachment to the nation presumably provides a reservoir of diffuse support that can maintain a political system through temporary periods of political stress. Feelings of national pride are displayed in table II.4. A clear majority of the public in each nation are proud of their country. Where comparisons are available to earlier timepoints (data not shown), there is little systematic evidence of decreasing system affect.

An intriguing cross-national pattern also emerges from table II.4. National pride is by far the highest in the United States; 87 percent of the public was proud to be an American in 1985. The chants of *USA! USA! USA!* are not limited to Olympic competition; they signify a persisting feeling among Americans. Europeans express their national pride in more moderate tones. West Germans, especially, are hesitant in their statements of national pride. A sense of national identity and a feeling of political community have become integrated into the West German political culture. Nevertheless, the trauma of the Third Reich burned a deep scar in the West German psyche. Especially among the young, there is a strong feeling that the nationalist excesses of the past should never be repeated. The Federal Republic therefore has avoided many of the emotional national symbols that are common in other industrial nations. There are few political holidays or memorials, the national anthem is seldom played, and even the anniversary of the founding of the Federal Republic attracts little public attention. Although most citizens are proud to be German, they avoid the unquestioning emotional attachment to state and nation.[4]

TABLE 11.5

SUPPORT FOR SOCIAL CHANGE (IN PERCENT)

	United States	Great Britain		West Germany		France	
	1981	1976	1983	1970	1983	1970	1983
Change society by revolutionary action	5	7	4	2	3	5	7
Improve society through reforms	66	60	59	70	48	78	64
Defend society against subversives	20	25	30	20	40	12	23
No opinion	9	8	7	8	9	5	6
Total	100	100	100	100	100	100	100
(N)	(2325)	(1351)	(2625)	(2021)	(2107)	(2046)	(2011)

SOURCES: European Community surveys; 1981 CARA Values Survey.

Another element of system support involves attitudes toward society and the political system. A standard question in several recent surveys measures public support for radical social change through revolutionary action; most Europeans favor a program of gradual social reform. Table 11.5 actually documents a trend away from radical social change in all three European nations and a growing preference for the status quo. A comparable question from the United States finds similarly high levels of system support.

The Future of Democratic Politics

Western publics have grown more critical of government and less positive toward political elites. The analyses of this chapter help to determine the present boundaries of these sentiments. The decline in political trust is most dramatic for evaluations of government incumbents and political elites in general. The deference to authority that once was common in many Western democracies has partially been replaced by public skepticism of elites.

Closer scrutiny of government actions by the public and media uncovers political scandals and policy failures that further erode political trust. Watergate began a string of exposes on abuse of power that has continued virtually without pause for the next decade. The Iran-Contra scandal then revived public distrust about policy makers in the White House. Giscard d'Estaing was voted out of office, in part, for assuming the trappings of an imperial French presidency. Under his successor, François Mitterrand, the French government sabotaged a Greenpeace ship in New Zealand, killing one crew member. Leaders of the three established West German political parties were recently implicated for accepting illegal party contributions while granting special legislative favors for their benefactors. The public's distrust of politicians has substantial supporting evidence.

Feelings of mistrust have gradually broadened to include evaluations of the political regime and other institutions in society. The lack of confidence in politics and political institutions is widespread. As yet, public skepticism has not significantly affected support for the political system and national community; but a continuing crisis of confidence can undermine even basic system support.

The consequences of declining political trust have become steadily more visible. A more skeptical public is more likely to question government policies, and this probably has contributed to the trend toward increased issue voting and growing electoral volatility. Dissatisfaction and political distrust are also related to the use of protest and other forms of unconventional political action (chapter 4; Barnes, Kaase, et al., 1979). These changes have often strained the democratic process, as demonstrators challenge established political elites and present government structures. Political systems are very robust and can withstand a great deal of pressure before their viability is threatened by popular dissatisfaction. Nevertheless, if the crisis of confidence erodes basic system support to a significant degree, pressure for more fundamental social change may not be containable within the democratic consensus.

The present crisis in confidence is partially the result of the policy failures of governments (especially in economic performance) and the corruption of elites displayed in episodes like Watergate, the Greenpeace bombing, and the Flick affair in West Germany. In addition, many analysts see deeper roots of this crisis in the imbalance between expanding popular demands and the relatively fixed capacities of governments to address citizen needs. The prime source of the demand-output imbalance is often traced to a set of structural changes in advanced industrial societies (Berger, 1979; Crozier et al., 1975; Huntington, 1981). Higher levels of social mobility and interaction weaken the influence of social networks that previously guided and channeled the behavior of individual citizens. Economic growth raises expectations among some sectors of the population while generating new bases of political conflict among other sectors. Institutions that traditionally moderated the pace of social change — such as the church and universities — are losing influence or becoming advocates for change. The growth of the mass media provides a new forum for critics of government and strips away the cloak of anonymity that once shielded government actions from popular scrutiny. These forces combine to create the new style of citizen politics described in this book, confronting governments with a more attentive, issue-oriented, active, and demanding public. A catchphrase of the 1970s maintained that governments were "overloaded" by the new demands of citizen action groups and issue-based politics. When governments failed to meet these demands—for a wide variety of reasons—a more assertive public became critical of the government itself.

What, then, can be done to bring the political process in Western democracies back into balance? At least a temporary improvement in political trust may occur as these nations weather the crises of the last decade. Vietnam is now long past, Western economies are gradually recovering from the recession created by OPEC price increases, and some attention is being devoted to the new issues of advanced industrial societies. The public relations efforts of governments to project a more positive image can mediate the problem. Yet it often seems that government's potential for scandalous behavior is unlimited. In addition, if the long-term structural conditions of these societies remain unchanged, a basic cause of the demand-output imbalance will continue.

Some conservative social critics have used the elitist theory of democracy (chapter 2) to offer a solution to this crisis. In a crude exaggeration of the theory, this approach maintains that if a supportive and quiescent public ensures a smoothly functioning political system, then we must redevelop these traits in contemporary publics. The centrifugal tendencies of democratic politics (and the demands of the public) must be controlled, and political authority must be reestablished. Samuel Huntington has assumed the ermine robes as spokesperson for this position:

> The problem of governance in the United States today stems from an "excess of democracy" . . . the effective operation of a democratic political system usually requires some measure of apathy and non-involvement on the part of some individuals and groups. The vulnerability of democratic government in the United States comes . . . from the internal dynamics of democracy itself in a highly educated, mobilized, and participatory society. (1975, pp. 37-38)

If more education, increased social mobility, the expansion of the mass media, and similar factors cause the excess of democracy, is not the solution obvious?

The elitist theorists contend that the crisis of democracy arises because too many people want to apply the creed of democracy and egalitarian values to themselves, whereas such values were intended only for a small core of political activists. These analysts contend that democracy is overloaded because minorities are no longer apathetic, women are demanding equality, students are no longer docile, and the working class is no longer deferential. If these groups would only leave politics to the politicians, and their expert advisers, "democracy" would again be secure.[5]

These words of caution sound suspiciously familiar. They echo a refrain that has accompanied the development of democracy throughout history. During the American Revolution there were numerous critics who argued that democratization should not proceed too quickly. Many members of the colonial establishment felt that Sam Adams's ideas were too radical and the Continental Congress was composed of extremists. Even after independence, they maintained that democracy was too extreme a departure from the past; instead, George Washington should begin a new American monarchy. These same arguments were used in reaction to "radical" nineteenth-century proposals in Europe to extend voting rights to all (male) citizens. Critics claimed that women were still not ready to vote in the early twentieth century (or the mid-twentieth century if they were French), and it was argued that American blacks were still unprepared in the 1960s. The respected British political theorist Walter Bagehot favored retention of the British House of Lords for fear of popular sovereignty. Does this history of cautious advice really reflect a concern for democracy?

The cure offered by the elitist theorists is worse than the problem it addresses, democracy's very goals are ignored in its defense. The critics of citizen politics forget that democracy means popular control of elites, not elite control over the populace. A leading West German sociologist, Ralf Dahrendorf, offered another view of our present situation:

> I do think that for democracies to cope with the new types of problems with which they are faced, they have to avoid a number of mistakes. They must avoid the belief that the very progress which they made possible for a large number of citizens must now be undone because it feels uncomfortable for some. They have to avoid the belief that a little more unemployment, a little less education, a little more deliberate discipline, and a little less freedom of expression would make the world a better place to live, in which it is possible to govern more effectively . . . what we have to do above all is to maintain that flexibility of democratic institutions which is in some ways their greatest virtue: the ability of democratic institutions to implement and effect change without revolution—the ability to react to new problems in new ways—the ability to develop institutions rather than change them all the time—the ability to keep the lines of communication open between leaders and led—and the ability to make individuals count above all. (1975, p. 194)

Democracies are indeed being challenged, but the crisis of confidence is not primarily a crisis of the public spirit, it is a crisis of the political process.

Part of the problem is that democratic political institutions are not effectively addressing the growing needs of modern societies. Government's demand a large share of the national wealth and possess tremendous potential. And yet, this potential is not always evident when important decisions must be made (see, for example, Feldman and Milch, 1982). European inaction over a damaging Common Agricultural Program (CAP) or American dismissal of destructive federal budget deficits reflects a style of government behavior that has become too familiar. Many people feel that governments are too concerned with preservation of the status quo and too little interested in present and future social needs. British opinion trends, for example, show a steady decrease in the belief that politicians are concerned with the national interest (Finer, 1980). The crisis of government is, first of all, a problem of raising the performance of government institutions to match their potential. If governments could (or would) take decisive action to meet economic problems, protect the environment, and address other issues of long-standing public concern, popular satisfaction with government would increase.

Another aspect of the problem is that democratic governments have not evolved to accommodate the expanding political interests of contemporary publics. The fundamental structure of contemporary democratic institutions was developed in the nineteenth century; society has changed a good deal since then.

The potential for citizen participation is now limited by the traditional definitions of democratic politics, especially in Western Europe. The opportunities for electoral input are scandalously low for most Europeans. An opportunity to cast only five or ten votes during a multiyear electoral cycle is not a record of citizen input that should still be admired. A large number of Europeans favor introduction of popular referendums and citizen initiatives, but established political elites resist this further democratization of society. Citizen groups could be granted greater representation in policymaking and administration (Kweit and Kweit, 1981; Foster, 1980). Another area of potential change is to decentralize the scale of government (Sharpe, 1979; Crozier, 1982, chap. 5). Measures of system support generally find that citizens are more positive toward local governments, which are more accessible and more responsive to local concerns. Benjamin Barber (1984) discusses these and other reforms under the concept of *Strong Democracy,* designed to maximize popular decision making rather than limit and channel citizen input (also see Margolis, 1979).

In the United States the number of voting opportunities is already quite large, but there are other ways of granting individuals greater say in the decisions affecting their lives. Democracy can be extended to the economic sector (Dahl, 1984). The West Germans have pioneered a system of co-determination that guarantees employees formal representation on the board of directors in large firms; the French have discussed a similar system of *autogestion.* Europeans also have made more progress than Americans in developing work councils that give employees more control over their working conditions. The critics may attack these forms of economic democracy as a threat to business efficiency; but these systems actually contributed to the West German "economic miracle" by involving workers in the operation of the system.

An emphasis on increased citizen action is not simply participation for participation's sake. One goal of expanding citizen participation is to open up political systems that have become sclerosed by corporatist policymaking and bureaucratized administration. The triumvirate of business-labor-government in many Western democracies often restricts the political interests of other groups. A political system that distorts access to the political process is necessarily inefficient in meeting all of society's needs. Expanding citizen access to politics is one method to ensure that governments become more responsive to a broader spectrum of political demands. In other words, this is not increasing the amount of political demands—the needs of the environment, women, consumers, and other groups exist—rather it is ensuring that these demands receive fair attention from the government and thereby improve the government's ability to address all societal needs.

Another goal of increased political involvement is to educate citizens in the democratic process. James Wright (1976, p. 260) noted a basic irony in the criticisms of citizen participation. The critics believe that governments can generate more support by convincing citizens of a lie (a sense of political efficacy that is fictitious) than by encouraging citizens to participate and learn of the necessary limits to their influence. The "big lie" may work for awhile, but as soon as someone points out the gap between myth and reality the political credibility of the system falters. Call it cooptation, pragmatism, or Jeffersonian idealism, involving citizens in the democratic process is one method to increase their identification with the process.

A final goal of increasing citizen input is to improve the quality of government decisionmaking. Citizen participation is not a panacea for all of society's modern ills. Even educated, informed, and politically involved citizens will still make errors in judgment. But as Benjamin Barber notes:

> Democracy does not place endless faith in the capacity of individuals to govern themselves, but it affirms with Machiavelli that the multitude will on the whole be as wise or wiser than princes, and with Theodore Roosevelt that "the majority of plain people will day in and day out make fewer mistakes in governing themselves than another smaller body of men will make in trying to govern them." (1984, p. 151)

There may, in fact, be some growing pains as the political process adjusts to increasing citizen participation, especially in the more tightly structured European political systems.[6] Ben Wattenberg's (1985) review of the development of participatory democracy in the United States concludes on an encouraging tone. Participatory democracy can generate political excesses, but it also contains within it an equilibrium mechanism to encourage political balance. In America this process has generally succeeded in retaining the benefits of new ideas while avoiding the dire predictions about the excesses of democracy. We should also keep in mind that democratic politics is not designed to maximize government efficiency and increase the autonomy of political elites. Just the opposite. Efficiency is partially sacrificed to ensure a more important goal: popular control of elites. Expanding participation is not a problem but an opportunity for the Western democracies to come closer to matching their democratic ideals.

In sum, the crisis of democracy is really a challenge. Democracies need to adapt to present-day politics and the new style of citizen politics. Thus Willy Brandt's concern about the future of democracies led him to believe that we must "risk more democracy." Change may be threatening to some, and it does present a risk—but change is necessary. The challenge to democracies is whether they can continue to evolve, to guarantee political rights, and to increase the ability of citizens to control their lives. Or, for the hope of greater government security, will Western nations turn their backs on this challenge?

Notes

1. Tocqueville made an interesting observation about American and European democracy that still has applicability today. He noted that European democracy was based on the premise that political institutions are a control mechanism, to limit the influence of traditional elites with counterbalancing popular pressure. Democracy in the United States was based on popular sovereignty, and was viewed as a method to allow citizens to control their own affairs.

2. The argument is also made that diffuse regime support existed in most other Western democracies. Consequently, dissatisfaction focused on the performance of political elites in these systems. These feelings were channeled within the political process, and the basic structure of democratic government went relatively unquestioned in the United States, Britain, and France.

3. These data are based on the Gallup question wording that measures confidence in the institutions per se. For a comparison of the different measures of confidence in institutions see Lipset and Schneider (1983, chap. 3).

4. Heavy stress has been placed on Almond and Verba's (1963) finding that few Germans took pride in their political system (7 percent), while many more (33 percent) were proud of their economic system. By 1978, almost a third of the West German public was openly proud of the political system and its democratic institutions, and another large group was proud of the policy accomplishments of the political system besides economics (Conradt, 1980). Among younger Germans, the political system is the major source of national pride.

5. Huntington's advice on limiting political demands overlooks the possibility of constraining the input of Harvard professors, corporate executives, and the upper class. His focus solely on the participation of average citizens suggests that he has confused the definitions of plutocracy and democracy.

6. One major problem is the possibility of a growing participation gap between sophisticated and unsophisticated citizens (see chapter 3).

Appendix
Major Data Sources

The establishment of scientific surveys of voters at election time began in the United States with local surveys during the 1940 election. In 1948 researchers at the University of Michigan conducted one of the first national election surveys based on scientific sampling methods. The four scholars who directed the early surveys—Angus Campbell, Philip Converse, Warren Miller, and Donald Stokes—wrote the landmark study of American public opinion, *The American Voter*. Since then, the Center for Political Studies (formerly part of the Survey Research Center) has continued this election study series at each biennial national election. The University of Michigan series has become a national resource in the social sciences and is used by researchers in hundreds of universities worldwide.

A comparable series of British election studies was begun by David Butler and Donald Stokes with the 1964 election. These scholars continued the series through the 1966 and 1970 elections, and then a team of researchers at the University of Essex, led by Ivor Crewe, continued the series in 1974 and 1979. In 1983 the British election study was conducted by Anthony Heath, Roger Jowell, and John Curtice of the SCPR in London.

Academic studies of West German elections trace their roots back to the 1961 study conducted by Gerhard Baumert, Erwin Scheuch, and Rudolf Wildenmann from the University of Cologne. The Cologne researchers and their students have continued this series to the present through the work of Max Kaase, Hans Klingemann, Franz Pappi, and the Forschungsgruppe Wahlen (Manfred Berger, Wolfgang Gibowski, and Dieter Roth) in Mannheim.

France presents the only case where a project of continuous monitoring and public dissemination of data on citizen electoral behavior has not developed. A number of individual scholars have conducted surveys of specific French elections: Roland Cayrol, Philip Converse, Georges Dupeux, Ronald Inglehart, and Roy Pierce. These independent studies provide a limited opportunity to track the evolution of French political behavior during the Fifth Republic.

Most of the data analyzed in this volume were drawn from the above data sources. A specific listing of these studies follows. The bulk of these data were acquired from the Inter-university Consortium for Political and Social Research (ICPSR) at the University of Michigan in Ann Arbor. Additional data were made available by the ESRC Archive at the University of Essex, England; the Zentralarchiv fuer empirische Sozialforschung (ZA), University of Cologne, West Germany; and the Banque de Donnees Socio-Politiques, University of Grenoble, France. Neither the archives nor the original collectors of the data bear responsibility for the analyses presented here.

American Election Studies

1948 American Election Study ($N = 622$). Angus Campbell and Robert Kahn. Available ICPSR.

1952 American Election Study ($N = 1899$). Angus Campbell, Gerald Gurin, et al. Available ICPSR.

1956 American Election Study ($N = 1762$). Angus Campbell, Philip Converse, et al. Available ICPSR.

1960 American Election Study ($N = 1181$). Angus Campbell, Philip Converse, et al. Available ICPSR.

1964 American Election Study ($N = 1571$). Political Behavior Program. Available ICPSR.

1968 American Election Study ($N = 1557$). Political Behavior Program. Available ICPSR.

1972 American Election Study ($N = 2705$). Warren Miller, Arthur Miller, et al. Available ICPSR.

1976 American Election Study ($N = 2248$). Warren Miller, Arthur Miller, et al. Available ICPSR.

1980 American Election Study ($N = 1614$). Warren Miller et al. Available ICPSR.

1984 American Election Study ($N = 2257$). Warren Miller et al. Available ICPSR.

British Election Studies

1964 British Election Study ($N = 1769$). David Butler and Donald Stokes. Available ICPSR and ESRC.

1966 British Election Study ($N = 1874$). David Butler and Donald Stokes. Available ICPSR and ESRC.

1970 British Election Study ($N = 1885$). David Butler and Donald Stokes. Available ICPSR and ESRC.

1974   British Election Study, February (N = 2462). Ivor Crewe, Bo Saarlvik, and James Alt. Available ICPSR and ESRC.

1974   British Election Study, October (N = 2365). Ivor Crewe, Bo Saarlvik, and James Alt. Available ICPSR and ESRC.

1979   British Election Study (N = 1893). Ivor Crewe, Bo Saarlik, and David Robertson. Available ICPSR and ESRC.

1983   British Election Study (N = 3955). Anthony Heath, Roger Jowell, and John Curtice. Available ICPSR and ESRC.

West German Election Studies

1953   The Social Bases of West German Politics (N = 3246). UNESCO Institute. Available ICPSR and ZA.

1961   West German Election Study (N = 1679, 1633, 1715). Gerhart Baumert, Erwin Scheuch, and Rudolf Wildenmann. Available ICPSR and ZA.

1965   West German Election Study, October (N = 1305). DIVO Institut. Available ICPSR and ZA.

1965   West German Election Study, September (N = 1411). Rudolf Wildenmann and Max Kaase. Available ICPSR and ZA.

1969   West German Election Study (N = 1158). Hans Klingemann and Franz Pappi. Available ICPSR and ZA.

1972   West German Election Study (N = 2052). Manfred Berger, Wolfgang Gibowski, Max Kaase, Dieter Roth, Uwe Schleth, and Rudolf Wildenmann. Available ICPSR and ZA.

1976   West German Election Study (N = 2076). Forschungsgruppe Wahlen. Available ICPSR and ZA.

1980   West German Election Study (N = 1620). Forschungsgruppe Wahlen. Available ICPSR and ZA.

1983   West German Election Study (N = 1622). Forschungsgruppe Wahlen. Available ICPSR and ZA.

1987   West German Election Study (N = 1545). Forschungsgruppe Wahlen. Available ZA.

French Election Studies

1958   French Election Study (N = 1650). Georges Dupeux. Available ICPSR.

1967   French Election Study (N = 2046). Philip Converse and Roy Pierce. Available ICPSR.

1968   French Election Study (N = 1905). Ronald Inglehart. Available ICPSR.

1978   French Election Study (N = 4507). Jacques Capdevielle, Elisabeth Dupoirier, Gerard Frunberg, Etienne Schweisguth, and Colette Ysmal. Available BDSP.

Crossnational Studies

1959   The Civic Culture Study (U.S.A. = 970, Great Britain = 963, West Germany = 955). Gabriel Almond and Sidney Verba. Available ICPSR.

1974   Political Action Study (U.S.A. = 1719, Great Britain = 1483, West Germany = 2307). Samuel Barnes, Max Kaase et al. Available ICPSR.

1981   European Values Survey and CARA Values Survey (U.S.A. = 1729, Great Britain = 1231, West Germany = 1305, France = 1200). Gallup Research.

1970– European Community Surveys/Eurobarometers (ongoing series of opinion surveys conducted by the Commission of the European Communities). Jacques-Rene Rabier, Ronald Inglehart, et al. Available ICPSR, ESRC, and ZA.

Bibliography

ABERBACH, JOEL, and WALKER, JACK. 1970. Political trust and racial ideology. *American Political Science Review* 64:1199-1219.

ABRAMSON, PAUL. 1974. Generational change in American electoral behavior. *American Political Science Review* 68:93-105.

_____. 1975. *Generational Change in American Politics.* Lexington, Mass.: Heath.

_____. 1979. Developing party identification. *American Journal of Political Science* 23:79-96.

_____. 1983. *Political Attitudes in America.* San Francisco: Freeman.

ABRAMSON, PAUL; ALDRICH, JOHN; and ROHDE, DAVID. 1986. *Change and Continuity in the 1984 Election.* Washington, D.C.: CQ Press.

ABRAMSON, PAUL, and INGLEHART, RONALD. 1986. Generational replacement and value change in six West European societies. *American Journal of Political Science* 30:1-25.

ACHEN, CHRISTOPHER. 1977. Measuring representation. *American Journal of Political Science* 21:805-15.

ALFORD, J., and LEEGE, J. 1984. Economic conditions and the individual vote in the Federal Republic of Germany. *Journal of Politics* 46:1168-81.

ALLARDT, ERIK. 1968. Past and emerging political cleavages. In O. Stammer, ed., *Party Organization and the Politics of the New Masses.* Berlin: Institute of Political Science at the Free University.

ALLERBECK, KLAUS, and ROSENMAYR, LEOPOLD, eds. 1971. *Aufstand Jugend?* Munich: Juventa Verlag.

ALMOND, GABRIEL, and POWELL, G. BINGHAM. 1980. *Comparative Politics.* Boston: Little, Brown.

_____, eds. 1988. *Comparative Politics Today.* 4th ed. Boston: Little, Brown.

ALMOND, GABRIEL, and VERBA, SIDNEY. 1963. *The Civic Culture.* Princeton: Princeton University Press.

_____, eds. 1980. *The Civic Culture Revisited.* Boston: Little, Brown.

ALT, JAMES. 1984. Dealignment and the dynamics of partisanship in Britain. In R. Dalton, S. Flanagan, and P. Beck, eds., *Electoral Change in Advanced Industrial Democracies.* Princeton: Princeton University Press.

ANDEWEG, RUDY. 1982. Dutch voters adrift. Ph.D. dissertation, University of Leiden.

ASHER, HERBERT. 1985. *Presidential Elections and American Politics.* 3d ed. Homewood, Ill.: Dorsey.

BAKER, KENDALL; DALTON, RUSSELL; and HILDEBRANDT, KAI. 1981. *Germany Transformed.* Cambridge, Mass.: Harvard University Press.

BAKER, KENDALL, and NORPOTH, HELMUT. Forthcoming. The media and the 1980 and

1983 elections. In K. Cerny, ed., *Germany at the Polls, 1980-1983*. Washington, D.C.: American Enterprise Institute.

BARBER, BENJAMIN. 1984. *Strong Democracy*. Berkeley: University of California Press.

BARNES, SAMUEL. 1977. *Representation in Italy*. Chicago: University of Chicago Press.

BARNES, SAMUEL; KAASE, MAX; et al. 1979. *Political Action*. Beverly Hills, Calif.: Sage.

BARNES, SAMUEL, and PIERCE, ROY. 1971. Public opinion and political preferences in France and Italy. *Midwest Journal of Political Science* 15:643-60.

BECK, PAUL. 1974. A socialization theory of party realignment. In R. Niemi et al., *The Politics of Future Citizens*. San Francisco: Jossey-Bass.

––––––. 1984. The dealignment era in America. In R. Dalton, S. Flanagan, and P. Beck, eds., *Electoral Change in Advanced Industrial Democracies*. Princeton: Princeton University Press.

BEER, SAMUEL. 1978. *The British Political System*. New York: Random House.

––––––. 1982. *Britain Against Itself*. New York: Norton.

BELL, DANIEL. 1960. *The End of Ideology*. New York: Free Press.

––––––. 1973. *The Coming of Post-Industrial Society*. New York: Basic Books.

BERELSON, BERNARD; LAZARSFELD, PAUL; and MCPHEE, WILLIAM. 1954. *Voting*. Chicago: University of Chicago Press.

BERGER, MANFRED. 1977. Stabilitaet und Intensitaet von Parteieneigung. *Politische Vierteljahresschrift* 18:501-9.

BERGER, SUZANNE. 1979. Politics and antipolitics in Western Europe in the 1970s. *Daedalus* 108:27-50.

BEYME, KLAUS VON. 1985. *Political Parties in Western Democracies*. New York: St. Martin's.

BISHOP, GEORGE, and FRANKOVIC, KATHLEEN. 1981. Ideological consensus and constraint among party leaders and followers in the 1978 election. *Micropolitics* 2: 87-111.

BISHOP, GEORGE; OLDENDICK, ROBERT; and TUCHFARBER, ALFRED. 1978. Effects of question wording and format on political attitude consistency. *Public Opinion Quarterly* 42:81-92.

BOELTKEN, FERDINAND, and JAGODZINSKI, WOLFGANG. 1984. Postmaterialism in the European Community, 1970-1980. *Comparative Political Studies* 17:453-484.

BORRE, OLE. 1984. Critical electoral change in Scandinavia. In R. Dalton, S. Flanagan, and P. Beck, eds., *Electoral Change in Advanced Industrial Democracies*. Princeton: Princeton University Press.

BORRE, OLE, and KATZ, DANIEL. 1973. Party identification and its motivational base in a multiparty system. *Scandinavian Political Studies* 8:69-111.

BRITTAN, SAMUEL. 1975. The economic consequences of democracy. *British Journal of Political Science* 5:129-59.

BROWN, BERNARD. 1974. *Protest in Paris*. Morristown, N.J.: General Learning Press.

BRZEZINSKI, ZBIGNIEW. 1970. *Between Two Ages*. New York: Viking.

BUDGE, IAN; CREWE, IVOR; and FARLIE, DAVID, eds. 1976. *Party Identification and Beyond*. New York: Wiley.

BUERKLIN, WILHELM. 1981. Die Grunen und die "Neue Politik." *Politische Vierteljahresschrift* 22:359-82.

––––––. 1985. The Greens: Ecology and the New Left. In H.G. Wallach and G. Romoser, eds., *West German Politics in the Mid-Eighties*. New York: Praeger.

BURNHAM, WALTER. 1980. The appearance and disappearance of the American voter. In R. Rose, ed., *Electoral Participation.* Beverly Hills, Calif.: Sage.

BUTLER, DAVID, and RANNEY, AUSTIN, eds. 1981. *Referendums.* Washington, D.C.: American Enterprise Institute.

BUTLER, DAVID, and STOKES, DONALD. 1969. *Political Change in Britain.* New York: St. Martin's.

———. 1974. *Political Change in Britain.* 2d ed. New York: St. Martin's.

CAMPBELL, ANGUS, et al. 1960. *The American Voter.* New York: Wiley.

———. 1966. *Elections and the Political Order.* New York: Wiley.

CAMPBELL, ANGUS; CONVERSE, PHILIP; and RODGERS, WILLARD. 1979. *The Quality of American Life.* New York: Russell Sage.

CAMPBELL, BRUCE. 1976. On the prospects of polarization in the French electorate. *Comparative Politics* 8:272-90.

CANTRIL, HADLEY. 1965. *The Patterns of Human Concerns.* New Brunswick, N.J.: Rutgers University Press.

CARMINES, EDWARD, and STIMSON, JAMES. 1988. *Race in America.* Princeton: Princeton University Press.

CAYROL, ROLAND. 1980. The mass media and the electoral campaign. In H. Penniman, ed., *The French National Assembly Elections of 1978.* Washington, D.C.: American Enterprise Institute.

CERNY, KARL, ed. 1978. *Germany at the Polls.* Washington, D.C.: American Enterprise Institute.

———, ed. Forthcoming. *Germany at the Polls, 1980-1983.* Washington, D.C.: American Enterprise Institute.

CERNY, PHILIP, ed. 1982. *Social Movements and Protest in France.* London: Pinter.

CHARLOT, MONICA. 1980. Women in politics in France. In H. Penniman, ed., *The French National Assembly Elections of 1978.* Washington, D.C.: American Enterprise Institute.

CITRIN, JACK. 1974. Comment. *American Political Science Review* 68:973-88.

CITRIN, JACK, and ELKINS, DAVID. 1975. *Political Disaffection among British University Students.* Berkeley: University of California Press.

CLUBB, JEROME; FLANIGAN, WILLIAM; and ZINGALE, NANCY. 1980. *Partisan Realignment.* Beverly Hills, Calif.: Sage.

CONRADT, DAVID. 1980. Changing German political culture. In G. Almond and S. Verba, eds., *The Civic Culture Revisited.* Boston: Little, Brown.

———. 1981. Political culture, legitimacy, and participation. *West European Politics* 4:18-34.

———. 1985. *The German Polity.* 3d ed. New York: Longman.

CONVERSE, PHILIP. 1964. The nature of belief systems in mass publics. In D. Apter, ed., *Ideology and Discontent.* New York: Free Press.

———. 1969a. Survey research and decoding patterns in ecological data. In M. Dogan and S. Rokkan, eds. *Quantitative Ecological Analysis in the Social Sciences.* Cambridge, Mass.: MIT Press.

———. 1969b. Of time and partisan stability. *Comparative Political Studies* 2:139-71.

———. 1970. Attitudes and nonattitudes. In E. Tufte, ed., *The Quantitative Analysis of Social Problems.* Reading, Mass.: Addison-Wesley.

———. 1972. Change in the American electorate. In A. Campbell and P. Converse, eds., *The Human Meaning of Social Change.* New York: Russell Sage.

———. 1975a. Public opinion and voting behavior. In F. Greenstein and N. Polsby, eds., *Handbook of Political Science.* Vol. 4. Reading, Mass.: Addison-Wesley.

———. 1975b. Some mass elite contrasts in the perception of political spaces. *Social Science Information* 14:49-83.

———. 1976. *The Dynamics of Party Support.* Beverly Hills, Calif.: Sage.

———. 1980. Comment: Rejoinder to Judd and Milburn. *American Sociological Review* 45:644-46.

CONVERSE, PHILIP, and DUPEUX, GEORGES. 1962. Politicization of the electorate in France and the United States. *Public Opinion Quarterly* 26:1-23.

CONVERSE, PHILIP, and MARKUS, GREG. 1979. Plus ça change . . . The new CPS election study panel. *American Political Science Review* 73:32-49.

CONVERSE, PHILIP, and PIERCE, ROY. 1986. *Representation in France.* Cambridge, Mass.: Harvard University Press.

CONWAY, M. MARGARET. 1985. *Political Participation in the United States.* Washington, D.C.: CQ Press.

CREWE, IVOR. 1981. Electoral participation. In D. Butler et al., eds., *Democracy at the Polls.* Washington, D.C.: American Enterprise Institute.

———. 1982. Is Britain's two-party system really about to crumble? *Electoral Studies* 1:275-313.

———. 1983. Dealignment and realignment in the British party system. Paper presented at the annual meeting of the American Political Science Association, Chicago.

CREWE, IVOR, and DENVER, D.T., eds. 1985. *Electoral Change in Western Democracies.* New York: St. Martin's.

CROZIER, MICHEL. 1982. *Strategies for Change.* Cambridge, Mass.: MIT Press.

CROZIER, MICHEL; HUNTINGTON, SAMUEL; and WATANUKI, JOJI. 1975. *The Crisis of Democracy.* New York: New York University Press.

CYERT, RICHARD, and MARCH, J.G. 1963. *A Behavioral Theory of the Firm.* Englewood Cliffs, N.J.: Prentice Hall.

DAALDER, HANS, and MAIR, PETER, eds. 1983. *Western European Party Systems.* Beverly Hills, Calif.: Sage.

DAHL, ROBERT. 1971. *Polyarchy.* New Haven: Yale University Press.

———. 1984. *A Preface to Economic Democracy.* Berkeley: University of California Press.

DAHL, ROBERT, and TUFTE, EDWARD. 1974. *Size and Democracy.* Stanford: Stanford University Press.

DAHRENDORF, RALF. 1959. *Class and Class Conflict in Industrial Society.* Stanford: Stanford University Press.

———. 1975. Excerpts from remarks on the ungovernability study. In M. Crozier et al., *The Crisis of Democracy.* New York: New York University Press.

DALTON, RUSSELL. 1977. Was there a revolution? *Comparative Political Studies* 9:459-73.

———. 1984a. Cognitive mobilization and partisan dealignment in advanced industrial democracies. *Journal of Politics* 46:264-84.

———. 1984b. The German party system between two ages. In R. Dalton et al., *Electoral Change in Advanced Industrial Democracies.* Princeton: Princeton University Press.

———. 1985. Political parties and political representation. *Comparative Political Studies* 17:267-99.

————. 1988. *Politics in West Germany*. Boston: Little, Brown.

————. Forthcoming. Religion and political behavior. In R. Inglehart et al., *People and their Polities*.

DALTON, RUSSELL, and BAKER, KENDALL. 1985. The contours of West German opinion. In H. G. Wallach and G. Romoser, eds., *West German Politics in the Mid-Eighties*. New York: Praeger.

DALTON, RUSSELL, and FLANAGAN, SCOTT. 1982. Social class, value priorities and partisan change. Manuscript, Florida State University.

DALTON, RUSSELL; FLANAGAN, SCOTT; and BECK, PAUL, eds. 1984. *Electoral Change in Advanced Industrial Democracies*. Princeton: Princeton University Press.

DAVIDSON, DOROTHY. 1982. Candidate evaluations. Ph.D. dissertation, Florida State University.

DECLERCQ, EUGENE, et al. 1976. Voting in American presidential elections. In S. Kirkpatrick, ed., *American Electoral Behavior*. Beverly Hills, Calif.: Sage.

DiPALMA, GIUSEPPE. 1970. *Apathy and Participation*. New York: Free Press.

DUNLEAVY, PATRICK, and HUSBANDS, CHRISTOPHER. 1985. *British Democracy at the Crossroads*. London: Allen and Unwin.

DYE, THOMAS, and ZEIGLER, HARMON. 1970. *The Irony of Democracy*. Belmont, Calif.: Duxbury.

EASTON, DAVID. 1965. *A Systems Analysis of Political Life*. New York: Wiley.

————. 1975. A reassessment of the concept of political support. *British Journal of Political Science* 5:435-57.

EASTON, DAVID, and DENNIS, JACK. 1969. *Children in the Political System*. New York: McGraw-Hill.

EDINGER, LEWIS. 1985. *Politics in West Germany*. New York: Columbia University Press.

EHRMANN, HENRY. 1983. *Politics in France*. 3d ed. Boston: Little, Brown.

EPSTEIN, LEON. 1980. *Political Parties in Western Democracies*. New Brunswick, N.J.: Transaction Books.

ERIKSON, ROBERT. 1978. Constituency opinion and congressional behavior. *American Journal of Political Science* 22:511-35.

ERIKSON, ROBERT; LUTTBEG, NORMAN; and TEDIN, KENT. 1980. *American Public Opinion*. New York: Wiley.

EULAU, HEINZ, and LEWIS-BECK, MICHAEL, eds. 1985. *Economic Conditions and Electoral Outcomes*. New York: Agathon Press.

FARAH, BARBARA. 1980. Political representation in West Germany. Ph.D. dissertation, University of Michigan.

FARAH, BARBARA, et al. 1979. Political dissatisfaction. In S. Barnes, M. Kaase, et al., *Political Action*. Beverly Hills, Calif.: Sage.

FELDMAN, ELLIOT, and MILCH, JEROME. 1982. *Technocracy versus Democracy*. Boston: Auburn House.

FIORINA, MORRIS. 1981. *Retrospective Voting in American National Elections*. New Haven: Yale University Press.

FINER, S.E. 1980. *The Changing British Party System*. Washington, D.C.: American Enterprise Institute.

FLANAGAN, SCOTT. 1982. Changing values in advanced industrial society. *Comparative Political Studies* 14:403-44.

FLANAGAN, SCOTT, and DALTON, RUSSELL. 1984. Parties under stress. *West European*

Studies 7:7-23.

FLORA, PETER. 1983. *State, Economy and Society in Western Europe, 1918-1975.* Frankfurt: Campus.

FLYNN, GREGORY, and RATTINGER, HANS, eds. 1985. *The Public and Atlantic Defense.* London: Croom Helm.

FOSTER, CHARLES, ed. 1980. *Comparative Public Policy and Citizen Participation.* New York: Praeger.

FRANKLIN, MARK. 1985. *The Decline of Class Voting in Britain.* Oxford: Oxford University Press.

GALLUP, GEORGE. 1976a. *International Public Opinion Polls: Britain.* New York: Random House.

———. 1976b. *International Public Opinion Polls: France.* New York: Random House.

GARNER, ROBERTA. 1977. *Social Movements in America.* 2d ed. Chicago: Rand McNally.

GEER, J. VAN DE, and MANN, H. DE. 1974. Analysis of response to issue statements by members of the Dutch parliament. Leiden: University of Leiden.

GRAHAM, HUGH, and GURR, T. ROBERT, eds. 1969. *Violence in America.* New York: Bantam.

GREENSTEIN, FRED, and TARROW, SIDNEY. 1969. The study of French political socialization. *World Politics* 22:95-137.

GURR, T. ROBERT. 1970. *Why Men Rebel.* Princeton: Princeton University Press.

HARDING, STEVE. 1986. *Contrasting Values in Western Europe.* London: Macmillan.

HARMEL, ROBERT, and JANDA, KENNETH. 1982. *Parties and their Environments.* New York: Longman.

HEATH, ANTHONY; JOWELL, ROGER; and CURTICE, JOHN. 1985. *How Britain Votes.* New York: Pergamon.

HEIDENHEIMER, ARNOLD, and FLORA, PETER. 1981. *The Development of the Welfare State.* New Brunswick, N.J.: Transaction Books.

HEIDENHEIMER, ARNOLD; HECLO, HUGH; and ADAMS, CAROLYN. 1983. *Comparative Public Policy.* 2d ed. New York: St. Martin's.

HEIDENHEIMER, ARNOLD, and KOMMERS, DONALD. 1975. *The Governments of Germany.* 4th ed. New York: Crowell.

HELM, JUTTA. 1980. Citizen action groups in West Germany. In P. Merkl, ed., *Western European Party Systems.* New York: Free Press.

HESS, ROBERT, and TORNEY, JUDITH. 1967. *The Development of Political Attitudes in Children.* Chicago: Aldine.

HILDEBRANDT, KAI, and DALTON, RUSSELL. 1978. The new politics. In M. Kaase and K. von Beyme, eds., *German Political Studies: Elections and Parties.* Vol. 3. Beverly Hills, Calif.: Sage.

HIMMELWEIT, HILDE, et al. 1981. *How Voters Decide.* London: Academic Press.

HOFFMANN, STANLEY. 1974. *Decline or Renewal?* New York: Viking.

HOFFMANN-LANGE, URSULA. 1984. The congruence of political beliefs among elites and voters as a measure of representation. Florence: European University Institute.

HOSKIN, MARILYN. 1982. Public opinion toward guestworkers. In M. Rosch and D. Frey, eds., *Guestworkers and other Immigrants in Industrial Societies.* New York: Academic Press.

HUNTINGTON, SAMUEL. 1974. Postindustrial politics: How benign will it be? *Comparative Politics* 6:147-77.

_____. 1975. The democratic distemper. *Public Interest* 41.

_____. 1981. *American Politics: The Promise of Disharmony.* Cambridge, Mass.: Harvard University Press.

INGLEHART, MARGARET. 1981. Political interest in West European women. *Comparative Political Studies* 13:299-326.

INGLEHART, RONALD. 1977. *The Silent Revolution.* Princeton: Princeton University Press.

_____. 1979a. Value priorities and socioeconomic change. In S. Barnes, M. Kaase, et al., *Political Action.* Beverly Hills, Calif.: Sage.

_____. 1979b. Political action. In S. Barnes, M. Kaase, et al., *Political Action.* Beverly Hills, Calif.: Sage.

_____. 1981. Post-materialism in an environment of insecurity. *American Political Science Review* 75:880-900.

_____. 1984a. New perspectives on value change. *Comparative Political Studies* 17: 485-532.

_____. 1984b. Changing cleavage alignments in Western democracies. In R. Dalton, S. Flanagan, and P. Beck, eds., *Electoral Change in Advanced Industrial Democracies.* Princeton: Princeton University Press.

_____. Forthcoming. Group sympathies, party ties and support for change. In R. Inglehart et al., *People and their Polities.*

INGLEHART, RONALD, and KLINGEMANN, HANS. 1976. Party identification, ideological preference and the left-right dimension among western publics. In I. Budge, I. Crewe, and D. Farlie, eds., *Party Identification and Beyond.* New York: Wiley.

JACOBS, DAN N., et al. 1983. *Comparative Politics.* Chatham, N.J.: Chatham House.

JAFFRE, JEROME. 1980. The French electorate in March 1978. In H. Penniman, ed., *The French National Assembly Elections of 1978.* Washington, D.C.: American Enterprise Institute.

JENNINGS, M. KENT, and MARKUS, GREG. 1984. Partisan orientations over the long haul. *American Political Science Review* 78:1000-1018.

JENNINGS, M. KENT, and NIEMI, RICHARD. 1973. *The Character of Political Adolescence.* Princeton: Princeton University Press.

_____. 1981. *Generations and Politics.* Princeton: Princeton University Press.

JENNINGS, M. KENT, et al. 1979. Generations and families. In S. Barnes, M. Kaase, et al. *Political Action.* Beverly Hills, Calif.: Sage.

JOWELL, ROGER, and AIREY, COLIN, eds. 1984. *British Social Attitudes.* London: Social and Community Planning Research.

JOWELL, ROGER, and WITHERSPOON, SHARON, eds. 1985. *British Social Attitudes.* Hants, England: Gower.

JUDD, CHARLES, and MILBURN, MICHAEL. 1980. The structure of attitude systems in the general public. *American Sociological Review* 45:627-43.

JUDD, CHARLES; KROSNICK, JON; and MILBURN, MICHAEL. 1981. Political involvement and attitude structure in the general public. *American Sociological Review* 46: 660-69.

KAASE, MAX. 1973. Findings from the Saarland panel, 1972-1973. Paper presented at the Conference on the Political Action Study. Bellagio, Italy.

KALTEFLEITER, WERNER, and PFALTZGRAFF, ROBERT, eds. 1985. *The Peace Movements in Europe and the United States.* London: Croom Helm.

KAVANAGH, DENNIS. 1980. Political culture in Great Britain. In G. Almond and S.

eds., *The Civic Culture Revisited*. Boston: Little, Brown.

KENISTON, KENNETH. 1968. *Young Radicals*. New York: Harcourt Brace.

KESSEL, HANS, and TISCHLER, WOLFGANG. 1982. *International Environment Survey.* Berlin: International Institute for Environment and Society.

KEY, V.O. 1966. *The Responsible Electorate*. Cambridge, Mass.: Belknap Press.

KIELMANSEGG, PETER, ed. 1976. Legitimationsprobleme politischer Systeme. *Politische Vierteljahresschrift,* special issue 7.

KIEWIET, D.R. 1983. *Macroeconomics and Micropolitics*. Chicago: University of Chicago Press.

KINDER, DONALD, and SEARS, DAVID. 1985. Political behavior. In G. Lindzey and E. Aronson, eds., *The Handbook of Social Psychology.* 3d ed. Reading, Mass.: Addison-Wesley.

KLEIN, ETHEL. 1987. The diffusion of consciousness in the United States and Western Europe. In M. Katzenstein and C. Mueller, eds., *The Women's Movements of the United States and Western Europe*. Philadelphia: Temple University Press.

KLINGEMANN, HANS. 1979. Measuring ideological conceptualizations. In S. Barnes, M. Kaase, et al. *Political Action*. Beverly Hills, Calif.: Sage.

———. 1983. Einstellungen zur SPD und CDU/CSU 1969-1980. In M. Kaase and H. Klingemann, eds., *Wahlen und Politisches System*. Opladen: Westdeutscher Verlag.

KORNHAUSER, WILLIAM. 1959. *The Politics of Mass Society*. New York: Free Press.

KUKLINSKI, JAMES. 1978. Representativeness and elections. *American Political Science Review* 72:165-77.

KWEIT, ROBERT, and KWEIT, MARY. 1981. *Implementing Citizen Participation in a Bureaucratic Society*. New York: Praeger.

LANE, ROBERT. 1962. *Political Ideology*. New York: Free Press.

———. 1965. The politics of consensus in an age of affluence. *American Political Science Review* 59:874-95.

———. 1973. Patterns of political belief. In J. Knutson, ed., *Handbook of Political Psychology*. San Francisco: Jossey-Bass.

LAZARSFELD, PAUL; BERELSON, BERNARD; and GAUDET, HAZEL. 1948. *The People's Choice*. New York: Columbia University Press.

LeDUC, LAWRENCE. 1981. The dynamic properties of party identification. *European Journal of Political Research* 9:257-68.

LEWIS-BECK, MICHAEL. 1984. France: The stalled electorate. In R. Dalton, S. Flanagan, and P. Beck, eds., *Electoral Change in Advanced Industrial Democracies*. Princeton: Princeton University Press.

LIJPHART, AREND. 1979. Religious vs. linguistic vs. class voting. *American Political Science Review* 73:442-58.

———. 1981. Political parties. In D. Butler et al., *Democracy at the Polls*. Washington, D.C.: American Enterprise Institute.

LIPPMANN, WALTER. 1922. *Public Opinion*. New York: Harcourt Brace.

LIPSET, S.M. 1963. *The First New Nation*. New York: Norton.

———. 1964. The changing class structure and contemporary European politics. *Daedalus* 93:271-303.

———. 1981a. *Political Man: The Social Bases of Politics*. Baltimore: Johns Hopkins University Press.

———. 1981b. The revolt against modernity. In P. Torsvik, ed., *Mobilization, Center-*

Periphery Structures and Nation-building. Bergen: Universitetsforlaget.

_____. 1985. Feeling better. *Public Opinion* 8:6ff.

LIPSET, S.M., and ROKKAN, STEIN. 1967. *Party Systems and Voter Alignments.* New York: Free Press.

LIPSET, S.M., and SCHNEIDER, WILLIAM. 1983. *The Confidence Gap.* New York: Free Press.

LIPSKY, MICHAEL. 1968. Protest as a political resource. *American Political Science Review* 62:1144-58.

LOWE, PHILIP, and GOYDER, JANE. 1983. *Environmental Groups in Politics.* London: Allen and Unwin.

McCLOSKY, HERBERT, et al. 1960. Issue conflict and consensus among party leaders and followers. *American Political Science Review* 54:406-27.

MacKUEN, MICHAEL. 1981. Social communication and the mass policy agenda. In M. MacKuen and S. Coombs, *More Than News.* Beverly Hills, Calif.: Sage.

MacRAE, DUNCAN. 1967. *Parliament, Parties, and Society in France, 1946-1958.* New York: St. Martin's.

MANN, THOMAS. 1978. *Unsafe at Any Margin.* Washington, D.C.: American Enterprise Institute.

MARGOLIS, MICHAEL. 1979. *Viable Democracy.* New York: St. Martin's.

MARKUS, GREG, and CONVERSE, PHILIP. 1979. A dynamic simultaneous equation model of electoral choice. *American Political Science Review* 73:1055-70.

MARSH, ALAN. 1974. Explorations in unorthodox political behavior. *European Journal of Political Research* 2:107-131.

_____. 1977. *Protest and Political Consciousness.* Beverly Hills, Calif.: Sage.

MARTIN, DAVID. 1978. *A General Theory of Secularization.* Oxford: Basil Blackwell.

MASLOW, ABRAHAM. 1954. *Motivation and Personality.* New York: Harper & Row.

MERKL, PETER, ed. 1980. *Western European Party Systems.* New York: Free Press.

MICHELAT, GUY, and SIMON, MICHEL. 1977a. *Classe, Religion, et Comportement Politique.* Paris: Fondation Nationale des Sciences Politiques.

_____. 1977b. Religion, class and politics. *Comparative Politics* 10:159-84.

MILBRATH, LESTER. 1984. *Environmentalists: Vanguard of a New Society.* Buffalo: State University of New York Press.

MILBRATH, LESTER, and GOEL, M.L. 1977. *Political Participation.* Skokie, Ill.: Rand McNally.

MILLER, ARTHUR. 1974a. Political issues and trust in government. *American Political Science Review* 68:951-72.

_____. 1974b. Rejoinder. *American Political Science Review* 68:989-1001.

MILLER, ARTHUR; GURIN, PATRICIA; and GURIN, GERALD. 1979. Electoral implications of group identification and consciousness. Paper presented at the annual meeting of the American Political Science Association, New York.

MILLER, ARTHUR, and WATTENBERG, MARTIN. 1985. Throwing the rascals out. *American Political Science Review* 79:359-72.

MILLER, MARK. 1981. *Foreign Workers in Western Europe.* New York: Praeger.

MILLER, WARREN E. 1976. The cross-national use of party identification as a stimulus to political inquiry. In I. Budge, I. Crewe, and D. Farlie, eds., *Party Identification and Beyond.* New York: Wiley.

MILLER, WARREN, and JENNINGS, M. KENT. 1987. *Party Leadership in Transition.* New

York: Russell Sage.

MILLER, WARREN E., and LEVITIN, TERESA. 1976. *Leadership and Change*. Boston: Winthrop.

MILLER, WARREN E., and STOKES, DONALD. 1963. Constituency influence in Congress. *American Political Science Review* 57:45-56.

MILLER, WILLIAM L. 1977. *Electoral Dynamics in Britain Since 1918*. London: Macmillan.

MILLER, WILLIAM L., et al. 1982. *Democratic or Violent Protest*. University of Strathclyde: Center for the Study of Public Policy.

MOSS, LOUIS. 1980. Some attitudes toward government. Paper presented at the Political Studies Association, Exeter.

MUELLER-ROMMEL, FERDINAND. 1982. Ecology parties in Western Europe. *West European Politics* 4:68-74.

MULLER, EDWARD. 1972. A test of a partial theory of potential for political violence. *American Political Science Review* 66:928-59.

―――. 1979. *Aggressive Political Participation*. Princeton: Princeton University Press.

MULLER, EDWARD, and JUKAM, THOMAS. 1977. On the meaning of political support. *American Political Science Review* 71:1561-95.

NAISBITT. JOHN. 1982. *Megatrends*. New York: Warner Books.

NELKIN, DOROTHY, and POLLACK, MICHAEL. 1981. *The Atom Besieged*. Cambridge, Mass.: MIT Press.

NIE, NORMAN, with ANDERSEN, KRISTI. 1974. Mass belief systems revisited. *Journal of Politics* 36:340-91.

NIE, NORMAN; POWELL, G. BINGHAM; and PREWITT, KENNETH. 1969. Social structure and participation: Developmental relationships, Parts 1 and 2. *American Political Science Review* 63:361-78, 808-32.

NIE, NORMAN, and RABJOHN, JOHN. 1979. Revisiting mass belief systems revisited. *American Journal of Political Science* 23:139-75.

NIE, NORMAN; VERBA, SIDNEY; and KIM, J.O. 1974. Participation and the life cycle. *Comparative Politics* 6:319-40.

NIE, NORMAN; VERBA, SIDNEY; and PETROCIK, JOHN. 1979. *The Changing American Voter*. Cambridge, Mass.: Harvard University Press.

NIEMI, RICHARD, and WESTHOLM, ANDERS. 1984. Issues, parties and attitudinal stability. *Electoral Studies* 3:65-83.

NOELLE-NEUMANN, ELISABETH. 1967. *The Germans, 1947-1966*. Allensbach: Institut fuer Demoskopie.

―――. 1981. *The Germans, 1967-1980*. Westport: Greenwood Press.

NOELLE-NEUMANN, ELISABETH, and PIEL, EDGAR, eds. 1984. *Allensbacher Jahrbuch der Demoskopie, 1978-1983*. Munich: Saur.

NORPOTH, HELMUT. 1978. Party identification in West Germany. *Comparative Political Studies* 11:36-61.

―――. 1983. The making of a more partisan electorate in West Germany. *British Journal of Political Science* 14:53-71.

NUNN, CLYDE, et al. 1978. *Tolerance for Nonconformity*. San Francisco: Jossey-Bass.

PAGE, BENJAMIN, and JONES, CHARLES. 1979. Reciprocal effects of policy preferences, party loyalties and the vote. *American Political Science Review* 73:1071-89.

PALMER, MONTE, and THOMPSON, WILLIAM. 1978. *The Comparative Analysis of Politics*. Itasca, Ill.: Peacock.

PARKIN, FRANK. 1968. *Middle Class Radicalism*. New York: Praeger.

PATEMAN, CAROLE. 1980. The civic culture: A philosophical critique. In G. Almond and S. Verba, eds., *The Civic Culture Revisited*. Boston: Little, Brown.

PENNIMAN, HOWARD, ed. 1975a. *Britain at the Polls*. Washington, D.C.: American Enterprise Institute.

———. 1975b. *France at the Polls*. Washington, D.C.: American Enterprise Institute.

———. 1980. *The French National Assembly Elections of 1978*. Washington, D.C.: American Enterprise Institute.

———. 1981. *Britain at the Polls, 1979*. Washington, D.C.: American Enterprise Institute.

PERCHERON, ANNICK, and JENNINGS, M. KENT. 1981. Political continuities in French families. *Comparative Politics* 13:421-36.

PIERCE, JOHN; BEATTY, KATHLEEN; and HAGNER, PAUL. 1982. *The Dynamics of American Public Opinion*. Glenview: Scott, Foresman.

POMPER, GERALD. 1975. *Voter's Choice*. New York: Dodd Mead.

———, ed. 1981. *The Election of 1980*. Chatham, N.J.: Chatham House.

———, ed. 1985. *The Election of 1984*. Chatham, N.J.: Chatham House.

POOLE, I. DE SOLA. 1983. *Technologies of Freedom*. Cambridge, Mass.: Belknap Press.

POWELL, G. BINGHAM. 1980. Voting turnout in thirty democracies. In R. Rose, ed., *Electoral Participation*. Beverly Hills, Calif.: Sage.

———. 1982. *Contemporary Democracies*. Cambridge, Mass.: Harvard University Press.

———. 1986. American voting turnout in comparative perspective. *American Political Science Review* 80:17-44.

RANNEY, AUSTIN. 1985. *Britain at the Polls, 1983*. Durham, N.C.: Duke University Press.

RASCHKE, JOACHIM, ed. 1982. *Buerger und Parteien*. Opladen: Westdeutscher Verlag.

REIF, KARLHEINZ, and CAYROL, ROLAND. Forthcoming. *Party Conference Delegates in Western Europe*.

RePASS, DAVID. 1971. Issue saliency and party choice. *American Political Science Review* 65:389-400.

RIESMAN, DAVID, et al. 1950. *The Lonely Crowd*. New Haven: Yale University Press.

ROBERTSON, DAVID. 1976. *A Theory of Party Competition*. New York: Wiley.

ROCHON, THOMAS. 1983. Political change in ordered societies. *Comparative Politics* 15:351-73.

ROKEACH, M. 1973. *The Nature of Human Values*. New York: Free Press.

ROKKAN, STEIN. 1970. *Citizens Elections Parties*. Oslo: Universitetsforlaget.

ROSE, RICHARD. 1974a. Comparability in electoral studies. In R. Rose, ed., *Electoral Behavior*. New York: Free Press.

———, ed. 1974b. *Electoral Behavior*. New York: Free Press.

———. 1974c. *The Problem of Party Government*. London: Macmillan.

———, ed. 1980a. *Challenge to Governance*. Beverly Hills, Calif.: Sage.

———. 1980b. *Politics in England*. 3d ed. Boston: Little, Brown.

———. 1982. *The Territorial Dimension in Politics*. Chatham, N.J.: Chatham House.

———. 1984. *Do Parties Make a Difference?* 2d ed. Chatham, N.J.: Chatham House.

———. 1985. *Politics in England*. 4th ed. Boston: Little, Brown.

———. 1986. *Voters Begin to Choose*. Beverly Hills, Calif.: Sage.

ROSE, RICHARD, and URWIN, DEREK. 1969. Social cohesion, political parties and strains in regimes. *Comparative Political Studies* 2:7-67.

———. 1970. Persistence and change in Western party systems since 1945. *Political Stud-*

ies 18:287-319.

SAARLVIK, BO, and CREWE, IVOR. 1983. *Decade of Dealignment.* New York: Cambridge University Press.

SANI, GIACOMO. 1974. Determinants of party preference in Italy. *American Journal of Political Science* 18:315-29.

SARTORI, GIOVANNI. 1968. Representational systems. *International Encyclopedia of the Social Sciences* 13:470-75.

_____. 1976. *Parties and Party Systems.* New York: Cambridge University Press.

SCHNEIDER, WILLIAM. 1985. Peace and strength. In G. Flynn and H. Rattinger, eds., *The Public and Atlantic Defense.* London: Croom Helm.

SCHUMACHER. E.F. 1973. *Small is Beautiful.* New York: Harper & Row.

SCHUMAN, HOWARD, and PRESSER, STANLEY. 1981. *Questions and Answers in Attitudinal Surveys.* New York: Academic Press.

SEARS, DAVID, and CITRIN, JACK. 1985. *Tax Revolt.* Cambridge, Mass.: Harvard University Press.

SHARPE, LEWIS, ed. 1979. *Decentralist Trends in Western Democracies.* Beverly Hills, Calif.: Sage.

SHIVELY, W. PHILIPS. 1979. The development of party identification among adults. *American Political Science Review* 73:1039-54.

SMITH, TOM, and SHEATSLEY, PAUL. 1984. American attitudes toward race relations. *Public Opinion* 7:14ff.

STOKES, DONALD, and MILLER, WARREN. 1962. Party government and the saliency of congress. *Public Opinion Quarterly* 26:531-46.

STRUMPEL, BURKHARDT, ed. 1976. *Economic Means for Human Needs.* Ann Arbor: Institute for Social Research.

SULLIVAN, JOHN, et al. 1982. *Political Tolerance and American Democracy.* Chicago: University of Chicago Press.

SULLIVAN, JOHN; PIERESON, JAMES; and MARCUS, GEORGE. 1978. Ideological constraint in the mass public. *American Journal of Political Science* 22:233-49.

SUNDQUIST, JAMES. 1973. *Dynamics of the Party System.* Washington, D.C.: Brookings Institution.

SZABO, STEPHEN, ed. 1983. *The Successor Generation.* London: Butterworth.

TAYLOR, CHARLES, and JODICE, DAVID. 1983. *World Handbook III.* New Haven: Yale University Press.

THOMAS, JOHN. 1980. Ideological trends in Western political parties. In P. Merkl, ed., *Western European Party Systems.* New York: Free Press.

THOMMASEN, JACQUES. 1976. *Kiezers en Gekozenen in een Representative Demokratie.* Alphen aan den Rijn: Samson.

TILLY, CHARLES. 1969. Collective violence in European perspective. In H. Graham and T. Gurr, eds., *Violence in America.* New York: Bantam.

_____. 1975. Revolutions and collective violence. In F. Greenstein and N. Polsby, eds., *Handbook of Political Science.* Vol. 3. Reading, Mass.: Addison-Wesley.

_____, et al. 1975. *The Rebellious Century.* Cambridge, Mass.: Harvard University Press.

TOCQUEVILLE, A. DE. 1966. *Democracy in America.* New York: Knopf.

TOFFLER, ALVIN. 1980. *The Third Wave.* New York: Morrow.

TOURAINE, ALAIN. 1971. *The Post-industrial Society.* New York: Random House.

VERBA, SIDNEY, and NIE, NORMAN. 1972. *Participation in America.* New York: Harper & Row.

VERBA, SIDNEY; NIE, NORMAN; and KIM, J.O. 1971. *The Modes of Democratic Participation.* Beverly Hills, Calif.: Sage Professional Papers in Comparative Politics.

_____. 1978. *Participation and Political Equality.* New York: Cambridge University Press.

VERBA, SIDNEY, and ORREN, GARY. 1985. *Equality in America.* Cambridge, Mass.: Harvard University Press.

WAHLKE, JOHN, et al. 1962. *The Legislative System.* New York: Wiley.

WALD, KENNETH. 1983. *Crosses on the Ballot.* Princeton: Princeton University Press.

WATTENBERG, BEN. 1984. As the dust settles. *Public Opinion* 7:2ff.

_____. 1985. *The Good News Is the Bad News Is Wrong.* New York: Simon & Schuster.

WATTENBERG, MARTIN. 1984. *The Decline of American Political Parties.* Cambridge, Mass.: Harvard University Press.

WEBB, NORMAN, and WYBROW, ROBERT. 1983. Friendly persuasion. *Public Opinion* 6:13ff.

WEIL, FREDERIC. 1979. On the conditions of liberalism in West Germany since world war II. Ph.D. dissertation. Harvard University.

WEISBERG, HERBERT, and BOWEN, BRUCE. 1977. *Survey Research and Data Analysis.* San Francisco: Freeman.

WEISSBERG, ROBERT. 1978. Collective versus dyadic representation in Congress. *American Political Science Review* 72:535-47.

WILSON, FRANK. 1979. The revitalization of French parties. *Comparative Political Studies* 12:82-103.

_____. 1988. The French party system. In P. Merkl and K. Lawson, eds., *Parties Under Challenge.* Princeton: Princeton University Press.

WOLFINGER, RAYMOND, and ROSENSTONE, STEVEN. 1980. *Who Votes?* New Haven: Yale University Press.

WRIGHT, JAMES. 1976. *The Dissent of the Governed.* New York: Academic Press.

ZUCKERMAN, ALAN. 1982. New approaches to political cleavage. *Comparative Political Studies* 15:131-44.

Index

About the Author

RUSSELL J. DALTON is a professor of political science at Florida State University at Tallahassee. He received his doctorate from the University of Michigan in 1978. He was co-director of the German Electoral Data Project at the Zentralarchiv fuer empirische Sozialforschung, University of Cologne; in 1980-81 he was a Fulbright guest professor at the Lehrstuhl fuer politische Wissenschaft und international vergleichende Sozialforschung, University of Mannheim.

His research interests include comparative political behavior, political parties, methodology, and political change in advanced industrial societies.

Among his publications are *Germany Transformed: Political Culture and the New Politics* (1981); *Electoral Change in Advanced Industrial Democracies: Realignment or Dealignment?* (1984); *Politics in West Germany* (1988); and *Challenging the Political Order: New Social and Political Movements in Advanced Industrial Democracies* (forthcoming). He is currently writing a book-length study of the environmental movement in Western Europe, based on a NSF-funded study of environmental groups in ten European democracies.